Get the eBook FREE!

(PDF, ePub, Kindle, and liveBook all included)

We believe that once you buy a book from us, you should be able to read it in any format we have available. To get electronic versions of this book at no additional cost to you, purchase and then register this book at the Manning website.

Go to https://www.manning.com/freebook and follow the instructions to complete your pBook registration.

That's it!
Thanks from Manning!

Five Lines of Code

Five Lines of Code

HOW AND WHEN TO REFACTOR

CHRISTIAN CLAUSEN

FOREWORD BY ROBERT C. MARTIN

MANNING

SHELTER ISLAND

Manning Publications Co.	Development editor: Helen Stergius
20 Baldwin Road	Technical development editor: Mark Elston
PO Box 761	Review editor: Mihaela Batinić
Shelter Island, NY 11964	Production editor: Keri Hales
	Copy editor: Tiffany Taylor
	Proofreader: Katie Tennant
	Technical proofreader: Jean François Morin
	Typesetter: Dennis Dalinnik
	Cover designer: Marija Tudor

ISBN: 9781617298318
Printed in the United States of America

To my university mentors, who told me

> *The key to being consistently brilliant is hard work every day.*
>
> *—Olivier Danvy*

and

> *You're missing the point.*
>
> *—Mayer Goldberg*

Thank you for teaching me to stop trying to do the right thing, and do the right thing.

brief contents

contents

foreword

Have you ever read a book on software and thought that the author was talking over your head? Did the book use unfamiliar vocabulary and overly complex concepts to make its points? Did it make you feel as though it was written for some elite inner circle of know-it-alls that didn't include you?

This is not that book. This book is down to earth, focused, and right on point.

Neither is this book a primer. It doesn't start at the atom and bore you with the basics of programming and languages. It doesn't try to coddle you and keep you safe. I guarantee that this book will challenge you. But it will challenge you without intimidating you and without insulting your intelligence.

Refactoring is the discipline of transforming bad code into good code without breaking it. When we consider that our entire civilization now depends on software for its further existence, it seems unlikely that there is a topic more worthy of study.

Perhaps you think that's hyperbolic. It's not. Look around you. How many processors running software are currently on your body? Your watch, your phone, your car keys, your headphones . . . how many are within 30 meters of you? Your microwave, your stove, your dishwasher, your thermostat, your clothes washer . . . and how about your car?

These days, nothing happens in our society without software. You can't buy or sell anything, or drive or fly anywhere, or cook a hot dog, or watch TV, or call someone on the phone without software.

And how much of that software is actually good code? Think of the systems you are working on right now. Are they clean? Or are they, like most, a mess in desperate need of refactoring?

This book does not present the kind of sterile and simplistic refactoring you may have heard or read about before. This book talks about *real* refactoring. Refactoring in *real* projects. Refactoring in legacy systems. Refactoring in the kinds of environments that we all face virtually every day.

What's more, this book won't make you feel guilty for not having automated tests. The author realizes that most inherited systems grew and evolved over time, and we are not so fortunate as to have such test suites.

This book lays down a set of simple rules that you can follow to reliably refactor complex, messy, tangled, untested systems. By learning and following these rules, you can make a real difference in the quality of the systems you maintain.

Don't get me wrong—it's not a silver bullet. Refactoring old, crufty, untested code is never easy. But armed with the rules and examples in this book, you will be able to make inroads against the cruft and tangle of systems that have bedeviled you for too long.

So I advise you to read this book carefully. Study the examples. Think hard about the abstractions and intentions the author presents. Get the codebase he offers, and refactor it along with him. Follow his refactoring journey from beginning to end.

It will take time. It will be frustrating. It will challenge you. But you'll come out the other side with a set of skills that will serve you well for the rest of your career. You'll also come out with a new intuition and understanding of what separates good code from bad code, and just what it is that makes code clean.

—Robert C. Martin (aka Uncle Bob)

preface

My father taught me to code at a very young age, so I have been thinking about structures for as long as I can remember. I was always motivated by helping people; that is why I got up in the morning. Therefore, teaching was naturally interesting to me. So when I was offered a teaching assistant position at university, I accepted immediately. I had a handful of these gigs, but unfortunately my luck ran out, and one semester there was nothing I could teach.

Being entrepreneurial, I decided to start a student organization where students would teach each other. Anyone was welcome to attend or speak, and the topics ranged from lessons learned from side projects to advanced topics not covered by the curriculum. I believed this would allow me to teach, and I was not wrong. As it turns out, computer scientists are timid, so I had to host almost 60 weeks in a row to get the ball rolling. I learned a great deal during this period, both about the topics I taught and about teaching. These talks also spawned a community of curious people where I met my best friends.

Some time after I left university, I was hanging out with one of those friends. We were bored, so he asked me if I could improvise a talk because I had done so many of them. I answered, "Let's find out." We opened a laptop, and without stopping for breath, I typed out what is essentially the overarching example of part 1 of this book.

When I took my fingers off the keyboard, he was awestruck. He thought that was the demonstration, but I had a different idea. I wanted to teach him refactoring.

My goal was that after one hour, he could code as though he were a master refactorer. Because refactoring and code quality are such intricate subjects, it was obvious that we had to fake it. So, I looked at the code and tried to come up with rules that would make him do the right thing while also being easy to remember. During the exercise, even though we were faking it, he made real improvements to the code. The results were so promising, and his improvement was so quick, that when I got home that evening, I wrote down everything we had covered. I repeated the exercise when we hired juniors at work, and slowly I collected, built, and refined the rules and refactoring patterns in this book.

Goal: The selected rules and refactoring patterns

Perfection is achieved, not when there is nothing more to add, but when there is nothing left to take away.

—Antoine de Saint-Exupéry

There are hundreds of refactoring patterns in the world; I chose to include only 13. I did so because I believe deep understanding is more valuable than broad familiarity. I also wanted to craft a complete, cohesive story because it helps add perspective and makes the subject matter easier to organize mentally. The same arguments apply to the rules.

There is no new thing under the sun.

—Book of Ecclesiastes

I don't claim to have come up with much novel stuff in this book, but I think I have combined things in a way that is both interesting and advantageous. Many of the rules are derived from Robert C. Martin's *Clean Code* (Pearson, 2008) but are modified to be easier to understand and apply. Many refactoring patterns originated in Martin Fowler's *Refactoring* (Addison-Wesley Professional, 1999) but are adapted to take advantage of the compiler instead of relying on strong test suites.

Audience and roadmap

This book consists of two parts with very different styles. The first builds a solid foundation of refactoring and is targeted at individuals. Instead of comprehensiveness, I focus on ease of learning. This part is for people who have yet to develop a solid foundation for refactoring, such as students and junior or self-taught developers. If you look at the book's source code and think, "This seems easy to improve," then part 1 is not for you.

In part 2, I focus more on the context and the team. I have selected what I believe to be the most valuable lessons about software development in the real world. Some topics are mostly theoretical, like "Collaborate with the compiler" and "Follow the structure in the code"; and some are primarily practical, like "Love deleting code" and "Make bad code look bad." Thus this part applies more widely, and even experienced developers should learn from these chapters.

Because the chapters of part 1 all use a single overarching example, they are linked tightly together and should be read one after the other. But in part 2, the chapters are largely self-contained, except for a few references to each other. If you do not have time to read the whole book, you can easily pick the most exciting topics in part 2 and read them in isolation.

About the teaching

I have spent much time reflecting on teaching. Transferring knowledge and skills presents many challenges. A teacher has to stimulate motivation, confidence, and reflection. But the student's brain would rather conserve the energy, so it constantly tries to distract from learning.

To overcome this struggling brain, we first need to stimulate motivation. I usually do this by posing a simple-looking exercise; when students realize that they cannot solve it, their natural curiosity takes over. This is the purpose of the code in part 1. "Improve this codebase" seems like a simple instruction; however, the code is already at a quality where many people don't know how to make progress.

The second stage is to give students confidence to experiment and apply new knowledge or skills. I first realized how important this is during extracurricular French lessons. When our teacher wanted to teach us a new phrase, she would go through the same steps:

1 She asked each of us to repeat the phrase verbatim. This pure imitation step would force us to say the phrase once.
2 She asked each of us a question. We did not always understand the question, but the intonation made it clear that it was a question. As we had no other tools available, we again repeated the phrase. This repetition built confidence and gave us the first bit of context for the phrase. Here, understanding started.
3 She asked us to use the phrase in a conversation. Being able to synthesize something new is the goal of teaching and requires both understanding and confidence.

I have learned that this approach follows the Japanese *Shuhari* concept from martial arts, which is becoming increasingly popular. It consists of three parts: "Shu" is imitation, with neither question nor understanding; "ha" is variation, doing something slightly novel; and "ri" is originality, departing entirely from the known.

Shuhari underlines all of part 1. I recommend first following the rules without understanding; then, once you understand their value, you can come up with variations. Finally, when you master them, you can move on to code smells. For the refactoring patterns, I show how to do something in the real code, and the reader should follow along (imitation). Then I show the same refactoring pattern in a different context (variation). Finally, I present another place to apply the pattern; here, I encourage the reader to attempt it on their own (synthesis).

You can use the book to verify the process and the Git tags to verify the code. If you are not following along in the code, this will feel overly repetitive, so I urge you to read part 1 with your hands on the keyboard.

About the code

This book contains many examples of source code both in numbered listings and in line with normal text. In both cases, source code is formatted in a `fixed-width font like this` to separate it from ordinary text. The code has been syntax highlighted with keywords set **in bold**, making the structure of the code easier to understand.

In many cases, the original source code has been reformatted; we've added line breaks and reworked indentation to accommodate the available page space in the book. Additionally, comments in the source code have often been removed from the listings when the code is described in the text. Code annotations accompany many of the listings, highlighting important concepts.

The code for the examples in this book is available for download from on the Manning website (https://www.manning.com/books/five-lines-of-code) or in my GitHub repository (https://github.com/thedrlambda/five-lines).

liveBook discussion forum

Purchase of *Five Lines of Code* includes free access to a private web forum run by Manning Publications where you can make comments about the book, ask technical questions, and receive help from the author and from other users. To access the forum, go to https://livebook.manning.com/#!/book/five-lines-of-code/discussion. You can also learn more about Manning's forums and the rules of conduct at https://livebook.manning.com/#!/discussion.

Manning's commitment to our readers is to provide a venue where a meaningful dialogue between individual readers and between readers and the author can take place. It is not a commitment to any specific amount of participation on the part of the author, whose contribution to the forum remains voluntary (and unpaid). We suggest you try asking him some challenging questions lest his interest stray! The forum and the archives of previous discussions will be accessible from the publisher's website as long as the book is in print.

Bonus project

To help you get an additional grasp of how to use the rules and refactoring patterns in this book, I've set up a bonus project. This project is slightly more advanced and comes without a solution; you can get it from Github: https://github.com/thedrlambda/bomb-guy. Good luck!

acknowledgments

First, I would not be the person I am, let alone have written this book, were it not for the two people to whom this book is dedicated: Olivier Danvy and Mayer Goldberg. I cannot thank each of you enough. You taught me type theory and lambda calculus, respectively, which form the very foundation of this work. But like any excellent teacher, you did much more. To Danvy: I know it was a surprise to you, but it is no surprise to me that you are the most thanked person in science. You earn that by offering advice that is immediately applicable and that can still be useful years later. To Mayer: Your inexhaustible enthusiasm, patience, and method for teaching arbitrarily complex topics in programming have shaped how I think about and teach programming.

I also want to extend a huge thank you to Robert C. Martin; if someone finds this book as inspiring as I found yours, I will be happy. I am also amazingly grateful that you took the time to look at this book and decided to write the foreword.

The last person who contributed to this book is my graphics designer: thank you, Lee McGorie. Your creativity and competence have pushed the quality of the graphics to the level of the content.

Deep-felt thanks go out to everyone on my Manning team. My acquisition editor, Andrew Waldron, offered fantastic feedback and enthusiasm that were the reasons I decided to work with Manning. My development editor, Helen Stergius, was my sensei throughout the enormous undertaking required to write a book like this one. Without her encouragement and excellent feedback, this book would not have reached this level of quality. My fantastic technical development editor was Mark Elston, whose comments were always very insightful and accurate; his perspective on the topics complement my own perfectly. Also, thanks go to the copy editor, the marketing team, and Manning itself for collaborating and being patient with me.

Another thank you goes out to the people who have mentored me in my work life. To Jacob Blom: You taught me by example how to be a technically brilliant consultant without sacrificing yourself or your values. Your passion for what you do is evident through the fact that you could recognize and recall code you worked on 10 years earlier—something that still baffles me. To Klaus Nørregaard: Your level of inner peace and goodness is something I aspire to every day. To Johan Abildskov: Never have I met a person who has so much technical breadth and depth at the same time, rivaled only by your kindness. Without you, this book would never have left my hard drive. Also, I thank all the people I have mentored or worked with closely.

I also want to thank all the people who have helped this book become what it is through feedback and countless technical discussions. I chose to spend time with you because you make my life better. To Hannibal Keblovszki: Your curiosity spawned the original idea for this book. To Mikkel Kringelbach: Thank you for helping any time I asked, challenging me intellectually, and sharing your insight and experiences, which benefited the book significantly. To Mikkel Brun Jakobsen: Your passion and competence in software craftsmanship inspire me and push me to be better. Thank you, everyone who at any point considered yourself part of the spare-time teaching community; your unquenchable thirst for knowledge kept me teaching. Notably: Sune Orth Sørensen, Mathias Vorreiter Pedersen, Jens Jensen, Casper Freksen, Mathias Bak, Frederik Brinck Truelsen, Kent Grigo, John Smedegaard, Richard Möhn, Kristoffer Nøddebo Knudsen, Kenneth Hansen, Rasmus Buchholdt, and Kristoffer Just Andersen.

Finally, to all the reviewers: Ben McNamara, Billy O'Callaghan, Bonnie Malec, Brent Honadel, Charles Lam, Christian Hasselbalch Thoudahl, Clive Harber, Daniel Vásquez, David Trimm, Gustavo Filipe Ramos Gomes, Jeff Neumann, Joel Kotarski, John Guthrie, John Norcott, Karthikeyarajan Rajendran, Kim Kjærsulf, Luis Moux, Marcel van den Brink, Marek Petak, Mathijs Affourtit, Orlando Méndez Morales, Paulo Nuin, Ronald Haring, Shawn Mehaffie, Sebastian Larsson, Sergiu Popa, Tan Wee, Taylor Dolezal, Tom Madden, Tyler Kowallis, and Ubaldo Pescatore—your suggestions helped make this a better book.

about the author

CHRISTIAN CLAUSEN holds a master's degree in computer science. He specialized in programming languages, specifically, software quality and how to code without bugs. He coauthored two peer-reviewed papers on the topic of software quality, published in some of the most prestigious journals and conferences. Christian has worked as a software engineer on a project called Coccinelle for a research group in Paris. He has taught introductory and advanced programming topics in both object-oriented and functional programming languages at two universities. Christian has worked as a consultant and tech lead for five years.

about the cover illustration

The figure on the cover of *Five Lines of Code* is captioned "Femme Samojede en habit d'Été," or a Samoyed woman in summer attire. The illustration is taken from a collection of dress costumes from various countries by Jacques Grasset de Saint-Sauveur (1757–1810), titled *Costumes Civils Actuels de Tous les Peuples Connus*, published in France in 1788. Each illustration is finely drawn and colored by hand. The rich variety of Grasset de Saint-Sauveur's collection reminds us vividly of how culturally apart the world's towns and regions were just 200 years ago. Isolated from each other, people spoke different dialects and languages. In the streets or in the countryside, it was easy to identify where they lived and what their trade or station in life was just by their dress.

The way we dress has changed since then and the diversity by region, so rich at the time, has faded away. It is now hard to tell apart the inhabitants of different continents, let alone different towns, regions, or countries. Perhaps we have traded cultural diversity for a more varied personal life—certainly for a more varied and fast-paced technological life.

At a time when it is hard to tell one computer book from another, Manning celebrates the inventiveness and initiative of the computer business with book covers based on the rich diversity of regional life of two centuries ago, brought back to life by Grasset de Saint-Sauveur's pictures.

Refactoring refactoring

This chapter covers

- Understanding the elements of refactoring
- Incorporating refactoring into your daily work
- The importance of safety for refactoring
- Introducing the overarching example for part 1

It is well known that high code quality leads to cheaper maintenance, fewer errors, and happier developers. The most common way to get high code quality is through refactoring. However, the way refactoring is usually taught—with *code smells* and *unit testing*—imposes an unnecessarily high barrier to entry. I believe that anyone can execute simple refactoring patterns safely with a little practice.

In software development, we place problems somewhere on the diagram shown in figure 1.1, indicating a lack of sufficient skills, culture, tools, or a combination of those. Refactoring is a sophisticated endeavor and therefore lies right in the middle. It requires each component:

- *Skills*—We need the skills to know what code is bad and needs refactoring. Experienced programmers can determine this through their knowledge of code smells. But the boundaries of code smells are blurry (requiring judgment and experience) or open to interpretation and therefore not easy to learn; and to a junior developer, understanding code smells can seem more like a sixth sense than a skill.

- *Culture*—We need a culture and workflow that encourage taking the time to perform refactoring. In many cases, this culture is implemented through the famous *red-green-refactor* loop used in test-driven development. However, test-driven development is a much more difficult craft, in my opinion. Red-green-refactor also does not easily give way to doing refactoring in a legacy codebase.
- *Tools*—We need something to help ensure that what we are doing is safe. The most common way to achieve this is through automated testing. But as already mentioned, learning to do effective automated testing is difficult in itself.

Figure 1.1   Skills, culture, and tools

The following sections dive into each of these areas and describe how we can begin our refactoring journey from a much simpler foundation without testing and abstract code smells. Learning refactoring this way can quickly catapult junior developers', students', and programming enthusiasts' code quality to the next level. Tech leads can also use the methods in this book as a basis for introducing refactoring in teams that are not routinely doing it.

1.1   What is refactoring?

I answer the question "What is refactoring?" in a lot more detail in the next chapter, but it is helpful to get an intuition for it up front before we dive into the different *hows* of refactoring. In its simplest form, *refactoring* means "changing code without changing what it does." Let's start with an example of refactoring to make it clear what I'm talking about. Here, we replace an expression with a local variable.

Listing 1.1   Before

```
return pow(base, exp / 2) * pow(base, exp / 2);
```

Listing 1.2   After

```
let result = pow(base, exp / 2);
return result * result;
```

There are many possible reasons to refactor:

- Making code faster (as in the previous example)
- Making code smaller
- Making code more general or reusable
- Making code easier to read or maintain

The last reason is so important and central that we equate it with good code.

> **DEFINITION** *Good code* is human-readable and easy to maintain, and it correctly performs what it set out to do.

As refactoring mustn't change what the code is doing, in this book we focus on human-readable and easy to maintain. We discuss these reasons to refactor in more detail in chapter 2. In this book, we only consider refactoring that results in good code; therefore, the definition we use is as follows.

> **DEFINITION** *Refactoring*—Changing code to make it more human-readable and maintainable without changing what it does.

I should also mention that the type of refactoring we consider relies heavily on working with an object-oriented programming language.

Many people think of programming as writing code; however, most programmers spend more time reading and trying to understand code than writing it. This is because we work in a complex domain, and changing something without understanding it can cause catastrophic failures.

So, the first argument for refactoring is purely economic: programmers' time is expensive, so if we make our codebase more readable, we free up time for implementing new features. The second argument is that making our code more maintainable means fewer, easier-to-fix bugs. Third, a good codebase is simply more fun. When we read code, we build a model in our heads of what the code is doing; the more we have to keep in our head at one time, the more exhausting it is. This is why it is much more fun to start from scratch—and why debugging can be dreadful.

1.2 Skills: What to refactor?

Knowing what you should refactor is the first barrier to entry. Usually, refactoring is taught alongside something called *code smells*. These "smells" are descriptions of things that might suggest our code is bad. While they are powerful, they are also abstract and difficult to get started with, and it takes time to develop a feel for them.

This book takes a different approach and presents easily recognizable, applicable rules to determine what to refactor. These rules are easy to use and quick to learn. They are also sometimes too strict and require you to fix code that is not smelly. On rare occasions, we might follow the rules and still have smelly code.

As figure 1.2 illustrates, the overlap between smells and rules is not perfect. My rules are not the be-all and end-all of good code. They are a head start on the road to developing a guru-like feeling for what good code is. Let's look at an example of the difference between a code smell and the rules in this book.

Figure 1.2   Rules and code smells

1.2.1   An example code smell

A well-known code smell is as follows: a function should do *one* thing. This is a great guideline, but it is not easy to know what the *one thing* is. Look again at the earlier code: is it smelly? Arguably, it divides, exponentiates, and then multiplies. Does that mean it does three things? On the other hand, it only returns one number and doesn't change any state, so is it doing only one thing?

```
let result = pow(base, exp / 2);
return result * result;
```

1.2.2   An example rule

Compare the preceding code smell to the following rule (covered in detail in chapter 3): a method should never have more than *Five Lines of Code*. We can determine this at a glance, with no further questions to ask. The rule is clear, concise, and easy to remember—especially since it is also the title of this book.

Remember, the rules presented in this book are like training wheels. As discussed earlier, they cannot guarantee good code in every situation; and on some occasions, it might be wrong to follow them. However, they are useful if you don't know where to start, and they motivate nice code refactoring.

Note that all the names of the rules are stated in absolute terms, using words like *never*, so they are easy to remember. But the detailed descriptions often specify exceptions: when *not* to apply the rules. The descriptions also state the rules' intentions. At the beginning of learning refactoring, we only need to use the absolute names; when those are internalized, we can start learning the exceptions as well, after which we can begin to use the intentions—then we'll be coding gurus.

1.3 Culture: When to refactor?

Refactoring is like taking a shower.

—Kent Beck

Refactoring works best—and costs least—if you do it regularly. So if you can, I recommend that you incorporate it into your daily work. Most of the literature suggests a red-green-refactor workflow; but as mentioned earlier, this approach ties refactoring to test-driven development—and in this book, we want to separate them and focus specifically on the refactoring part. Therefore, I recommend a more general six-step workflow to solve any programming task, as shown in figure 1.3:

1 *Explore.* Often, we are not completely sure what we need to build right from the start. Sometimes the customer does not know what they want us to build; other times, the requirements are written in ambiguous prose; sometimes we do not even know if the task can be solved. So, always start by experimenting. Implement something quickly, and then you can validate with the customer that you agree on what they need.

2 *Specify.* Once you know what you need to build, make it explicit. Optimally, this results in some form of automated test.

3 *Implement.* Implement the code.

4 *Test.* Make sure the code passes the specification from step 2.

5 *Refactor.* Before delivering the code, make sure it is easy for the next person to work with (and that next person might be you).

6 *Deliver.* There are many ways to deliver; the most common are through a pull request or by pushing to a specific branch. The most important thing is that your code gets to the users. Otherwise, what's the point?

Figure 1.3   Workflow

Because we are doing *rule-based* refactoring, the workflow is straightforward and easy to get started with. Figure 1.4 zooms in on step 5: *refactor.*

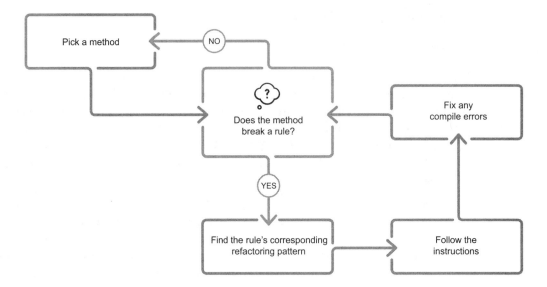

Figure 1.4   Detailed view of the refactoring step

I have designed the rules so they are easy to remember and so that it's easy to spot when to use them without any assistance. This means finding a method that breaks a rule is usually trivial. Every rule also has a few refactoring patterns linked with it, making it easy to know exactly how to fix a problem. The refactoring patterns have explicit step-by-step instructions to ensure that you do not accidentally break something. Many of the refactoring patterns in this book intentionally use compile errors to help make sure you don't introduce errors. Once we've practiced a little, both the rules and the refactoring patterns will become second nature.

1.3.1   *Refactoring in a legacy system*

Even if we are starting from a large legacy system, there is a clever way to incorporate refactoring into our daily work without having to stop everything and refactor the whole codebase first. Simply following this awesome quote:

> *First make the change easy, then make the easy change.*

—Kent Beck

Whenever we are about to implement something new, we start by refactoring, so it is easy to add our new code. This is similar to getting all the ingredients ready before you start baking.

1.3.2   *When should you not refactor?*

Mostly, refactoring is awesome, but it has a few downsides. Refactoring can be time consuming, especially if you don't do it regularly. And as mentioned earlier, programmer time is expensive.

There are three types of codebases where refactoring probably isn't worth it:

- Code you are going to write, run only once, and then delete. This is what is known as a *spike* in the Extreme Programming community.
- Code that is in maintenance mode before it is going to be retired.
- Code with strict performance requirements, such as an embedded system or a high-end physics engine in a game.

In any other case, I argue that investing in refactoring is the smart choice.

1.4   Tools: How to refactor (safely)

I like automated tests as much as anybody. However, learning how to test software effectively is a complicated skill in itself. So if you already know how to do automated testing, feel free to use it throughout this book. If you don't, don't worry.

We can think about testing this way: automated testing is to software development what brakes are to cars. Cars don't have brakes because we want to go slowly—they have brakes so we feel safe going fast. The same is true for software: automated tests make us feel safe going fast. In this book, we are learning a completely new skill, so we don't need to go fast.

Instead, I propose relying more heavily on other tools, such as these:

- Detailed, step-by-step, structured refactoring patterns akin to recipes
- Version control
- The compiler

I believe that if the refactoring patterns are carefully designed and performed in tiny steps, it is possible to refactor without breaking anything. This is especially true in cases where our IDE can perform the refactoring for us.

To remedy the fact that we don't talk about testing in this book, we use the compiler and types to catch a lot of the common mistakes we might make. Even so, I recommend that you regularly open the application you are working on and check that it is not completely broken. Whenever we have verified this, or when we know the compiler is happy, we make a commit so that if at some point the application is broken and we don't know how to immediately fix it, we can easily jump back to the last time it was working.

If we are working on a real-world system without automated tests, we can still perform refactoring, but we need to get our confidence from somewhere. Confidence can come from using an IDE to perform the refactoring; testing manually; taking truly tiny steps; or something else. However, the extra time we would spend on these activities probably makes it more cost effective to do automated testing.

1.5   Tools you need to get started

As I said earlier, the types of refactoring discussed in this book need an object-oriented language. That is the primary thing you need in order to read and understand this book. Coding and refactoring are both crafts that we perform with our fingers.

Therefore, they are best learned through the fingers by following along with the examples, experimenting, and having fun while your hands learn the routines. To follow along with the book, you need the tools described next. For installation instructions, see the appendix.

1.5.1   *Programming language: TypeScript*

All the coding examples presented in this book are written in TypeScript. I chose TypeScript for multiple reasons. Most important, it looks and feels similar to the most commonly used programming languages—Java, C#, C++, and JavaScript—and thus, people familiar with any of those languages should be able to read TypeScript without any problem. TypeScript also provides a way to go from completely "un-object-oriented" code (that is, code without a single class) to highly object-oriented code.

> **NOTE**   To better utilize space in the printed book, this book uses a programming style that avoids line breaks while still being readable. I'm not advocating that you use the same style—unless you are coincidentally also writing a book containing lots of TypeScript code. This is also why indentation and braces are sometimes formatted differently in the book than in the project code.

If you are unfamiliar with TypeScript, I'll explain any gotchas as they appear, in boxes like the following.

> **In TypeScript ...**
>
> We use identity (===) to check equality, because it acts more like what we expect from equality than double equals (==). Consider the following:
>
> - `0 == ""` is true.
> - `0 === ""` is false.

Even though the examples are in TypeScript, all refactoring patterns and rules are general and apply to any object-oriented language. In rare cases, TypeScript helps or hinders us; these cases are explicitly stated, and we discuss how to handle these situations in other common languages.

1.5.2   *Editor: Visual Studio Code*

I do not assume that you are using a specific editor; however, if you don't have a preference, I recommend Visual Studio Code. It works well with TypeScript. Also, it supports running `tsc -w` in a background terminal that does the compiling so we don't forget to do it.

> **NOTE**   *Visual Studio Code* is an entirely different tool than *Visual Studio.*

1.5.3   *Version control: Git*

Although you are not required to use version control to follow along with this book, I strongly recommend it, as it makes it much easier to undo something if you get lost in the middle.

> **Resetting to the reference solution**
>
> At any point, you can jump to the code as it should look at the beginning of a major section with a command like
>
> ```
> git reset --hard section-2.1
> ```
>
> *Caution*: You will lose any changes you have made.

1.6   *Overarching example: A 2D puzzle game*

Finally, let's discuss how I am going to teach all these wonderful rules and amazing refactoring patterns. The book is built around a single overarching example: a 2D block-pushing puzzle game, similar to the classic game Boulder Dash (figure 1.5).

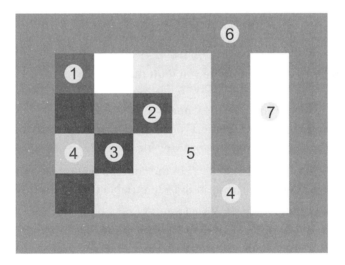

Figure 1.5   A screenshot of the game out of the box

This means we have one substantial codebase to play with throughout part 1 of the book. Having one example saves time because we don't have to become familiar with a new example in every chapter.

The example is written in a realistic style, similar to what is used in the industry. It is by no means an easy exercise unless you have the skills learned in this book. The code already adheres to the *DRY* (Don't Repeat Yourself) *KISS* (Keep It Simple, Stupid) principles; even so, it is no more pleasant than a dry kiss.

I chose a computer game because when we test manually, it is easy to spot if something behaves incorrectly: we have an intuition for how it should behave. It is also slightly more fun to test than looking at something like logs from a financial system.

The user controls the player square using the arrow keys. The objective of the game is to get the box (labeled 2 in figure 1.5) to the lower-right corner. Although the colors don't appear in the printed book, the game elements are different colors as follows:

1 The red square is the player.
2 Brown squares are boxes.
3 Blue squares are stones.
4 Yellow squares are keys *or* locks—we fix this later.
5 Greenish squares are called *flux.*
6 Gray squares are walls.
7 White squares are air (empty).

If a box or stone is not supported by anything, it falls. The player can push one stone or box at a time, provided it is not obstructed or falling. The path between the box and the lower-right corner is initially obstructed by a lock, so the player has to get a key to remove it. Flux can be "eaten" (removed) by the player by stepping on it.

Now would be a great time to get the game and play around with it:

1 Open a console where you want the game to be stored.
  a `git clone https://github.com/thedrlambda/five-lines` downloads the source code for the game.
  b `tsc -w` compiles the TypeScript to JavaScript every time it changes.
2 Open index.html in a browser.

It is possible to change the level in the code, so feel free to have fun creating your own maps by updating the array in the `map` variable (for an example, see the appendix):

1 Open the folder in Visual Studio Code.
2 Select Terminal and then New Terminal.
3 Run the command `tsc -w`.
4 TypeScript is now compiling your changes in the background, and you can close the terminal.
5 Every time you make a change, wait for a moment while TypeScript compiles, and then refresh your browser.

This is the same procedure you'll use when coding along with the examples in part 1. Before we get to that, though, we build a more detailed foundation of refactoring in the next chapter.

1.6.1 Practice makes perfect: A second codebase

As I am a strong believer in practice, I have made another project, provided without a solution. You can use this project on rereading, if you want a challenge; or as exercises for students, if you are a teacher. This project is a 2D action game. Both codebases use the same style and structure, they have the same elements, and it takes the same steps to refactor them. Although this second codebase is slightly more advanced, carefully following the rules and refactoring patterns should yield the desired result. To get this project, use the same steps as described with the URL `https://github .com/thedrlambda/bomb-guy`.

1.7 A note on real-world software

It is important to reiterate that the focus of this book is introducing refactoring. The focus is *not* on providing specific rules that you can apply to production code in all circumstances. The way to use the rules is to first learn their names and follow them. Once this is easy for you, learn the descriptions with their exceptions; finally, use this to build an understanding of the underlying code smell. This journey is illustrated in figure 1.6.

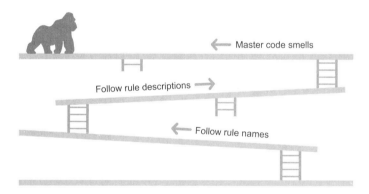

Figure 1.6   How to use the rules

This also answers why we cannot make an automatic refactoring program. (We might be able to make a plugin to highlight *possibly problematic* areas in the code, based on the rules.) The purpose of the rules is to build understanding. In short: follow the rules until you know better.

Also note that because we focus only on learning refactoring, and we have a safe environment, we can get away without automated tests—but this probably is not true for real systems. We do so because it is much easier to learn automated testing and refactoring separately.

Summary

- Executing refactoring requires a combination of *skills* to know what to refactor, *culture* to know when to refactor, and *tools* to know how to refactor.
- Conventionally, code smells are used to describe what to refactor. These are difficult for junior programmers to internalize because they are fuzzy. This book provides concrete rules to replace code smells while learning. The rules have three levels of abstraction: very concrete names, descriptions that add nuance in the form of exceptions, and, finally, the intention of the smells they are derived from.
- I believe that automated testing and refactoring can be learned separately to further lower the barrier to entry. Instead of automated testing, we utilize the compiler, version control, and manual testing.
- The workflow of refactoring is connected with test-driven development in the red-green-refactor loop. But this again implies a dependency on automated testing. Instead, I suggest using a six-step workflow (explore, specify, implement, test, refactor, deliver) for new code or doing refactoring right before changing code.
- Throughout part 1 of this book, we use Visual Studio Code, TypeScript, and Git to transform the source code of a 2D puzzle game.

Looking under
the hood of refactoring

This chapter covers

- Using readability to communicate intent
- Localizing invariants to improve maintainability
- Enabling change by addition to speed up development
- Making refactoring part of daily work

In the last chapter, we took a look at the different elements involved in refactoring. In this chapter, we dive into the technical details to form a solid foundation of what refactoring is and why it is important from a technical perspective.

2.1 Improving readability and maintainability

We start by reiterating the definition of refactoring that we use in this book: *refactoring* is making code better without changing what it does. Let's break down the two main components of this definition: *making code better* and *without changing what it does.*

2.1.1 Making code better

We already saw that better code excels in readability and maintainability and why that matters. But we did not discuss what readability and maintainability are, or how refactoring affects them.

READABILITY

Readability is the code's aptitude for communicating its intent. This means that if we assume the code works as intended, it is very easy to figure out what the code does. There are many ways to communicate intent in code: having and following conventions; writing comments; variable, method, class, and file naming; using whitespace; and so on.

These techniques can be more or less effective, and we discuss them in detail later. For now, let's look at a simple artificial function that breaks all the communication methods I just described. On the right is the same method without breaking them. One version is hard to read, and the other is easy to read.

Listing 2.1   Example of really unreadable code

```
function checkValue(str: boolean) {
    // Check value

    if (str !== false)
        // return
        return true;

    else; // otherwise
        return str;

}
```

Bad method name: a parameter named str that is a boolean

Comment that just repeats the code

Easy-to-miss semicolon (;) and a trivial comment

Double negation is hard to read.

Comment that just repeats a name

Misleading indentation; and at this point, str can only be false, so it's clearer to just put that.

Listing 2.2   Same code written more readably

```
function isTrue(bool: boolean) {

    if (bool)
        return true;

    else
        return false;

}
```

Cleaned up like this, it is clear that we could have simply written the following.

Listing 2.3   Same code, simplified

```
function isTrue(bool: boolean) {
    return bool;
}
```

MAINTAINABILITY

Whenever we need to change some functionality, whether to fix a bug or add a feature, we often start by investigating the context of where we suspect the new code should go. We try to assess what the code is currently doing and how we can safely, quickly, and easily modify it to accommodate our new goal. *Maintainability* is an expression of how much we need to investigate.

It is easy to see that the more code we need to read and include in our investigation, the longer it takes—and the more likely we are to miss something. Therefore, maintainability is closely tied to the risk that is inherent any time we make a change.

Many programmers at every level are deliberate and careful during the investigation phase. Everyone has accidentally missed something at some point and seen the consequences. Being careful also means that if we cannot readily determine whether something is important, we usually err on the side of caution. Having a long investigation phase is a symptom that code maintainability is bad, and we should strive to improve it.

In some systems, when we change something in one location, something breaks somewhere seemingly unrelated. Imagine an online store where making a change to the recommendation feature breaks the payment subsystem. We call such systems *fragile*.

The root of this fragility is usually *global state*. Here, *global* means outside the scope we are considering. From the perspective of a method, fields are global. The concept of *state* is a bit more abstract; it is anything that can change while our program is running. This includes all the variables, but also the data in a database, the files on the hard drive, and the hardware itself. (Technically, even the user's intention and all of reality are state in some sense, but they're unimportant for our purposes.)

A useful trick to help think about global state is to look for braces: { ... }. Everything outside the braces is considered global state for everything inside the braces.

The problem with global state is that we often associate properties with our data. The danger is that when data is global, it can be accessed or modified by someone who associates different properties with it, thereby inadvertently breaking our properties. Properties that we do not explicitly check in the code (or check only with assertions) are called *invariants*. "This number will never be negative" and "This file definitely exists" are examples of invariants. Unfortunately, it is nearly impossible to ensure that invariants remain valid, especially as the system changes, programmers forget, and new people are added to the team.

How nonlocal invariants corrupt

Say we are working on an application for a grocery store. The store sells fruits and vegetables, so in our system, all items have a `daysUntilExpiry` property. We implement a feature that runs every day, subtracts one from `daysUntilExpiry`, and automatically removes items if the value reaches zero. We now have an invariant that `daysUntilExpiry` is always positive.

In our system, we also want an `urgency` property to show how important it is to sell each item. Items with higher `value` should have higher `urgency`, and so should items with fewer `daysUntilExpiry`. We therefore implement `urgency = value / daysUntilExpiry`. This cannot go wrong since we *know* that `daysUntilExpiry` is always positive.

Two years later, we are asked to update the system because the store has started selling light bulbs. We quickly add light bulbs. Light bulbs do not have an expiry date,

> **(continued)**
>
> and we remember the feature that subtracts days and removes items if their `days-UntilExpiry` reaches zero—but we completely forget the invariant. We decide to set `daysUntilExpiry` to zero to start with; this way, it will not be zero after the function subtracts one.
>
> We have violated the invariant, and this results in the system crashing when it tries to calculate the `urgency` of any light bulb: `Error: Division by zero`.

We can improve maintainability by explicitly checking properties, thereby removing invariants. However, doing so changes what the code does, which refactoring is not allowed to do, as we will see in the next section. Instead, refactoring tends to improve maintainability by moving the invariants closer together so they are easier to see. This is called *localizing invariants*: things that change together should be together.

2.1.2 *Maintaining code . . . without changing what it does*

"What does the code do?" is an interesting, albeit somewhat metaphysical, question. Our first instinct is to think of code as a *black box* and say that we may change whatever goes on inside as long as it is indistinguishable from the outside. If we put a value in, we should get the same result before and after a refactoring—even if the result is an exception.

This is mostly true, with one notable exception: we may change performance. Specifically, we rarely care if the code gets slower while refactoring. There are multiple reasons for this. First, in most systems, performance is less valuable than readability and maintainability. Second, if performance is important, it should be handled in a separate phase from refactoring, guided by profiling tools or performance experts. We discuss optimization in much more detail in chapter 12.

When we refactor, we need to consider the boundaries of our black box. How much code do we intend to change? The more code we include, the more things we can change. This is especially important when working with other people, because if someone makes changes to code we are refactoring, we can end up with nasty merge conflicts. We essentially need to *reserve* the code we are refactoring so no one else changes it. The less code we reserve, the lower the risk of our changes conflicting. As such, determining the appropriate scope of our refactoring is a difficult and important balancing act.

To sum up, the three pillars of refactoring are

1. Improving readability by communicating intent
2. Improving maintainability by localizing invariants
3. Doing 1 and 2 without affecting any code outside our scope

2.2   *Gaining speed, flexibility, and stability*

I already mentioned the advantages of working in a clean codebase: we are more productive, we make fewer mistakes, and it is more fun. Higher maintainability comes with a few extra perks, which we discuss in this section.

There are several levels of refactoring patterns, from concrete and local (like variable renaming) to abstract and global (like introducing design patterns). While I agree that variable naming can add to or subtract from readability, I believe the most significant impact on code quality comes from architectural changes. In this book, the closest we come to intra-method-level refactoring is discussing good method naming.

2.2.1   *Favoring composition over inheritance*

The fact that nonlocal invariants are hard to maintain is not new. The endearingly named Gang of Four (Erich Gamma, Richard Helm, Ralph Johnson, and John Vlissides) published the book *Design Patterns* (Addison-Wesley) back in 1994, and all those years ago, they recommended against a common way to accidentally introduce nonlocal invariants: inheritance. Their most famous sentence even tells us how to avoid it: "Favor object composition over inheritance."

That advice is at the center of this book, and most of the refactoring patterns and rules we describe exist specifically to help with *object composition*: that is, objects having references to other objects. Here is a tiny library for birds (the ornithological details are not important). On the left, it uses inheritance; and on the right, it uses composition.

Listing 2.4   Using inheritance

```
interface Bird {
  hasBeak(): boolean;
  canFly(): boolean;
}
class CommonBird implements Bird {
  hasBeak() { return true; }
  canFly() { return true; }
}
class Penguin extends CommonBird {      ◁
  canFly() { return false; }
}
                                    Inheritance
```

Listing 2.5   Using composition

```
interface Bird {
  hasBeak(): boolean;
  canFly(): boolean;
}
class CommonBird implements Bird {
  hasBeak() { return true; }
  canFly() { return true; }
}
                                    Composition
class Penguin implements Bird {
  private bird = new CommonBird();    ◁
  hasBeak() { return bird.hasBeak(); } ◁
  canFly() { return false; }
}
                               We have to
                           manually forward calls.
```

In this book, we talk a lot more about the advantages of the right side. But to give a bit of foreshadowing, imagine adding a new method to `Bird` called `canSwim`. In both cases, we add this method to `CommonBird`.

Listing 2.6   Using inheritance

```
class CommonBird implements Bird {
  // ...
  canSwim() { return false; }
}
```

In listing 2.5, the example with composition, we still have a compiler error in Penguin because it does not implement the new canSwim method, so we have to manually add it and decide whether a penguin can swim or not. In the case where we simply want Penguin to behave like other birds, this is trivial to implement, like hasBeak. Conversely, the inheritance example silently assumes that a Penguin cannot swim, so we have to remember to override canSwim. Human memory has often proven to be a fragile dependency, especially when our focus is consumed by the new feature we are working on.

FLEXIBILITY

A system that is built around composition allows us to combine and reuse code in a much more fine-grained manner than we could otherwise. Working with systems that use composition heavily is like playing with LEGO blocks. When everything is built to fit together, it is amazingly fast to swap out parts or build new things by combining existing components. This flexibility becomes more important when we realize that most systems end up being used in ways the original programmers didn't imagine.

2.2.2   *Changing code by addition rather than modification*

Perhaps the greatest advantage of composition is that it enables *change by addition*. This means it is possible to add or change functionality without affecting other existing functionality—in some cases, without even changing any existing code. We return to how this is technically possible throughout the book; here, we consider some of the implications of change by addition. This property is also sometimes referred to as the *open-closed principle*, which means components should be open for extension (addition) but closed for modification.

PROGRAMMING SPEED

As described earlier, one of the first things we do when we need to implement something new or fix a bug is consider the surrounding code, to ensure that we do not break anything. However, if we can make our changes without touching any of the other code, we can save all that time.

Of course, if we just keep adding code, our codebase quickly grows, which can also be a problem. We need to pay extra attention to which code is being used and which is not. We should delete unused code as quickly as possible. We will return to this point also throughout the book.

STABILITY

When we follow a change-by-addition mindset, it is always possible to preserve the existing code. It is easy to implement functionality to fall back on the old functionality if the new code fails. This way, we can ensure that we never introduce new errors in existing functionality. Adding that on top of making fewer errors due to localizing invariants leads to much more stable systems.

2.3 *Refactoring and your daily work*

I said in the introduction that refactoring should be part of any programmer's daily routine. If we deliver unrefactored code, we are only borrowing time from the next programmer. Even worse, due to the negative factors described up to this point, there is an interest rate on poor software architecture. Therefore, we usually call it *technical debt*; we discuss this concept in greater detail in chapter 9. I already stated the two variants of daily refactoring that I recommend:

- In a legacy system, start by refactoring before making any changes. Then follow the regular workflow.
- After making any changes to the code, refactor.

Making sure you refactor before you deliver code is also sometimes referred to as

Always leave a place better than you found it.

—The Boy Scout rule

2.3.1 *Refactoring as a method for learning*

A final point about refactoring is that, like many things, it takes time to learn; but eventually, it becomes automatic. Seeing and experiencing the advantages of better code changes the way we write and think about code. Once we have a little more stability, we start thinking about how we can exploit this stability. One example is increasing our deployment frequency, which usually gives even more stability. With flexibility, it is possible to build configuration management or feature-toggling systems, the maintenance of which would be infeasible without the flexibility.

Refactoring is a completely different way to study code. It gives us a unique perspective. Sometimes we're given code that would take hours or days to understand. The next chapter demonstrates that refactoring allows us to improve code even without understanding it. This way, we can digest small portions while we are working on the code until the final result is very easy to understand.

> **Refactoring as an intro task**
> Refactoring is often used as an introductory task for new team members, so they can work with the code and learn in a safe environment without having to deal with customers right away. While this is a nice practice, it is only possible if we have neglected our daily due diligence—which I, of course, do not condone.

As I have said, there are many advantages to both learning and practicing refactoring. I hope you are excited to go on this journey with me into the world of refactoring!

2.4 *Defining the "domain" in a software context*

Software is a model of specific aspects of real life, whether it is code to automate a process, track or simulate real-world events, or do something else. There is always a real-world counterpart to software. We call this real-world component the *domain* of software. This domain typically comes with users and experts, its own language, and its own culture.

In part 1 of the book, the domain is the 2D puzzle game. The users are players, and the domain experts are the game or level designers. We have already seen how the game uses its own language by introducing words such as "flux" that the player can "eat." Finally, video games come with a lot of culture in the form of expectations for how we can interact with them. An example is that people familiar with video games readily accept that some game objects are subject to gravity (stones and boxes) while others are not (keys and the player).

When developing software, we often have to work closely with domain experts, which means we must learn their language and culture. Programming languages do not allow for any ambiguity; therefore, we sometimes have to explore new corner cases unfamiliar even to the experts. As a result, programming is primarily about learning and communicating.

Summary

- Refactoring is about making the code communicate its intention and localizing invariants without changing the functionality.
- Favoring composition over inheritance leads to change by addition, by which we gain developer speed, flexibility, and stability.
- We should make refactoring part of our daily work to prevent accumulating technical debt.
- Practicing refactoring gives us a unique perspective on code, which leads us to come up with better solutions.

Part 1

Learn by refactoring a computer game

In part 1, we go through a reasonable-looking codebase and improve it step by step. While doing so, we introduce a set of rules and build a small catalog of powerful refactoring patterns.

We improve the code in four phases, each with a dedicated chapter: shattering long functions, making type codes work, fusing similar code together, and, finally, defending the data. Each chapter builds on the previous one, so some transformations are temporary. If the code or an instruction feels weird or looks ugly, be patient; it will probably change.

Don't panic.

—Douglas Adams, *The Hitchhiker's Guide to the Galaxy*

Shatter long functions

This chapter covers

- Identifying overly long methods with FIVE LINES
- Working with code without looking at the specifics
- Breaking up long methods with EXTRACT METHOD
- Balancing abstraction levels with EITHER CALL OR PASS
- Isolating `if` statements with `if` ONLY AT THE START

Code can easily get messy and confusing, even when following the Don't Repeat Yourself (DRY) and Keep It Simple, Stupid (KISS) guidelines. Some strong contributors to this messiness are as follows:

- Methods are doing multiple different things.
- We use low-level primitive operations (array accesses, arithmetic operations, etc.).
- We lack human-readable text, like comments and good method and variable naming.

Unfortunately, knowing these issues is not enough to determine exactly what is wrong, let alone how to deal with it.

In this chapter, we describe a concrete way to identify methods that likely have too many responsibilities. As an example, we look at a specific method in our 2D puzzle game that is doing too much: draw. We show a structured, safe way to improve the method while eliminating comments. Then, we generalize this process to a reusable refactoring pattern: EXTRACT METHOD (P3.2.1). Continuing with the same example draw method, we learn how to identify another problem of mixing different levels of abstraction and how EXTRACT METHOD can also alleviate this issue. In the process, we learn about good method-naming habits.

After concluding our work with draw, we continue with another example—the update method—and repeat the process, refining how we work with the code without diving into the details of it. This example teaches us to identify a different symptom that a method is doing too much; and through EXTRACT METHOD, we learn how to improve readability by renaming variables.

We should also note that we often distinguish between methods (defined on objects) and functions (static or outside classes). This can be a little confusing. Luckily, TypeScript helps us because we have to put **function** when we define functions and not when we define methods. If you still find this distinction distracting, you can simply replace *function* with *method*, as all rules and refactorings apply equally to both.

Assuming you have set up the tools and downloaded the code as described in the appendix, let's jump into the code in the file index.ts. Remember, you can always check whether your code is up to date with any top-level section in the book by running, for instance, git diff section-3.1. If you get lost, you can use, for instance, git reset --hard section-3.1 to get a clean copy of the code at a top-level section. Once we have the code in front of us, we want to improve its quality. But where do we begin?

3.1   *Establishing our first rule: Why five lines?*

To answer this question, we introduce the most fundamental rule in this book: FIVE LINES. This is a simple rule stating that no method should have more than five lines. In this book, FIVE LINES is the ultimate goal, because adhering to this rule is a huge improvement all on its own.

3.1.1   *Rule: FIVE LINES*

STATEMENT
A method should not contain more than five lines, excluding { and }.

EXPLANATION
A line, sometimes called a *statement*, refers to an **if**, a **for**, a **while**, or anything ending with a semicolon: that is, assignments, method calls, **return**, and so on. We discount whitespace and braces: { and }.

We can transform any method so it adheres to this rule. Here's an easy way to see how this is possible: if we have a method with 20 lines, we can create a helper method with the first 10 lines and a method with the last 10 lines. The original method is now 2 lines: one calling the first helper and one calling the second. We can repeat this process until we have as few as 2 lines in each method.

The specific limit is less important than having a limit. In my experience, it works to set the limit to whatever value is required to implement a pass through your fundamental data structure.

In this book, we are working in a 2D setting, which means our fundamental data structure is a 2D array. The following two functions do a pass through a 2D array: one checks whether the array contains an even number, and the other finds the array's minimum element, each in exactly five lines.

Listing 3.1 Function to check whether a 2D array contains an even number

```
function containsEven(arr: number[][]) {
  for (let x = 0; x < arr.length; x++) {
    for (let y = 0; y < arr[x].length; y++) {
      if (arr[x][y] % 2 === 0) {
        return true;
      }
    }
  }
  return false;
}
```

In TypeScript ...

We do not have different types for integers and floating points. We have only one type to cover both: `number`.

Listing 3.2 Function to find the minimum element in a 2D array

```
function minimum(arr: number[][]) {
  let result = Number.POSITIVE_INFINITY;
  for (let x = 0; x < arr.length; x++) {
    for (let y = 0; y < arr[x].length; y++) {
      result = Math.min(arr[x][y], result);
    }
  }
  return result;
}
```

In TypeScript ...

We use `let` to declare variables. `let` tries to infer the type, but we can specify it with, for example, `let a: number = 5;`. We *never* use `var`, due to its weird scoping rules: we can define variables after their use. Here, the code on the left is valid, but probably not what we meant. The code on the right gives an error, as we expect.

Bad	Good
`a = 5;` `var a: number;`	`a = 5;` `let a: number;`

To clarify how we count lines, here is the same example we saw at the beginning of chapter 2. We count four lines: one for each `if` (including `else`) and one for each semicolon.

Listing 3.3   Four-line method from chapter 2

```
function isTrue(bool: boolean) {
  if (bool)
    return true;
  else      return false;
}
```

SMELL

Having long methods is a smell in itself. This is because long methods are difficult to work with; you have to keep all of a method's logic in your head at once. But "long methods" begs the question: what is *long*?

To answer this question, we draw from another smell: Methods should do one thing. If FIVE LINES is exactly what is necessary to do one meaningful thing, then this limit also prevents us from breaking that smell. We sometimes work in settings where the fundamental data structure is different in different places in the code. Once we are comfortable with this rule, we can start varying the number of lines to fit specific examples. This is fine; but in practice, the number of lines often ends up being around five.

INTENT

Left unchecked, methods tend to grow over time as we add more and more functionality to them. This makes them increasingly difficult to understand. Imposing a size limit on our methods prevents us from sliding into this bad territory.

I argue that four methods, each with 5 lines of code, can be much more quickly and easily understood than one method with 20 lines. This is because each method's name is an opportunity to communicate the intent of the code. Essentially, method naming is equivalent to putting a comment at least every 5 lines. Plus, if small methods are properly named, finding a good name for a big function is easier, too.

REFERENCES

To help achieve this rule, see the refactoring EXTRACT METHOD. You can read more about the smell "Methods should do one thing" in Robert C. Martin's book *Clean Code* (Pearson, 2008) and the "Long methods" smell in Martin Fowler's book *Refactoring* (Addison-Wesley Professional, 1999).

3.2　*Introducing a refactoring pattern to break up functions*

While the FIVE LINES rule is easy to understand, achieving it isn't always. Therefore we return to it many times, tackling increasingly difficult examples throughout this part of the book.

With the rule in hand, we are ready to dive into the code. We start with a function named `draw`. Our first stab at understanding the code should always be to consider the function name. The danger is getting bogged down trying to understand every single line—that would take a lot of time and be unproductive. Instead, we begin by looking at the "shape" of the code.

We are trying to identify groups of lines related to the same thing. To make these groups clear, we add blank lines where we think the group should be. Sometimes we add comments to help us remember what the grouping is related to. In general, we strive to avoid comments, as they tend to go out of date, or they are used like deodorant on bad code; but in this case, the comments are temporary, as we'll see in a moment.

Often, the original programmers had groupings in mind and inserted blank lines. Sometimes they included comments. At this point, it is tempting to look at what the code is doing—but since the code is not in a pristine state, that would be counterproductive! You may have heard the saying "The best way to eat an elephant is one bite at a time." This is what we are doing now. Without digesting the entire function, we cut it up and process each piece while it is small and easy to understand.

In figure 3.1, to help avoid getting distracted by the details, we have blurred out all the nonessential lines so we can focus on the structure. (We only do this here in the beginning.) Even without being able to see any specifics, we notice the two groupings, each starting with a comment: `// Draw map` and `// Draw player`.

We can take advantage of those comments by doing the following:

1　Create a new (empty) method, `drawMap`.

2　Where the comment is, put a call to `drawMap`.

3　Select all the lines in the group we identified, and then cut them and paste them as the body of `drawMap`.

Figure 3.1   Initial draw function

Repeating the same process for drawPlayer results in the transformation shown in figures 3.2 and 3.3.

Figure 3.2 Before

```
function draw() {
```

// Draw map

// Draw player

}

Figure 3.3 After

```
function draw() {
```

```
    drawMap(g);
    drawPlayer(g);
}
function drawMap(g: Canvas          ) {
```

```
    }
}
function drawPlayer(g: Canvas          ) {
```

```
}
```

Now let's take a look at how that works with actual code. We begin with the code in listing 3.4; notice that we can see the same structure, still without looking at what any individual line does.

Listing 3.4 Initial

```
function draw() {
  let canvas = document.getElementById("GameCanvas") as HTMLCanvasElement;
  let g = canvas.getContext("2d");

  g.clearRect(0, 0, canvas.width, canvas.height);

  // Draw map                              ⟵——      Comments marking
  for (let y = 0; y < map.length; y++) {            the start of a logical
    for (let x = 0; x < map[y].length; x++) {       grouping of lines
```

```
    if (map[y][x] === Tile.FLUX)
      g.fillStyle = "#ccffcc";
    else if (map[y][x] === Tile.UNBREAKABLE)
      g.fillStyle = "#999999";
    else if (map[y][x] === Tile.STONE || map[y][x] === Tile.FALLING_STONE)
      g.fillStyle = "#0000cc";
    else if (map[y][x] === Tile.BOX || map[y][x] === Tile.FALLING_BOX)
      g.fillStyle = "#8b4513";
    else if (map[y][x] === Tile.KEY1 || map[y][x] === Tile.LOCK1)
      g.fillStyle = "#ffcc00";
    else if (map[y][x] === Tile.KEY2 || map[y][x] === Tile.LOCK2)
      g.fillStyle = "#00ccff";

    if (map[y][x] !== Tile.AIR && map[y][x] !== Tile.PLAYER)
      g.fillRect(x * TILE_SIZE, y * TILE_SIZE, TILE_SIZE, TILE_SIZE);
  }
}
// Draw player
g.fillStyle = "#ff0000";
g.fillRect(playerx * TILE_SIZE, playery * TILE_SIZE, TILE_SIZE, TILE_SIZE);
}
```

Comments marking the start of a logical grouping of lines

In TypeScript …

We use **as** to convert between types, like casts in other languages. It does not return `null` when a conversion is invalid, like **as** in C#.

We follow the steps described earlier:

1 Create a new (empty) method `drawMap`.
2 Where the comment is, put a call to `drawMap`.
3 Select all the lines in the grouping we identified, and then cut them and paste them as the body of `drawMap`.

When we try to compile now, we get quite a few errors. This is because the variable g is no longer in scope. We can fix this by first hovering our cursor over g in the original draw method. This lets us know its type, which we use to introduce a parameter g: `CanvasRenderingContext2D` in `drawMap`.

Compiling again tells us that there is an error where we call `drawMap` because we are missing the parameter g. Again, this is easy to fix: we pass g as an argument.

Now we repeat the same process for `drawPlayer`, and this is what we end up with—exactly as we expected. Notice that there is still no need to examine what the code is doing any deeper than the method names.

Listing 3.5   After EXTRACT METHOD

```
function draw() {
  let canvas = document.getElementById("GameCanvas") as HTMLCanvasElement;
  let g = canvas.getContext("2d");
```

```
        g.clearRect(0, 0, canvas.width, canvas.height);

        drawMap(g);
        drawPlayer(g);
    }

    function drawMap(g: CanvasRenderingContext2D) {
        for (let y = 0; y < map.length; y++) {
            for (let x = 0; x < map[y].length; x++) {
                if (map[y][x] === Tile.FLUX)
                    g.fillStyle = "#ccffcc";
                else if (map[y][x] === Tile.UNBREAKABLE)
                    g.fillStyle = "#999999";
                else if (map[y][x] === Tile.STONE || map[y][x] === Tile.FALLING_STONE)
                    g.fillStyle = "#0000cc";
                else if (map[y][x] === Tile.BOX || map[y][x] === Tile.FALLING_BOX)
                    g.fillStyle = "#8b4513";
                else if (map[y][x] === Tile.KEY1 || map[y][x] === Tile.LOCK1)
                    g.fillStyle = "#ffcc00";
                else if (map[y][x] === Tile.KEY2 || map[y][x] === Tile.LOCK2)
                    g.fillStyle = "#00ccff";

                if (map[y][x] !== Tile.AIR && map[y][x] !== Tile.PLAYER)
                    g.fillRect(x * TILE_SIZE, y * TILE_SIZE, TILE_SIZE, TILE_SIZE);
            }
        }
    }

    function drawPlayer(g: CanvasRenderingContext2D) {
        g.fillStyle = "#ff0000";
        g.fillRect(playerx * TILE_SIZE, playery * TILE_SIZE, TILE_SIZE, TILE_SIZE);
    }
```

New function and call corresponding to the first comment

New function and call corresponding to the second comment

We have completed our first two refactorings. Congratulations! The process we just went through is a standard pattern—a refactoring pattern—that we call EXTRACT METHOD.

> **NOTE** Because we are only moving lines around, the risk of introducing errors is minimal, especially since the compiler told us when we forgot parameters.

We use the comments as the method names; therefore, the functions' names and the comments convey the same information. Thus we eliminate the comments. We also eliminate the now-obsolete blank lines that we used to group the lines.

3.2.1 *Refactoring pattern: EXTRACT METHOD*

DESCRIPTION

EXTRACT METHOD takes part of one method and extracts it into its own method. This can be done mechanically, and indeed, many modern IDEs have this refactoring pattern built right in. This alone probably makes it safe; computers rarely mess up such things. But there is also a safe way to do it by hand.

Doing so can get complicated if we assign to multiple parameters or **return** only in some paths and not all. We do not consider these situations here as they are rare, and we can usually simplify them by reordering or duplicating lines in the methods.

> **Pro tip**
> As **returning** in only some branches of an **if** can prevent us from extracting a method, I recommend starting from the bottom of the method and working upward. This has the effect of pushing the **return** upward, so we eventually **return** in all branches.

PROCESS

1. Mark the lines to extract by placing blank lines around them, and possibly comments as well.
2. Create a new (empty) method with the desired name.
3. At the top of the grouping, put a call to the new method.
4. Select all the lines in the group, and then cut them and paste them as the body of the new method.
5. Compile.
6. Introduce parameters, thus causing errors.
7. If we assign to *one* of these parameters (let's call it p):
   a. Put **return** p; as the last thing in the new method.
   b. Put the assignment p = newMethod(...); at the call site.
8. Compile.
9. Pass arguments, thus fixing the errors.
10. Remove obsolete blank lines and comments.

EXAMPLE

Let's see an example of how the full process works. Here we again have a function to find the minimum element in a 2D array. We have determined that it is too long, so we want to extract the part between the blank lines.

Listing 3.6   Function to find the minimum element of a 2D array

```
function minimum(arr: number[][]) {
  let result = Number.POSITIVE_INFINITY;
  for (let x = 0; x < arr.length; x++)
    for (let y = 0; y < arr[x].length; y++)

      if (result > arr[x][y])        Lines we want
        result = arr[x][y];          to extract

  return result;
}
```

We follow the process:

1   Mark the lines to extract by placing blank lines around them, and possibly comments as well.

2   Create a new method, `min`.

3   At the top of the grouping, put a call to `min`.

4   Cut and paste the lines in the group into the body of the new method.

Listing 3.7 Before

```
function minimum(arr: number[][]) {
  let result = Number.POSITIVE_INFINITY;
  for (let x = 0; x < arr.length; x++)
    for (let y = 0; y < arr[x].length; y++)


      if (result > arr[x][y])
        result = arr[x][y];

  return result;
}
```

Listing 3.8 After (1/3)

```
function minimum(arr: number[][]) {
  let result = Number.POSITIVE_INFINITY;
  for (let x = 0; x < arr.length; x++)
    for (let y = 0; y < arr[x].length; y++)


      min();

  return result;
}

function min() {
  if (result > arr[x][y])
    result = arr[x][y];
}
```

New method and call

Extracted lines from before

5   Compile.

6   Introduce parameters for `result`, `arr`, `x`, and `y`.

7   The extracted function assigns to `result`. So, we need to

   a   Put **return** `result;` as the last thing in `min`.

   b   Put the assignment `result = min(...);` at the call site.

Listing 3.9 Before

```
function minimum(arr: number[][]) {
  let result = Number.POSITIVE_INFINITY;
  for (let x = 0; x < arr.length; x++)
    for (let y = 0; y < arr[x].length; y++)

      min();

  return result;
}

function min() {


  if (result > arr[x][y])
    result = arr[x][y];


}
```

Listing 3.10 After (2/3)

```
function minimum(arr: number[][]) {
  let result = Number.POSITIVE_INFINITY;
  for (let x = 0; x < arr.length; x++)
    for (let y = 0; y < arr[x].length; y++)

      result = min();

  return result;
}

function min(
  result: number, arr: number[][],
  x: number, y: number)
{
  if (result > arr[x][y])
    result = arr[x][y];
  return result;
}
```

Assignment to result

Added parameters

Added return statement

8 Compile.

9 We pass the arguments causing errors result, arr, x, and y.

10 Finally, we remove the obsolete blank lines.

Listing 3.11 Before

```
function minimum(arr: number[][]) {
  let result = Number.POSITIVE_INFINITY;
  for (let x = 0; x < arr.length; x++)
    for (let y = 0; y < arr[x].length; y++)
      result = min();
  return result;
}

function min(
  result: number, arr: number[][],
  x: number, y: number)
{
  if (result > arr[x][y])
    result = arr[x][y];
  return result;
}
```

Listing 3.12 After (3/3)

```
function minimum(arr: number[][]) {
  let result = Number.POSITIVE_INFINITY;
  for (let x = 0; x < arr.length; x++)
    for (let y = 0; y < arr[x].length; y++)
      result = min(result, arr, x, y);    ←─┐
  return result;                             Arguments added
}                                            and blank lines
                                             removed
function min(
  result: number, arr: number[][],
  x: number, y: number)
{
  if (result > arr[x][y])
    result = arr[x][y];
  return result;
}
```

You may be thinking that it would be better to use the built-in Math.min or arr[x][y] as an argument instead of all three separately. If you can get there safely, that may be a better approach for you. But the important lesson to take from this example is that the transformation, although slightly cumbersome, is *safe*. We can easily get into trouble trying to be clever, which often isn't worth it.

We can trust that this process does not break anything. The confidence that we have not broken anything is more valuable than perfect output, especially when we have not yet studied what the code does. The more things we have to keep track of, the more likely we are to forget something. The compiler does not forget, and this process is specialized to exploit that fact. We would rather produce unusual-looking code safely than pretty code with less confidence. (If we were feeling confident as a result of something else, like lots of automated testing, we could take more risks; but this isn't the case here.)

FURTHER READING

If we want to get a pretty result, we can combine a few other refactoring patterns. We do not go into depth about these, as we only consider inter-method refactoring patterns in this book. But we outline the process here if you want to investigate it further on your own:

1 Execute another small refactoring pattern, "Extract common subexpression," which in this case introduces a temporary variable **let** tmp = arr[x][y]; outside the grouping and replaces the occurrences of arr[x][y] inside the grouping with tmp.

2 Use EXTRACT METHOD as described earlier.

3 Perform INLINE LOCAL VARIABLE, where we undo the work of "Extract common subexpression" by replacing `tmp` with `arr[x][y]`, and delete the temporary variable `tmp`.

You can read more about all of these patterns, including EXTRACT METHOD, in Martin Fowler's book, *Refactoring*.

3.3 *Breaking up functions to balancing abstraction*

We have achieved the goal of five lines for our seed function, `draw`. Of course, `drawMap` conflicts with the rule; we return to fix this in chapter 4. But we are not quite done with `draw`: it also conflicts with another rule.

3.3.1 *Rule: EITHER CALL OR PASS*

STATEMENT

A function should either call methods on an object or pass the object as an argument, but not both.

EXPLANATION

Once we start introducing more methods and passing things around as parameters, we can end up with uneven responsibilities. For example, a function might be both performing low-level operations, such as setting an index in an array, and also passing the same array as an argument to a more complicated function. This code would be difficult to read because we would need to switch between low-level operations and high-level method names. It is much easier to stay at one level of abstraction.

Consider this function, which finds the average of an array. Notice that it uses both the high-level abstraction `sum(arr)` and the low-level `arr.length`.

Listing 3.13 Function to find the average of an array

```
function average(arr: number[]) {
  return sum(arr) / arr.length;
}
```

This code violates our rule. Here is a better implementation that abstracts away how to find the length.

Listing 3.14 Before

```
function average(arr: number[]) {
  return sum(arr) / arr.length;
}
```

Listing 3.15 After

```
function average(arr: number[]) {
  return sum(arr) / size(arr);
}
```

SMELL

The statement "The content of a function should be on the same level of abstraction" is so powerful that it is a smell in its own right. However, as with most other smells, it is hard to quantify what it means, let alone how to address it. It is trivial to spot whether something is passed as an argument and just as easy to spot if it has a . next to it.

INTENT

When we introduce abstraction by extracting some details out of a method, this rule forces us to also extract other details. This way, we make sure the level of abstraction inside the method always stays the same.

REFERENCES

To help achieve this rule, see the refactoring EXTRACT METHOD. You can read more about the smell "The content of a function should be on the same level of abstraction" in Robert C. Martin's book *Clean Code.*

3.3.2   *Applying the rule*

Again without looking at the specifics, if we examine our draw method as it currently looks, in figure 3.4, we quickly spot that we violate this rule. The variable g is passed as a parameter, and we also call a method on it.

```
function draw() {
    [                                    ]
    [                    ]

    g.[                              ]

    [        ](g);
    [          ](g);
}
```

Figure 3.4   g being both passed and called

We fix violations of this rule by using EXTRACT METHOD. But what do we extract? Here we need to look a bit at the specifics. There are blank lines in the code, but if we extract the line with g.clearRect, we end up passing canvas as an argument and also calling canvas.getContext—thus violating the rule again.

Listing 3.16   draw as it currently looks

```
function draw() {
    let canvas = document.getElementById("GameCanvas") as HTMLCanvasElement;
    let g = canvas.getContext("2d");

    g.clearRect(0, 0, canvas.width, canvas.height);          ◁──┐ Calls a
                                                                 │ method on g
    drawMap(g);              g is passed as
    drawPlayer(g);           an argument.
}
```

Instead, we decide to extract the first three lines together. Every time we perform EXTRACT METHOD, it's a great opportunity to make the code more readable by introducing a good method name. So, before we extract the lines, let's discuss what a good name actually is.

3.4   *Properties of a good function name*

I cannot supply universal rules for a *good name*, but I can provide a few properties that a good name should have:

- It should be honest. It should describe the function's intention.
- It should be complete. It should capture everything the function does.
- It should be understandable for someone working in the domain. Use words from the domain you are working in. This also has the advantage of making communication more efficient and making it easier to talk about the code with teammates and customers.

For the first time, we need to consider what the code is doing, because we have no comments to follow. Luckily, we have already significantly reduced the number of lines we need to consider: only three.

The first line fetches the HTML element to draw onto, the second line instantiates the graphics to draw on, and the third clears the canvas. In short, the code creates a graphics object.

Listing 3.17   Before

```
function draw() {
  let canvas = document
      .getElementById("GameCanvas")
      as HTMLCanvasElement;
  let g = canvas.getContext("2d");

  g.clearRect(0, 0,
    canvas.width, canvas.height);

  drawMap(g);
  drawPlayer(g);
}
```

New method and call

Listing 3.18   After

```
function createGraphics() {
  let canvas = document
      .getElementById("GameCanvas")
      as HTMLCanvasElement;
  let g = canvas.getContext("2d");
  g.clearRect(0, 0,
    canvas.width, canvas.height);
  return g;
}

function draw() {
  let g = createGraphics();
  drawMap(g);
  drawPlayer(g);
}
```

Original lines

Notice that we no longer need any of the blank lines, as the code is easy to understand even without them.

draw is finished, and we can move on. Let's start over and go through the same process with another long function: update. Again, even without reading any of the code, we can identify two clear groups of lines separated by a blank line.

Listing 3.19   Initial

```
function update() {
  while (inputs.length > 0) {
    let current = inputs.pop();
    if (current === Input.LEFT)
      moveHorizontal(-1);
    else if (current === Input.RIGHT)
      moveHorizontal(1);
    else if (current === Input.UP)
      moveVertical(-1);
    else if (current === Input.DOWN)
      moveVertical(1);
  }

  for (let y = map.length - 1; y >= 0; y--) {
    for (let x = 0; x < map[y].length; x++) {
      if ((map[y][x] === Tile.STONE || map[y][x] === Tile.FALLING_STONE)
        && map[y + 1][x] === Tile.AIR) {
        map[y + 1][x] = Tile.FALLING_STONE;
        map[y][x] = Tile.AIR;
      } else if ((map[y][x] === Tile.BOX || map[y][x] === Tile.FALLING_BOX)
        && map[y + 1][x] === Tile.AIR) {
        map[y + 1][x] = Tile.FALLING_BOX;
        map[y][x] = Tile.AIR;
      } else if (map[y][x] === Tile.FALLING_STONE) {
        map[y][x] = Tile.STONE;
      } else if (map[y][x] === Tile.FALLING_BOX) {
        map[y][x] = Tile.BOX;
      }
    }
  }
}
```

Blank line separating
two groupings

We can naturally split this code into two smaller functions. What should we call them? Both groups are still pretty complex, so we want to postpone understanding them further. We notice superficially that in the first group, the predominant word is input, and in the second, the predominant word is map. We know we are splitting a function called update, so as a first draft, we can combine these words to get the function names updateInputs and updateMap. updateMap is fine; however, we probably do not "update" the inputs. So, we decide to use another naming trick and use handle, instead: handleInputs.

NOTE   When choosing names like this, always come back later, when the functions are smaller, to assess whether you can improve the names.

Listing 3.20   After EXTRACT METHOD

```
function update() {
  handleInputs();
  updateMap();
}

function handleInputs() {
  while (inputs.length > 0) {
    let current = inputs.pop();
    if (current === Input.LEFT)
      moveHorizontal(-1);
    else if (current === Input.RIGHT)
      moveHorizontal(1);
    else if (current === Input.UP)
      moveVertical(-1);
    else if (current === Input.DOWN)
      moveVertical(1);
  }
}

function updateMap() {
  for (let y = map.length - 1; y >= 0; y--) {
    for (let x = 0; x < map[y].length; x++) {
      if ((map[y][x] === Tile.STONE || map[y][x] === Tile.FALLING_STONE)
          && map[y + 1][x] === Tile.AIR) {
        map[y + 1][x] = Tile.FALLING_STONE;
        map[y][x] = Tile.AIR;
      } else if ((map[y][x] === Tile.BOX || map[y][x] === Tile.FALLING_BOX)
          && map[y + 1][x] === Tile.AIR) {
        map[y + 1][x] = Tile.FALLING_BOX;
        map[y][x] = Tile.AIR;
      } else if (map[y][x] === Tile.FALLING_STONE) {
        map[y][x] = Tile.STONE;
      } else if (map[y][x] === Tile.FALLING_BOX) {
        map[y][x] = Tile.BOX;
      }
    }
  }
}
```

Extracted
first grouping
and call

Extracted
second
grouping
and call

Already, update is compliant with our rules. We are finished with it. This may not seem like a big deal, but we are getting closer to the magic five lines we are going for.

3.5   *Breaking up functions that are doing too much*

We're finished with update, so we can continue with, for instance, one of the functions we just introduced: updateMap. In this function, it is not natural to add more whitespace. Therefore, we need another rule: place **if** ONLY AT THE START of a function.

3.5.1 *Rule:* IF ONLY AT THE START

STATEMENT

If you have an `if`, it should be the first thing in the function.

EXPLANATION

We have already discussed that functions should do only one thing. Checking something is one thing. So, if a function has an `if`, it should be the first thing in the function. It should also be the *only* thing, in the sense that we should not do anything after it; but we can avoid having something after it by extracting that separately, as we have seen multiple times.

When we say that `if` should be the only thing a method does, we do not need to extract its body, and we also should not separate it from its `else`. Both the body and the `else` are part of the code structure, and we rely on this structure to guide our efforts so we do not have to understand the code. Behavior and structure are closely tied, and as we are refactoring, we are not supposed to change the behavior—so we shouldn't change the structure, either.

The following example shows a function that prints the primes from 2 to *n*.

Listing 3.21 Function to print all primes from 2 to *n*

```
function reportPrimes(n: number) {
  for (let i = 2; i < n; i++)
    if (isPrime(i))
      console.log(`${i} is prime`);
}
```

We have at least two clear responsibilities:

- Loop over the numbers.
- Check whether a number is prime.

Therefore, we should have at least two functions.

Listing 3.22 Before

```
function reportPrimes(n: number) {
  for (let i = 2; i < n; i++)
    if (isPrime(i))
      console.log(`${i} is prime`);
}
```

Listing 3.23 After

```
function reportPrimes(n: number) {
  for (let i = 2; i < n; i++)
    reportIfPrime(i);
}

function reportIfPrime(n: number) {
  if (isPrime(n))
    console.log(`${n} is prime`);
}
```

Every time we check something, it is a responsibility, and it should be handled by one function. Therefore we have this rule.

SMELL

SMELL

This rule—like FIVE LINES—exists to help prevent the smell of functions doing more than one thing.

INTENT

This rule intends to isolate `if` statements because they have a single responsibility, and a chain of `else ifs` represents an atomic unit that we cannot split up. This means the fewest lines we can achieve with EXTRACT METHOD in the context of an `if` with `else ifs` is to extract exactly only that `if` along with its `else ifs`.

REFERENCES

To help achieve this rule, see the refactoring EXTRACT METHOD. You can read more about the smell "Methods should do one thing" in Robert C. Martin's book *Clean Code*.

3.5.2 Applying the rule

It's easy to spot violations of this rule without looking at the specifics of the code. In figure 3.5, there is one big `if` group in the middle of the function.

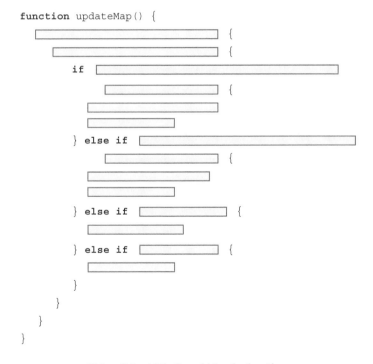

Figure 3.5 `if` in the middle of a function

To figure out what to name the function that we want to extract, we need to take a superficial look at the code we are extracting. There are two predominant words in this group of lines: map and tile. We already have updateMap, so we call the new function updateTile.

Listing 3.24   After EXTRACT METHOD

```
function updateMap() {
  for (let y = map.length - 1; y >= 0; y--) {
    for (let x = 0; x < map[y].length; x++) {
      updateTile(x, y);                                    ←——————┐
    }                                                              │   Extracted
  }                                                                │   method
}                                                                  │   and call
                                                                   │
function updateTile(x: number, y: number) {        ←———————————————┘
  if ((map[y][x] === Tile.STONE || map[y][x] === Tile.FALLING_STONE)
      && map[y + 1][x] === Tile.AIR) {
    map[y + 1][x] = Tile.FALLING_STONE;
    map[y][x] = Tile.AIR;
  } else if ((map[y][x] === Tile.BOX || map[y][x] === Tile.FALLING_BOX)
      && map[y + 1][x] === Tile.AIR) {
    map[y + 1][x] = Tile.FALLING_BOX;
    map[y][x] = Tile.AIR;
  } else if (map[y][x] === Tile.FALLING_STONE) {
    map[y][x] = Tile.STONE;
  } else if (map[y][x] === Tile.FALLING_BOX) {
    map[y][x] = Tile.BOX;
  }
}
```

Now updateMap is within our five-line limit, and we are content with it. We are starting to feel the momentum, so let's quickly perform the same transformation on handle-Inputs.

Listing 3.25   Before

```
function handleInputs() {
  while (inputs.length > 0) {
    let current = inputs.pop();
    if (current === Input.RIGHT)
      moveHorizontal(1);
    else if (current === Input.LEFT)
      moveHorizontal(-1);
    else if (current === Input.DOWN)
      moveVertical(1);
    else if (current === Input.UP)
      moveVertical(-1);
  }
}
```

Listing 3.26   After

```
function handleInputs() {
  while (inputs.length > 0) {
    let current = inputs.pop();
    handleInput(current);            ←——————┐
  }                                          │   Extracted
}                                            │   method
                                             │   and call
function handleInput(input: Input) {  ←——————┘
  if (input === Input.RIGHT)
    moveHorizontal(1);
  else if (input === Input.LEFT)
    moveHorizontal(-1);
  else if (input === Input.DOWN)
    moveVertical(1);
  else if (input === Input.UP)
    moveVertical(-1);
}
```

That completes `handleInputs`. Here we see another readability advantage of EXTRACT METHOD: it lets us give parameters new names that are more informative in their new context. `current` is a fine name for a variable in a loop, but in the new `handleInput` function, `input` is a much better name.

We did introduce a function that seems problematic. `handleInput` is already compact, and it is hard to see how we can make it compliant with the five-line rule. This chapter has only considered EXTRACT METHOD and rules for when to apply it. But since the body of each **if** is already a single line, and we cannot extract part of an **else if** chain, we cannot apply EXTRACT METHOD to `handleInput`. However, as we will see in the next chapter, there is an elegant solution.

Summary

- The FIVE LINES rule states that methods should have five lines or fewer. It helps identify methods that do more than one thing. We use the refactoring pattern EXTRACT METHOD to break up these long methods, and we eliminate comments by making them method names.

- The EITHER CALL OR PASS rule states that a method should either call methods on an object or pass the object as a parameter, but not both. It helps us identify methods that mix multiple levels of abstraction. We again use EXTRACT METHOD to separate different levels of abstraction.

- Method names should be honest, complete, and understandable. EXTRACT METHOD allows us to rename parameters to further improve readability.

- The rule **if** ONLY AT THE START states that checking a condition using **if** does one thing, so a method should not do anything else. This rule also helps us identify methods that do more than one thing. We use EXTRACT METHOD to isolate these **if**s.

Make type codes work 4

At the end of the last chapter, we had just introduced a handleInput function that we could not use EXTRACT METHOD (P3.2.1) on because we did not want to break up the **else if** chain. Unfortunately, handleInput is not compliant with our fundamental FIVE LINES (R3.1.1) rule, so we cannot leave it as is.

Here's the function.

Listing 4.1 Initial

```
function handleInput(input: Input) {
  if (input === Input.LEFT) moveHorizontal(-1);
  else if (input === Input.RIGHT) moveHorizontal(1);
  else if (input === Input.UP) moveVertical(-1);
  else if (input === Input.DOWN) moveVertical(1);
}
```

4.1 Refactoring a simple if statement

We are stuck. To show how we deal with **else if** chains like this, we start by introducing a new rule.

4.1.1 Rule: NEVER USE IF WITH ELSE

STATEMENT

Never use **if** with **else**, unless we are checking against a data type we do not control.

EXPLANATION

Making decisions is hard. In life, many people try to avoid and postpone making decisions; but in code, we seem eager to use **if-else** statements. I won't dictate what is best in real life, but in code, waiting is definitely better. When we use an **if-else**, we lock in the point at which a decision is made in the code. This makes the code less flexible, as it is not possible to introduce any variation any later than where the **if-else** is located.

We can view **if-else**s as hardcoded decisions. Just as we do not like hardcoded constants in our code, we also do not like hardcoded decisions.

We would prefer never to hardcode a decision—that is, never to use **if**s with **else**s. Unfortunately, we have to pay attention to what we are checking against. For example, we use e.key to check which key is pressed, and it has type string. We cannot modify the implementation of string, so we cannot avoid an **else if** chain.

This should not discourage us, though, because these cases typically occur at the edges of a program, where we get input from outside the application: the user typing something, fetching values from a database, and so on. In these cases, the first thing to do is map the third-party data types into the data types we have control over. In our example game, one such **else if** chain reads the user's input and maps it to our types.

Listing 4.2 Mapping user input into a data type we control

```
window.addEventListener("keydown", e => {
  if (e.key === LEFT_KEY || e.key === "a") inputs.push(Input.LEFT);
  else if (e.key === UP_KEY || e.key === "w") inputs.push(Input.UP);
  else if (e.key === RIGHT_KEY || e.key === "d") inputs.push(Input.RIGHT);
  else if (e.key === DOWN_KEY || e.key === "s") inputs.push(Input.DOWN);
});
```

We don't have control over any of the two data types in the conditions: KeyboardEvent and string. As mentioned, these **else if** chains should be directly connected to I/O, which should be separated from the rest of the application.

Note that we consider standalone **if**s to be *checks* and **if-else**s to be *decisions*. This allows for simple validation at the start of methods where it would be difficult to extract an early **return**, as in the next example. So, this rule specifically targets **else**.

Other than that, this rule is easy to validate: simply look for **else**. Let's revisit an earlier function that takes an array of numbers and gives the average. If we call the previous implementation with an empty array, we get a "division by zero" error. This makes sense because we know the implementation, but it is not helpful for the user; so, we would like to throw a more informative error. Here are two ways to fix that.

Listing 4.3 Before	Listing 4.4 After

```
function average(ar: number[]) {
  if (size(ar) === 0)
    throw "Empty array not allowed";
  else
    return sum(ar) / size(ar);
}
```

```
function assertNotEmpty(ar: number[]) {
  if (size(ar) === 0)
    throw "Empty array not allowed";
}
function average(ar: number[]) {
  assertNotEmpty(ar);
  return sum(ar) / size(ar);
}
```

SMELL

This rule relates to *early binding*, which is a smell. When we compile our program, a behavior—like **if-else** decisions—is resolved and locked into our application and cannot be modified without recompiling. The opposite of this is *late binding*, where the behavior is determined at the last possible moment when the code is run.

Early binding prevents change by addition because we can only change the **if** statement by modifying it. The late-binding property allows us to use change by addition, which is desirable, as discussed in chapter 2.

INTENT

ifs are control-flow operators. This means they determine what code to run next. However, object-oriented programming has much stronger control-flow operators: objects. If we use an interface with two implementations, then we can determine what code to run based on which class we instantiate. In essence, this rule forces us to look for ways to use objects, which are stronger, more flexible tools.

REFERENCES

We discuss late binding in more detail when we look at the REPLACE TYPE CODE WITH CLASSES (P4.1.3) and INTRODUCE STRATEGY PATTERN (P5.4.2) refactoring patterns.

4.1.2 Applying the rule

The first step to get rid of the **if-else** in handleInput is to replace the Input *enum* with an Input *interface*. The values are then replaced with classes. Finally—and this is the brilliant part—because the values are now objects, we can move the code inside the **if**s to methods in each of the classes. It takes a few sections to get there, so be patient. Let's go through it step by step:

1 Introduce a new interface with the temporary name Input2, with methods for the four values in our enum.

Listing 4.5 New interface

```
enum Input {
  RIGHT, LEFT, UP, DOWN
}
interface Input2 {
  isRight(): boolean;
  isLeft(): boolean;
  isUp(): boolean;
  isDown(): boolean;
}
```

2 Create the four classes corresponding to the four enum values. All the methods except the one corresponding to the class should **return false**. Note: These methods are temporary, as we will see later.

Listing 4.6 New classes

```
class Right implements Input2 {
  isRight() { return true; }      ←┐  isRight returns true in
  isLeft() { return false; }       └   the Right class.
  isUp() { return false; }
  isDown() { return false; }       The other methods
}                                  return false.
class Left implements Input2 { ... }
class Up implements Input2 { ... }
class Down implements Input2 { ... }
```

3 Rename the enum to something like RawInput. This causes the compiler to report an error in all the places where we use the enum.

Listing 4.7 Before

```
enum Input {
  RIGHT, LEFT, UP, DOWN
}
```

Listing 4.8 After (1/3)

```
enum RawInput {
  RIGHT, LEFT, UP, DOWN
}
```

4 Change the types from Input to Input2, and replace the equality checks with the new methods.

Listing 4.9   Before

```
function handleInput(input: Input) {
  if (input === Input.LEFT)
    moveHorizontal(-1);
  else if (input === Input.RIGHT)
    moveHorizontal(1);
  else if (input === Input.UP)
    moveVertical(-1);
  else if (input === Input.DOWN)
    moveVertical(1);
}
```

Listing 4.10   After (2/3)

```
function handleInput(input: Input2) {
  if (input.isLeft())
    moveHorizontal(-1);
  else if (input.isRight())
    moveHorizontal(1);
  else if (input.isUp())
    moveVertical(-1);
  else if (input.isDown())
    moveVertical(1);
}
```

Changes type to use the interface

Uses the new methods instead of equality checks

5 Fix the last errors by changing.

Listing 4.11   Before

```
Input.RIGHT
Input.LEFT
Input.UP
Input.DOWN
```

Listing 4.12   After (3/3)

```
new Right()
new Left()
new Up()
new Down()
```

6 Finally, rename `Input2` to `Input` everywhere.

At this point, here is what the code looks like.

Listing 4.13   Before

```
window.addEventListener("keydown", e =>
{
  if (e.key === LEFT_KEY
      || e.key === "a")
    inputs.push(Input.LEFT);
  else if (e.key === UP_KEY
      || e.key === "w")
    inputs.push(Input.UP);
  else if (e.key === RIGHT_KEY
      || e.key === "d")
    inputs.push(Input.RIGHT);
  else if (e.key === DOWN_KEY
      || e.key === "s")
    inputs.push(Input.DOWN);
});

function handleInput(input: Input) {
  if (input === Input.LEFT)
    moveHorizontal(-1);
  else if (input === Input.RIGHT)
    moveHorizontal(1);
  else if (input === Input.UP)
    moveVertical(-1);
  else if (input === Input.DOWN)
    moveVertical(1);
}
```

Listing 4.14   After

```
window.addEventListener("keydown", e =>
{
  if (e.key === LEFT_KEY
      || e.key === "a")
    inputs.push(new Left());
  else if (e.key === UP_KEY
      || e.key === "w")
    inputs.push(new Up());
  else if (e.key === RIGHT_KEY
      || e.key === "d")
    inputs.push(new Right());
  else if (e.key === DOWN_KEY
      || e.key === "s")
    inputs.push(new Down());
});

function handleInput(input: Input) {
  if (input.isLeft())
    moveHorizontal(-1);
  else if (input.isRight())
    moveHorizontal(1);
  else if (input.isUp())
    moveVertical(-1);
  else if (input.isDown())
    moveVertical(1);
}
```

We capture this process of making enums into classes in the refactoring pattern REPLACE TYPE CODE WITH CLASSES.

4.1.3   *Refactoring pattern: REPLACE TYPE CODE WITH CLASSES*

DESCRIPTION

This refactoring pattern transforms an enum into an interface, and the enums' values become classes. Doing so enables us to add properties to each value and localize functionality concerning that specific value. This leads to change by addition in collaboration with another refactoring pattern, discussed next: PUSH CODE INTO CLASSES (P4.1.5). The reason is that we often use enums via `switch`es or `else if` chains spread throughout the application. A `switch` states how each possible value in an enum should be handled at this location.

When we transform values into classes, we can instead group together functionality concerning that value without having to consider any other enum values. This process brings functionality and data together; it localizes the functionality to the data, i.e., the specific value. Adding a new value to an enum means verifying logic connected to that enum across many files, whereas adding a new class that implements an interface only asks us to implement methods in that file—no modification of any other code is required (until we want to use the new class).

Note that *type codes* also come in flavors other than enums. Any integer type, or any type that supports the exact equality check ===, can act as a type code. Most commonly, we use `int`s and **enums**. Here is an example of such a type code for t-shirt sizes.

Listing 4.15   Initial

```
const SMALL = 33;
const MEDIUM = 37;
const LARGE = 42;
```

It is trickier to track down uses of a type code when it is an `int`, because someone might have used the number without reference to a central constant. So we always immediately transform type codes to enums when we see them. Only then can we apply this refactoring pattern safely.

Listing 4.16   Before

```
const SMALL = 33;
const MEDIUM = 37;
const LARGE = 42;
```

Listing 4.17   After

```
enum TShirtSizes {
  SMALL = 33,
  MEDIUM = 37,
  LARGE = 42
}
```

PROCESS

1 Introduce a new interface with a temporary name. The interface should contain methods for each of the values in our enum.

2 Create classes corresponding to each of the enum values; all the methods from the interface except the one corresponding to the class should **return false**.

3 Rename the enum to something else. Doing so causes the compiler to report an error in all the places where we use the enum.

4 Change types from the old name to the temporary name, and replace equality checks with the new methods.

5 Replace the remaining references to the enum values with instantiating the new classes, instead.

6 When there are no more errors, rename the interface to its permanent name everywhere.

EXAMPLE

Consider this tiny example with a traffic light enum and a function to determine whether we can drive.

Listing 4.18   Initial

```
enum TrafficLight {
  RED, YELLOW, GREEN
}
const CYCLE = [TrafficLight.RED, TrafficLight.GREEN, TrafficLight.YELLOW];
function updateCarForLight(current: TrafficLight) {
  if (current === TrafficLight.RED)
    car.stop();
  else
    car.drive();
}
```

We follow the process:

1 Introduce a new interface with a temporary name. The interface should contain methods for each of the values in our enum.

Listing 4.19   New interface

```
interface TrafficLight2 {
  isRed(): boolean;
  isYellow(): boolean;
  isGreen(): boolean;
}
```

2 Create classes corresponding to each of the enum values; all the methods from the interface except the one corresponding to the class should **return false**.

Listing 4.20   New classes

```
class Red implements TrafficLight2 {
  isRed() { return true; }
  isYellow() { return false; }
  isGreen() { return false; }
}
```

```
class Yellow implements TrafficLight2 {
  isRed() { return false; }
  isYellow() { return true; }
  isGreen() { return false; }
}
class Green implements TrafficLight2 {
  isRed() { return false; }
  isYellow() { return false; }
  isGreen() { return true; }
}
```

3 Rename the enum to something else. This causes the compiler to error all the places where we use the enum.

Listing 4.21 Before	Listing 4.22 After (1/4)

```
enum TrafficLight {
  RED, YELLOW, GREEN
}
```

```
enum RawTrafficLight {
  RED, YELLOW, GREEN
}
```

4 Change types from the old name to the temporary name, and replace equality checks with the new methods.

Listing 4.23 Before	Listing 4.24 After (2/4)

```
function updateCarForLight(
  current: TrafficLight)
{
  if (current === TrafficLight.RED)
    car.stop();
  else
    car.drive();
}
```

```
function updateCarForLight(
  current: TrafficLight2)
{
  if (current.isRed())
    car.stop();
  else
    car.drive();
}
```

5 Replace the remaining references to the enum values with instantiating the new classes, instead.

Listing 4.25 Before	Listing 4.26 After (3/4)

```
const CYCLE = [
  TrafficLight.RED,
  TrafficLight.GREEN,
  TrafficLight.YELLOW
];
```

```
const CYCLE = [
  new Red(),
  new Green(),
  new Yellow()
];
```

6 Finally, when there are no more errors, rename the interface to its permanent name everywhere.

Listing 4.27 Before	Listing 4.28 After (4/4)

```
interface TrafficLight2 {
  // ...
}
```

```
interface TrafficLight {
  // ...
}
```

This refactoring pattern in itself does not add much value, but it enables fantastic improvements later. Having is methods for all the values is a smell, too, so we have replaced one smell with another. But we can handle these methods one by one, whereas the enum values were tightly connected. It is important to note that most of the is methods are temporary and do not exist for long—in this case, we get rid of some of them in this chapter and many more in chapter 5.

FURTHER READING

This refactoring pattern can also be found in Martin Fowler's book *Refactoring*.

4.1.4 *Pushing code into classes*

Now the magic is about to happen. All conditions in handleInput have to do with the input parameter, which means the code should be in that class. Luckily, there is a simple way to do this:

1 Copy handleInput, and paste it into all the classes. Remove **function**, because it is now a method, and replace the input parameter with **this**. It still has the wrong name, so we still get errors.

Listing 4.29   After

```
class Right implements Input {        Remove "function"
  // ...                              and the parameter.
  handleInput() {
    if (this.isLeft())
      moveHorizontal(-1);
    else if (this.isRight())          Change
      moveHorizontal(1);              input to
    else if (this.isUp())             "this."
      moveVertical(-1);
    else if (this.isDown())
      moveVertical(1);
  }
}
```

2 Copy the method signature into the Input interface, and give it a slightly different name than the source method handleInput. In this case, we are already in Input, so there is no point in writing it twice.

Listing 4.30   New interface

```
interface Input {
  // ...
  handle(): void;
}
```

3 Go through the handleInput methods in all four classes. The process is identical, so we show only one:

a Inline the return values of the methods isLeft, isRight, isUp, and isDown.

Listing 4.31 Before

```
class Right implements Input {
  // ...
  handleInput() {
    if (this.isLeft())
      moveHorizontal(-1);
    else if (this.isRight())
      moveHorizontal(1);
    else if (this.isUp())
      moveVertical(-1);
    else if (this.isDown())
      moveVertical(1);
  }
}
```

Listing 4.32 After (1/4)

```
class Right implements Input {
  // ...
  handleInput() {
    if (false)
      moveHorizontal(-1);
    else if (true)
      moveHorizontal(1);
    else if (false)
      moveVertical(-1);
    else if (false)
      moveVertical(1);
  }
}
```

After inlining the is methods

b Remove all the **if** (**false**) { ... } and the **if** part of **if** (**true**).

Listing 4.33 Before

```
class Right implements Input {
  // ...
  handleInput() {
    if (false)
      moveHorizontal(-1);
    else if (true)
      moveHorizontal(1);
    else if (false)
      moveVertical(-1);
    else if (false)
      moveVertical(1);
  }
}
```

Listing 4.34 After (2/4)

```
class Right implements Input {
  // ...
  handleInput() {



      moveHorizontal(1);



  }
}
```

c Change the name to handle to signal that we are finished with this method. The compiler should accept the method at this point.

Listing 4.35 Before

```
class Right implements Input {
  // ...
  handleInput() { moveHorizontal(1); }
}
```

Listing 4.36 After (3/4)

```
class Right implements Input {
  // ...
  handle() { moveHorizontal(1); }
}
```

4 Replace the body of handleInput with a call to our new method.

Listing 4.37 Before

```
function handleInput(input: Input) {
  if (input.isLeft())
    moveHorizontal(-1);
  else if (input.isRight())
    moveHorizontal(1);
  else if (input.isUp())
    moveVertical(-1);
  else if (input.isDown())
    moveVertical(1);
}
```

Listing 4.38 After (4/4)

```
function handleInput(input: Input) {
  input.handle();
}
```

After going through this process, we arrive at this nice improvement. All the `ifs` are gone, and these methods easily fit in five lines.

Listing 4.39 Before

```
function handleInput(input: Input) {
  if (input.isLeft())
    moveHorizontal(-1);
  else if (input.isRight())
    moveHorizontal(1);
  else if (input.isUp())
    moveVertical(-1);
  else if (input.isDown())
    moveVertical(1);
}
```

Listing 4.40 After

```
function handleInput(input: Input) {
  input.handle();
}

interface Input {
  // ...
  handle(): void;
}
class Left implements Input {
  // ...
  handle() { moveHorizontal(-1); }
}
class Right implements Input {
  // ...
  handle() { moveHorizontal(1); }
}
class Up implements Input {
  // ...
  handle() { moveVertical(-1); }
}
class Down implements Input {
  // ...
  handle() { moveVertical(1); }
}
```

This is my favorite refactoring pattern: it is so structured that we can perform it with little cognitive load, but we end up with very nice code. I call it PUSH CODE INTO CLASSES.

4.1.5 Refactoring pattern: PUSH CODE INTO CLASSES

DESCRIPTION

This refactoring pattern is a natural continuation of REPLACE TYPE CODE WITH CLASSES, as it moves functionality into classes. As a result, `if` statements are often eliminated, and functionality is moved closer to the data. As discussed earlier, this helps localize the invariants because functionality connected with a specific value is moved into the class corresponding to that value.

In its simplest form, we always assume that we move an entire method into the classes. This is not a problem because, as we have seen, we usually start by extracting methods. It is possible to move code without extracting it first, but doing so requires more care to verify that we have not broken anything.

PROCESS

1 Copy the source function, and paste it into all the classes. Remove `function`, as it is now a method; replace the context with `this`; and remove the unused parameters. The method still has the wrong name, so we still get errors.

2 Copy the method signature into the target interface. Give it a slightly different name than the source method.

3 Go through the new method in all the classes:

  a Inline the methods that return a constant expression.

  b Perform all the computations we can up front, which usually amounts to removing `if (true)` and `if (false) { ... }` but may also require simplifying the conditions first (for example, `false || true` becomes `true`).

  c Change the name to its proper name, to signal that we are finished with this method. The compiler should accept it.

4 Replace the body of the original function with a call to our new method.

EXAMPLE

As this refactoring pattern is so closely related to REPLACE TYPE CODE WITH CLASSES, we continue with the traffic light example.

Listing 4.41 Initial

```
interface TrafficLight {
  isRed(): boolean;
  isYellow(): boolean;
  isGreen(): boolean;
}
class Red implements TrafficLight {
  isRed() { return true; }
  isYellow() { return false; }
  isGreen() { return false; }
}
class Yellow implements TrafficLight {
  isRed() { return false; }
  isYellow() { return true; }
  isGreen() { return false; }
}
class Green implements TrafficLight {
  isRed() { return false; }
  isYellow() { return false; }
  isGreen() { return true; }
}
function updateCarForLight(current: TrafficLight) {
  if (current.isRed())
```

```
    car.stop();
  else
    car.drive();
}
```

We follow the process:

1 Make a new method in the target interface. Give it a slightly different name than the source method.

Listing 4.42 New method

```
interface TrafficLight {
  // ...
  updateCar(): void;
}
```

2 Copy the source function, and paste it into all the classes. Remove **function**, as it is now a method; replace the context with **this**; and remove the unused parameters. It still has the wrong name, so we still get errors.

Listing 4.43 Duplicating the method into the classes

```
class Red implements TrafficLight {
  // ...
  updateCarForLight() {
    if (this.isRed())
      car.stop();
    else
      car.drive();
  }
}
class Yellow implements TrafficLight {
  // ...
  updateCarForLight() {
    if (this.isRed())
      car.stop();
    else
      car.drive();
  }
}
class Green implements TrafficLight {
  // ...
  updateCarForLight() {
    if (this.isRed())
      car.stop();
    else
      car.drive();
  }
}
```

3 Go through the new method in all the classes:

  a Inline the methods that return a constant expression.

  b Perform all the computations we can up front.

Listing 4.44 Before

```
class Red implements TrafficLight {
  // ...
  updateCarForLight() {
    if (this.isRed())
      car.stop();
    else
      car.drive();
  }
}
class Yellow implements TrafficLight {
  // ...
  updateCarForLight() {
    if (this.isRed())
      car.stop();
    else
      car.drive();
  }
}
class Green implements TrafficLight {
  // ...
  updateCarForLight() {
    if (this.isRed())
      car.stop();
    else
      car.drive();
  }
}
```

Listing 4.45 After (1/4)

```
class Red implements TrafficLight {
  // ...
  updateCarForLight() {
    if (true)
      car.stop();
    else
      car.drive();
  }
}
class Yellow implements TrafficLight {
  // ...
  updateCarForLight() {
    if (false)
      car.stop();
    else
      car.drive();
  }
}
class Green implements TrafficLight {
  // ...
  updateCarForLight() {
    if (false)
      car.stop();
    else
      car.drive();
  }
}
```

Listing 4.46 Before

```
class Red implements TrafficLight {
  // ...
  updateCarForLight() {
    if (true)
      car.stop();
    else
      car.drive();
  }
}
class Yellow implements TrafficLight {
  // ...
  updateCarForLight() {
    if (false)
      car.stop();
    else
      car.drive();
  }
}
class Green implements TrafficLight {
  // ...
  updateCarForLight() {
    if (false)
      car.stop();
    else
```

Listing 4.47 After (2/4)

```
class Red implements TrafficLight {
  // ...
  updateCarForLight() {

    car.stop();

  }
}
class Yellow implements TrafficLight {
  // ...
  updateCarForLight() {


    car.drive();
  }
}
class Green implements TrafficLight {
  // ...
  updateCarForLight() {
```

```
        car.drive();                              car.drive();
    }                                         }
}                                         }
```

    c Change the name to its proper name, to signal that we are finished with this method.

Listing 4.48 Before

```
class Red implements TrafficLight {
    // ...
    updateCarForLight() { car.stop(); }
}
class Yellow implements TrafficLight {
    // ...
    updateCarForLight() { car.drive(); }
}
class Green implements TrafficLight {
    // ...
    updateCarForLight() { car.drive(); }
}
```

Listing 4.49 After (3/4)

```
class Red implements TrafficLight {
    // ...
    updateCar() { car.stop(); }
}
class Yellow implements TrafficLight {
    // ...
    updateCar() { car.drive(); }
}
class Green implements TrafficLight {
    // ...
    updateCar() { car.drive(); }
}
```

    4 Replace the body of the original function with a call to our new method.

Listing 4.50 Before

```
function updateCarForLight(
    current: TrafficLight)
{
    if (current.isRed())
        car.stop();
    else        car.drive();
}
```

Listing 4.51 After (4/4)

```
function updateCarForLight(
    current: TrafficLight)
{
    current.updateCar();
}
```

We mentioned earlier that the `is` methods become a smell if they remain, so it is worth noting that at this point, we do not need any of them in this tiny example. This is an extension of the advantages of this refactoring pattern.

FURTHER READING

In this simple form, this refactoring is essentially the same as Martin Fowler's "Move method." However, I think this rebranding better conveys the intention and force behind it.

4.1.6 *Inlining a superfluous method*

At this point, we can see another amusing effect of refactoring. Even though we just introduced the `handleInput` function, that does not necessarily mean it should stay. Refactoring is often circular, adding things that enable further refactoring and then removing them again. So, never be afraid of adding code.

When we introduced `handleInput`, it had a clear purpose. Now, however, it does not add any readability to our program, and it takes up space, so we can remove it:

1 Change the method name to `handleInput2`. This makes the compiler error wherever we use the function.

2 Copy the body `input.handle();`, and note that `input` is the parameter.

3 We use this function in only one place, where we replace the call with the body.

Listing 4.52 Before	Listing 4.53 After

```
handleInput(current);
```

```
current.handle();
```

After this, and after a quick renaming of `current` to `input`, `handleInputs` looks like this.

Listing 4.54 Before	Listing 4.55 After

```
function handleInputs() {
  while (inputs.length > 0) {
    let current = inputs.pop();
    handleInput(current);
  }
}

function handleInput(input: Input) {
  input.handle();
}
```

```
function handleInputs() {
  while (inputs.length > 0) {
    let input = inputs.pop();
    input.handle();    ◁── Inlining
  }                          method
}

          ◁── handleInput
                 deleted
```

This refactoring pattern, INLINE METHOD, is the exact inverse of EXTRACT METHOD (P3.2.1) from chapter 3.

4.1.7 Refactoring pattern: INLINE METHOD

DESCRIPTION

Two great themes of this book are adding code (usually to support classes) and removing code. This refactoring pattern supports the latter: it removes methods that no longer add readability to our program. It does so by moving code from a method to all call sites. This makes the method unused, at which point we can safely delete it.

Notice that we differentiate between inlining methods and the refactoring pattern INLINE METHOD. In the previous sections, we inlined the `is` methods while we were pushing code into classes, and then we used INLINE METHOD to eliminate the original function. When we inline methods (without the emphasis), we don't do it at every call site, so we preserve the original method. This is usually to simplify the call site. When we INLINE METHOD (emphasized), we do it at every call site and then delete the method.

In this book, we often do this when methods have only a single line. This is because of our strict five-line limit; inlining a method with a single line cannot break this rule. We can also apply this refactoring pattern to methods with more than one line.

Another consideration is whether the method is too complex to be inlined. The following method gives the absolute value of a number; we have optimized it for performance, so it is branch-free. It is a single line. It relies on low-level operations to achieve its purpose, so having the method adds readability, and we should not inline it. In this case, inlining it would also go against the smell "Operations should be on the same level of abstraction," which motivated our EITHER CALL OR PASS (R3.1.1) rule.

Listing 4.56   Method that should not be inlined

```
const NUMBER_BITS = 32;
function absolute(x: number) {
  return (x ^ x >> NUMBER_BITS-1) - (x >> NUMBER_BITS-1);
}
```

PROCESS

1 Change the method name to something temporary. This makes the compiler error wherever we use the function.
2 Copy the body of the method, and note its parameters.
3 Wherever the compiler gives errors, replace the call with the copied body, and map the arguments to the parameters.
4 Once we can compile without errors, we know the original method is unused. Delete the original method.

EXAMPLE

As we have already seen an example on the game code, let's examine an example from a different domain. In this example, we discover that we have split the two parts of a bank transaction: withdrawing money from one account and depositing it into another. This means we can accidentally deposit money without withdrawing it if we call the wrong method. To remedy the situation, we decide to join the two methods.

Listing 4.57   Initial

```
function deposit(to: string, amount: number) {
  let accountId = database.find(to);
  database.updateOne(accountId, { $inc: { balance: amount } });
}

function transfer(from: string, to: string, amount: number) {
  deposit(from, -amount);
  deposit(to, amount);
}
```

> **In TypeScript ...**
> The symbol $ is treated like any other character, similar to _. Thus it can be part of a name and has no special meaning. $inc could just as well be do_inc.

We follow the process:

1 Change the method name to something temporary. This makes the compiler error wherever we use the function.

Listing 4.58 Before

```
function deposit(to: string,
    amount: number) {
  // ...
}
```

Listing 4.59 After (1/2)

```
function deposit2(to: string,
    amount: number) {
  // ...
}
```

2 Copy the body of the method, and note its parameters.
3 Wherever the compiler gives errors, replace the call with the copied body, and map the arguments to the parameters.

Listing 4.60 Before

```
function transfer(
  from: string,
  to: string,
  amount: number)
{
  deposit(from, -amount);


  deposit(to, amount);


}
```

Listing 4.61 After (2/2)

```
function transfer(
  from: string,
  to: string,
  amount: number)
{
  let fromAccountId = database.find(from);
  database.updateOne(fromAccountId,
    { $inc: { balance: -amount } });
  let toAccountId = database.find(to);
  database.updateOne(toAccountId,
    { $inc: { balance: amount } });
}
```

4 Once we can compile without errors, we know the original method is unused. Delete the original method.

At this point, money cannot be created from nothing in the code. It is debatable whether having this code duplication is a bad idea; in chapter 6, we see another solution that uses encapsulation.

FURTHER READING

This refactoring pattern can be found in Martin Fowler's book *Refactoring*.

4.2   *Refactoring a large if statement*

Let's go through the same process, but with a bigger method: drawMap.

Listing 4.62   Initial

```
function drawMap(g: CanvasRenderingContext2D) {
  for (let y = 0; y < map.length; y++) {
    for (let x = 0; x < map[y].length; x++) {
      if (map[y][x] === Tile.FLUX)
        g.fillStyle = "#ccffcc";
      else if (map[y][x] === Tile.UNBREAKABLE)
        g.fillStyle = "#999999";
      else if (map[y][x] === Tile.STONE || map[y][x] === Tile.FALLING_STONE)
        g.fillStyle = "#0000cc";
      else if (map[y][x] === Tile.BOX || map[y][x] === Tile.FALLING_BOX)
        g.fillStyle = "#8b4513";
      else if (map[y][x] === Tile.KEY1 || map[y][x] === Tile.LOCK1)
        g.fillStyle = "#ffcc00";
      else if (map[y][x] === Tile.KEY2 || map[y][x] === Tile.LOCK2)
        g.fillStyle = "#00ccff";

      if (map[y][x] !== Tile.AIR && map[y][x] !== Tile.PLAYER)
        g.fillRect(x * TILE_SIZE, y * TILE_SIZE, TILE_SIZE, TILE_SIZE);
    }
  }
}
```

Immediately we notice a major violation of our **if** ONLY AT THE START (R3.5.1) rule from the last chapter: there is a long **else if** chain right in the middle of the code. So, the first thing we do is extract the **else if** chain to its own method.

Listing 4.63   After EXTRACT METHOD (P3.2.1)

```
function drawMap(g: CanvasRenderingContext2D) {
  for (let y = 0; y < map.length; y++) {
    for (let x = 0; x < map[y].length; x++) {
      colorOfTile(g, x, y);
      if (map[y][x] !== Tile.AIR && map[y][x] !== Tile.PLAYER)
        g.fillRect(x * TILE_SIZE, y * TILE_SIZE, TILE_SIZE, TILE_SIZE);
    }
  }
}

function colorOfTile(g: CanvasRenderingContext2D, x: number, y: number) {
  if (map[y][x] === Tile.FLUX)
    g.fillStyle = "#ccffcc";
  else if (map[y][x] === Tile.UNBREAKABLE)
    g.fillStyle = "#999999";
  else if (map[y][x] === Tile.STONE || map[y][x] === Tile.FALLING_STONE)
    g.fillStyle = "#0000cc";
  else if (map[y][x] === Tile.BOX || map[y][x] === Tile.FALLING_BOX)
    g.fillStyle = "#8b4513";
  else if (map[y][x] === Tile.KEY1 || map[y][x] === Tile.LOCK1)
```

Extracted method and call

```
    g.fillStyle = "#ffcc00";
  else if (map[y][x] === Tile.KEY2 || map[y][x] === Tile.LOCK2)
    g.fillStyle = "#00ccff";
}
```

For now, drawMap complies with our FIVE LINES rule, so we continue with colorOf-Tile. colorOfTile violates NEVER USE **if** WITH **else**. As we did earlier, to solve this issue, we replace the Tile enum with a Tile interface:

1 Introduce a new interface with the temporary name Tile2, with methods for all the values in our enum.

Listing 4.64   New interface

```
interface Tile2 {
  isFlux(): boolean;
  isUnbreakable(): boolean;         Methods for all
  isStone(): boolean;               the values of
  // ...              ◁─────────    the enum
}
```

2 Create classes corresponding to each of the enum values.

Listing 4.65   New classes

```
class Flux implements Tile2 {
  isFlux() { return true; }
  isUnbreakable() { return false; }
  isStone() { return false; }
  // ...
}
class Unbreakable implements Tile2 { ... }      Similar classes for
class Stone implements Tile2 { ... }            the rest of the values
/// ...                       ◁─────────        of the enum
```

3 Rename the enum to RawTile, making the compiler show us wherever it is used.

Listing 4.66   Before

```
enum Tile {
  AIR,
  FLUX,
  UNBREAKABLE,
  PLAYER,
  STONE, FALLING_STONE,
  BOX, FALLING_BOX,
  KEY1, LOCK1,
  KEY2, LOCK2
}
```

Listing 4.67   After (1/2)

```
enum RawTile {        ◁──┐   Changing the
  AIR,                    │   name to get
  FLUX,                   │   compile errors
  UNBREAKABLE,
  PLAYER,
  STONE, FALLING_STONE,
  BOX, FALLING_BOX,
  KEY1, LOCK1,
  KEY2, LOCK2
}
```

4 Replace equality checks with the new methods. We have to make this change in a lot of places throughout the application; here, we show only colorOfTile.

Listing 4.68 Before	Listing 4.69 After (2/2)

```
function colorOfTile(
  g: CanvasRenderingContext2D,
  x: number, y: number)
{
  if (map[y][x] === Tile.FLUX)
    g.fillStyle = "#ccffcc";
  else if (map[y][x] === Tile.UNBREAKABLE)
    g.fillStyle = "#999999";
  else if (map[y][x] === Tile.STONE
        || map[y][x] === Tile.FALLING_STONE)
    g.fillStyle = "#0000cc";
  else if (map[y][x] === Tile.BOX
        || map[y][x] === Tile.FALLING_BOX)
    g.fillStyle = "#8b4513";
  else if (map[y][x] === Tile.KEY1
        || map[y][x] === Tile.LOCK1)
    g.fillStyle = "#ffcc00";
  else if (map[y][x] === Tile.KEY2
        || map[y][x] === Tile.LOCK2)
    g.fillStyle = "#00ccff";
}
```

```
function colorOfTile(
  g: CanvasRenderingContext2D,
  x: number, y: number)
{
  if (map[y][x].isFlux())
    g.fillStyle = "#ccffcc";
  else if (map[y][x].isUnbreakable())
    g.fillStyle = "#999999";
  else if (map[y][x].isStone()
        || map[y][x].isFallingStone())
    g.fillStyle = "#0000cc";
  else if (map[y][x].isBox()
        || map[y][x].isFallingBox())
    g.fillStyle = "#8b4513";
  else if (map[y][x].isKey1()
        || map[y][x].isLock1())
    g.fillStyle = "#ffcc00";
  else if (map[y][x].isKey2()
        || map[y][x].isLock2())
    g.fillStyle = "#00ccff";
}
```

Use new methods instead of equality checks.

WARNING Take care that `map[y][x] === Tile.FLUX` becomes `map[y][x].isFlux()`, and `map[y][x] !== Tile.AIR` becomes `!map[y][x].isAir()`. Pay attention to the `!`.

5 Replace uses of `Tile.FLUX` with **new** `Flux()`, `Tile.AIR` with **new** `Air()`, and so forth.

At this point last time, we had no errors and could rename the temporary `Tile2` to the permanent `Tile`. But now the situation is different: we still have two places with errors showing that we are using `Tile`. This is why we use a temporary name; otherwise, we probably would not have spotted the issue in `remove` and would have assumed it was working—which it is not.

Listing 4.70 Last two errors

```
let map: Tile[][] = [
  [2, 2, 2, 2, 2, 2, 2, 2],
  [2, 3, 0, 1, 1, 2, 0, 2],
  [2, 4, 2, 6, 1, 2, 0, 2],
  [2, 8, 4, 1, 1, 2, 0, 2],
  [2, 4, 1, 1, 1, 9, 0, 2],
  [2, 2, 2, 2, 2, 2, 2, 2],
];

function remove(tile: Tile) {
  for (let y = 0; y < map.length; y++) {
    for (let x = 0; x < map[y].length; x++) {
      if (map[y][x] === tile) {
```

Errors because we refer to Tile

```
        map[y][x] = new Air();
      }
    }
  }
}
```

Both of these errors require special treatment, so we go through them in turn.

4.2.1 *Removing generality*

The problem with `remove` is that it takes a tile type and removes it from everywhere on the map. That is, it does not check against a specific instance of `Tile`; instead, it checks that the instances are similar.

Listing 4.71 Initial

```
function remove(tile: Tile) {
  for (let y = 0; y < map.length; y++) {
    for (let x = 0; x < map[y].length; x++) {
      if (map[y][x] === tile) {
        map[y][x] = new Air();
      }
    }
  }
}
```

In other words, the problem is that `remove` is too general. It can remove any type of tile. This generality makes it less flexible and more difficult to change. Therefore, we prefer specialization: we make a less general version and switch to using that, instead.

Before we can make a general version, we need to investigate how it is used. We want to make the parameter less general, so we look for what arguments are passed to it in practice. We use our familiar process and rename `remove` to a temporary name, `remove2`. We find that `remove` is used in four places.

Listing 4.72 Before

```
/// ...
remove(new Lock1());
/// ...
remove(new Lock2());
/// ...
remove(new Lock1());
/// ...
remove(new Lock2());
/// ...
```

We can see that even though `remove` supports removing any type of tile, in practice it is only removing `Lock1` or `Lock2`. We can take advantage of this:

1 Duplicate `remove2`.

Listing 4.73 Before

```
function remove2(tile: Tile) {
  // ...
}
```

Listing 4.74 After (1/4)

```
function remove2(tile: Tile) {
  // ...
}
function remove2(tile: Tile) {
  // ...
}
```
They have
the same
body.

2 Rename one of them to `removeLock1`, remove its parameter, and replace `===` `tile` with `===` `Tile.LOCK1` temporarily. We do this even though we have renamed `Tile` to `RawTile` because it makes the code identical to the code we handled earlier.

Listing 4.75 Before

```
function remove2(tile: Tile) {
  for (let y = 0; y < map.length; y++)
    for (let x = 0; x < map[y].length; x++)
      if (map[y][x] === tile)
        map[y][x] = new Air();
}
```
**Replace
tile with
Tile.LOCK1.**

Listing 4.76 After (2/4)

```
function removeLock1() {
  for (let y = 0; y < map.length; y++)
    for (let x = 0; x < map[y].length; x++)
      if (map[y][x] === Tile.LOCK1)
        map[y][x] = new Air();
}
```
**Rename and remove
the parameter.**

3 This is exactly the type of equality we know how to eliminate. So, as we did before, we replace it with the method call.

Listing 4.77 Before

```
function removeLock1() {
  for (let y = 0; y < map.length; y++)
    for (let x = 0; x < map[y].length; x++)
      if (map[y][x] === Tile.LOCK1)
        map[y][x] = new Air();
}
```

Listing 4.78 After (3/4)

```
function removeLock1() {
  for (let y = 0; y < map.length; y++)
    for (let x = 0; x < map[y].length; x++)
      if (map[y][x].isLock1())
        map[y][x] = new Air();
}
```
**Uses a method instead
of an equality check**

4 This function has no more errors, so we can switch the old calls to use the new ones.

Listing 4.79 Before

```
remove(new Lock1());
```

Listing 4.80 After (4/4)

```
removeLock1();
```

We do the same thing for `removeLock2`. After that, we have `removeLock1` and `remove-Lock2` with no errors. `remove2` still has an error, but it is no longer called, so we simply delete it. In total, we performed the following change.

Listing 4.81 Before

```
function remove(tile: Tile) {
  for (let y = 0; y < map.length; y++)
    for (let x = 0; x < map[y].length; x++)
      if (map[y][x] === tile)
        map[y][x] = new Air();
}
```

Listing 4.82 After

```
function removeLock1() {
  for (let y = 0; y < map.length; y++)
    for (let x = 0; x < map[y].length; x++)
      if (map[y][x].isLock1())
        map[y][x] = new Air();
}
function removeLock2() {
  for (let y = 0; y < map.length; y++)
    for (let x = 0; x < map[y].length; x++)
      if (map[y][x].isLock2())
        map[y][x] = new Air();
}
```

◁─┐ **Original remove**
   │ **is deleted**

We call the process of introducing less-general versions of a function SPECIALIZE METHOD.

4.2.2 Refactoring pattern: SPECIALIZE METHOD

DESCRIPTION

This refactoring is more esoteric because it goes against the instincts of many programmers. We have a natural desire to generalize and reuse, but doing so can be problematic because it blurs responsibilities and means our code can be called from a variety of places. This refactoring pattern reverses these effects. More specialized methods are called from fewer places, which means they become unused sooner, so we can remove them.

PROCESS

1 Duplicate the method we want to specialize.
2 Rename one of the methods to a new permanent name, and remove (or replace) the parameter we are using as the basis of our specialization.
3 Correct the method accordingly so it has no errors.
4 Switch the old calls over to use the new ones.

EXAMPLE

Imagine that we are implementing a chess game. As part of our move-checker, we have come up with a brilliantly general expression to test whether a move fits a piece's pattern.

Listing 4.83 Initial

```
function canMove(start: Tile, end: Tile, dx: number, dy: number) {
  return dx * abs(start.x - end.x) === dy * abs(start.y - end.y)
    || dy * abs(start.x - end.x) === dx * abs(start.y - end.y);
}
```

```
/// ...
  if (canMove(start, end, 1, 0)) // Rook
/// ...
  if (canMove(start, end, 1, 1)) // Bishop
/// ...
  if (canMove(start, end, 1, 2)) // Knight
/// ...
```

We follow the process:

1 Duplicate the method we want to specialize.

Listing 4.84   Before

```
function canMove(start: Tile, end: Tile,
  dx: number, dy: number)
{
  return dx * abs(start.x - end.x)
    === dy * abs(start.y - end.y)
    || dy * abs(start.x - end.x)
    === dx * abs(start.y - end.y);
}
```

Listing 4.85   After (1/4)

```
function canMove(start: Tile, end: Tile,
  dx: number, dy: number)
{
  return dx * abs(start.x - end.x)
    === dy * abs(start.y - end.y)
    || dy * abs(start.x - end.x)
    === dx * abs(start.y - end.y);
}
function canMove(start: Tile, end: Tile,
  dx: number, dy: number)
{
  return dx * abs(start.x - end.x)
    === dy * abs(start.y - end.y)
    || dy * abs(start.x - end.x)
    === dx * abs(start.y - end.y);
}
```

2 Rename one of the methods to a new permanent name, and remove (or replace) the parameter(s) we are using as the basis of our specialization.

Listing 4.86   Before

```
function canMove(start: Tile, end: Tile,
  dx: number, dy: number)
{
  return dx * abs(start.x - end.x)
    === dy * abs(start.y - end.y)
    || dy * abs(start.x - end.x)
    === dx * abs(start.y - end.y);
}
```

Listing 4.87   After (2/4)

```
function rookCanMove(
  start: Tile, end: Tile)
{
  return 1 * abs(start.x - end.x)
    === 0 * abs(start.y - end.y)
    || 0 * abs(start.x - end.x)
    === 1 * abs(start.y - end.y);
}
```

3 Correct the method accordingly, so it has no errors. Since there are no errors here, we merely simplify.

```
Listing 4.88    Before
```

```
function rookCanMove(
  start: Tile, end: Tile)
{
  return 1 * abs(start.x - end.x)
    === 0 * abs(start.y - end.y)
    || 0 * abs(start.x - end.x)
    === 1 * abs(start.y - end.y);
}
```

```
Listing 4.89    After (3/4)
```

```
function rookCanMove(
  start: Tile, end: Tile)
{
  return abs(start.x - end.x)
    === 0
    || 0
    === abs(start.y - end.y);
}
```

4 Switch the old calls over to use the new ones.

```
Listing 4.90    Before
```

```
if (canMove(start, end, 1, 0)) // Rook
```

```
Listing 4.91    After (4/4)
```

```
if (rookCanMove(start, end))
```

Notice that we no longer need the comment. rookCanMove is also much easier to understand: a rook can make a move if the change on either x or y is zero. We could even remove the abs part to simplify further.

I leave it to you to perform the same refactoring for the other pieces in the initial code. Are their methods as easy to understand?

FURTHER READING

To my knowledge, the preceding description is the first of this as a refactoring pattern, although Jonathan Blow discussed the advantages of specialized methods versus general ones in his speech "How to program independent games" at UC Berkeley's Computer Science Undergraduate Association 2011.

4.2.3   *The only switch allowed*

Only one error remains: we create our map using the enum indices, which no longer works. Indices like these are commonly used to store things in databases or files. In the case of a game, it would be logical to store levels in files using indices, as they are easier to serialize than objects. In practice, it is often not possible to change existing external data to accommodate refactoring. So instead of changing the entire map, it is better to make a new function to take us from enum indices to the new classes. Luckily, this is straightforward to implement.

```
Listing 4.92    Introducing transformTile
```

```
let rawMap: RawTile[][] = [
  [2, 2, 2, 2, 2, 2, 2, 2],
  [2, 3, 0, 1, 1, 2, 0, 2],
  [2, 4, 2, 6, 1, 2, 0, 2],
  [2, 8, 4, 1, 1, 2, 0, 2],
  [2, 4, 1, 1, 1, 9, 0, 2],
```

```
      [2, 2, 2, 2, 2, 2, 2, 2],
];
let map: Tile2[][];
function assertExhausted(x: never): never {
  throw new Error("Unexpected object: " + x);
}
function transformTile(tile: RawTile) {
  switch (tile) {
    case RawTile.AIR: return new Air();
    case RawTile.PLAYER: return new Player();
    case RawTile.UNBREAKABLE: return new Unbreakable();
    case RawTile.STONE: return new Stone();
    case RawTile.FALLING_STONE: return new FallingStone();
    case RawTile.BOX: return new Box();
    case RawTile.FALLING_BOX: return new FallingBox();
    case RawTile.FLUX: return new Flux();
    case RawTile.KEY1: return new Key1();
    case RawTile.LOCK1: return new Lock1();
    case RawTile.KEY2: return new Key2();
    case RawTile.LOCK2: return new Lock2();
    default: assertExhausted(tile);
  }
}
function transformMap() {
  map = new Array(rawMap.length);
  for (let y = 0; y < rawMap.length; y++) {
    map[y] = new Array(rawMap[y].length);
    for (let x = 0; x < rawMap[y].length; x++) {
      map[y][x] = transformTile(rawMap[y][x]);
    }
  }
}
window.onload = () => {
  transformMap();
  gameLoop();
}
```

TypeScript trick, explained shortly

New method for transforming a RawTile enum into a Tile2 object

New method for mapping the entire map

Remember to call the new method.

In TypeScript ...

An enum is a name for a number, as in C#, not a class, as in Java. So, we do not need any conversion between numbers and enums, and we can simply use the enum indices as in the previous code.

transformMap exactly fits within our five-line limit. With that, our application compiles without error. Now we can check that the game still works, rename Tile2 to Tile everywhere, and commit our changes.

transformTile violates our five-line rule. It also almost violates another rule, NEVER USE switch, but we narrowly fall into the exception.

4.2.4 *Rule: NEVER USE SWITCH*

STATEMENT

Never use `switch` unless you have no `default` and return in *every* case.

EXPLANATION

Switches are evil, as they allow for two "conveniences," each of which leads to bugs. First, when we do case analysis with `switch`, we don't always have to do something for every value; `switch` supports `default` for this purpose. With `default`, we can address many values without duplication. What we handle and what we don't is now invariant. However, like any default value, this stops the compiler from asking us to revalidate the invariant when we add a new value. To the compiler, there is no difference between us forgetting to handle a new value and us wanting it to fall under `default`.

The other unfortunate convenience of `switch` is fall-through logic, where our program continues executing cases until it hits a `break`. It is easy to forget to include it and to not notice `break` is missing.

In general, I strongly recommend staying away from `switch`. But as specified in the detailed statement of the rule, we can remedy these maladies. The first way is easy: don't put functionality in `default`. In most languages, we should not have a `default`. Not all languages allow omitting `default`, and if the language we are using doesn't, we should not use `switch` at all.

We address the fall-through concern by returning in every case. As a result, there is no fall-through, so there is no `break` to overlook.

> **In TypeScript ...**
> Switches are particularly helpful, as we can make the compiler check that we have mapped all the enum values. We do need to introduce a "magic function" to make this work, but it is TypeScript-specific, so why it works is out of scope for this book. Luckily, the function never changes, and this pattern always works in TypeScript.

Listing 4.93 `assertExhausted` trick

```
function assertExhausted(x: never): never {
  throw new Error("Unexpected object: " + x);
}
/// ...
  switch (t) {
    case ...: return ...;
    // ...
    default: assertExhausted(t);
  }
```

This type of function is also one of the few that we cannot transform to fit in five lines if we want the compiler to check that we have mapped all the values.

SMELL

In Martin Fowler's book *Refactoring*, switch is the name of a smell. Switch focuses on context: how to handle value X *here*. In contrast, pushing functionality into classes focuses on data: how this value (object) handles situation X. Focusing on context means moving invariants further from their data, thereby globalizing the invariants.

INTENT

An elegant side effect of this rule is that we transform switches to else if chains, which we then make into classes. We push code eliminating the ifs, and in the end, they disappear while preserving the functionality and making it easier and safer to add new values.

REFERENCES

As mentioned earlier, you can read more about the smell in Martin Fowler's book *Refactoring*.

4.2.5 *Eliminating the if*

Where were we? We are working on the colorOfTile function, and here is how it currently looks.

Listing 4.94 Initial

```
function colorOfTile(g: CanvasRenderingContext2D, x: number, y: number) {
  if (map[y][x].isFlux())
    g.fillStyle = "#ccffcc";
  else if (map[y][x].isUnbreakable())
    g.fillStyle = "#999999";
  else if (map[y][x].isStone()
        || map[y][x].isFallingStone())
    g.fillStyle = "#0000cc";
  else if (map[y][x].isBox()
        || map[y][x].isFallingBox())
    g.fillStyle = "#8b4513";
  else if (map[y][x].isKey1()
        || map[y][x].isLock1())
    g.fillStyle = "#ffcc00";
  else if (map[y][x].isKey2()
        || map[y][x].isLock2())
    g.fillStyle = "#00ccff";
}
```

colorOfTile violates the rule NEVER USE if WITH else. We see that all the conditions in colorOfTile look at map[y][x]. This is the same condition we had earlier, so as before, we apply PUSH CODE INTO CLASSES:

1 Copy colorOfTile, and paste it into all the classes. Remove **function**; in this case, remove the parameters y and x, and replace map[y][x] with **this**.

2 Copy the method signature into the Tile interface. Let's also rename it to color.

3 Go through the new method in all classes:

    a Inline all the `is` methods.

    b Remove `if (true)` and `if (false) { ... }`. Most of the new methods are left with a single line, and `Air` and `Player` are empty.

    c Change the name to `color` to signal that we are finished with this method.

4 Replace the body of `colorOfTile` with a call to `map[y][x].color`.

At this point, the `if` is gone, and we are no longer violating any rules.

Listing 4.95 Before	Listing 4.96 After

```
function colorOfTile(
  g: CanvasRenderingContext2D,
  x: number, y: number)
{
  if (map[y][x].isFlux())
    g.fillStyle = "#ccffcc";
  else if (map[y][x].isUnbreakable())
    g.fillStyle = "#999999";
  else if (map[y][x].isStone()
        || map[y][x].isFallingStone())
    g.fillStyle = "#0000cc";
  else if (map[y][x].isBox()
        || map[y][x].isFallingBox())
    g.fillStyle = "#8b4513";
  else if (map[y][x].isKey1()
        || map[y][x].isLock1())
    g.fillStyle = "#ffcc00";
  else if (map[y][x].isKey2()
        || map[y][x].isLock2())
    g.fillStyle = "#00ccff";
}
```

```
function colorOfTile(
  g: CanvasRenderingContext2D,
  x: number, y: number)
{
  map[y][x].color(g);
}
interface Tile {
  // ...
  color(g: CanvasRenderingContext2D): void;
}
class Air implements Tile {
  // ...
  color(g: CanvasRenderingContext2D) {

  }
}
class Flux implements Tile {
  // ...
  color(g: CanvasRenderingContext2D) {
    g.fillStyle = "#ccffcc";
  }
}
```

color is empty in Air and Player because all the ifs were false.

All other classes have only their specific color.

`colorOfTile` has only a single line, so we decide to INLINE METHOD:

1 Change the method name to `colorOfTile2`.

2 Copy the body `map[y][x].color(g);`, and note that the parameters are `x`, `y`, and `g`.

3 We use this function in only one place, where we replace the call with the body.

Listing 4.97 Before	Listing 4.98 After

```
colorOfTile(g, x, y);
```

```
map[y][x].color(g);
```

In the end, we have the following.

Listing 4.99   Before

```
function drawMap(
  g: CanvasRenderingContext2D)
{
  for (let y = 0; y < map.length; y++) {
    for (let x = 0; x < map[y].length; x++){
      colorOfTile(g, x, y);
      if (map[y][x] !== Tile.AIR
          && map[y][x] !== Tile.PLAYER)
        g.fillRect(
          x * TILE_SIZE,
          y * TILE_SIZE,
          TILE_SIZE,
          TILE_SIZE);
    }
  }
}
function colorOfTile(
  g: CanvasRenderingContext2D,
  x: number, y: number)
{
  map[y][x].color(g);
}
```

Listing 4.100   After

```
function drawMap(
  g: CanvasRenderingContext2D)
{
  for (let y = 0; y < map.length; y++) {
    for (let x = 0; x < map[y].length; x++){
      map[y][x].color(g);                    ◁──┐ Inlined
      if (!map[y][x].isAir()                    │ body
          && !map[y][x].isPlayer())
        g.fillRect(
          x * TILE_SIZE,
          y * TILE_SIZE,
          TILE_SIZE,
          TILE_SIZE);
    }
  }
}
```

◁──┐ **colorOfTile**
    │ **is deleted.**

We have eliminated the large **if** from drawMap. But drawMap still does not comply with our rules, so we continue.

4.3   *Addressing code duplication*

drawMap is in violation because it has an **if** in the middle. We can solve this by extracting the **if** as we have done many times. But this is the chapter of PUSH CODE INTO CLASSES, so we can also be adventurous and try that. Doing so makes sense because both the **if** and the line before it concern map[y][x].

> **TIP** If you want to be a bit daring, you can skip extracting the method and inlining it in the following process, and push it directly into the classes. Make sure you have committed first so you can return to this point if something breaks.

The procedure is the same as for handleInput and colorOfTile, except that we are not just extracting an **if**. We start with EXTRACT METHOD (P3.2.1) on the body of the **fors**.

Listing 4.101 Before

```
function drawMap(
  g: CanvasRenderingContext2D)
{
  for (let y = 0; y < map.length; y++) {
    for (let x = 0; x < map[y].length; x++){
      map[y][x].color(g);
      if (!map[y][x].isAir()
            && !map[y][x].isPlayer())
        g.fillRect(
          x * TILE_SIZE, y * TILE_SIZE,
          TILE_SIZE, TILE_SIZE);
    }
  }
}
```

Listing 4.102 After

```
function drawMap(
  g: CanvasRenderingContext2D)
{
  for (let y = 0; y < map.length; y++) {
    for (let x = 0; x < map[y].length; x++){
      drawTile(g, x, y);
    }
  }
}
function drawTile(
  g: CanvasRenderingContext2D,
  x: number, y: number)
{
  map[y][x].color(g);
  if (!map[y][x].isAir()
        && !map[y][x].isPlayer())
    g.fillRect(
      x * TILE_SIZE, y * TILE_SIZE,
      TILE_SIZE, TILE_SIZE);
}
```

We can now use PUSH CODE INTO CLASSES to move this method into the Tile classes.

Listing 4.103 Before

```
function drawTile(
  g: CanvasRenderingContext2D,
  x: number, y: number)
{
  map[y][x].color(g);
  if (!map[y][x].isAir()
        && !map[y][x].isPlayer())
    g.fillRect(
      x * TILE_SIZE,
      y * TILE_SIZE,
      TILE_SIZE,
      TILE_SIZE);
}
```

Listing 4.104 After

```
function drawTile(
  g: CanvasRenderingContext2D,
  x: number, y: number)
{
  map[y][x].draw(g, x, y);
}
interface Tile {
  // ...
  draw(g: CanvasRenderingContext2D,
    x: number, y: number): void;
}
class Air implements Tile {
  // ...
  draw(g: CanvasRenderingContext2D,
    x: number, y: number)
  {
  
  }
}
class Flux implements Tile {
  // ...
  draw(g: CanvasRenderingContext2D,
    x: number, y: number)
  {
```

⟵ **draw ends up being empty in Air and Player.**

<table>
<tr><td style="text-align:right">All other classes
end up with two
lines after inlining
color and isAir
and deleting
the if (true).</td><td>

```
g.fillStyle = "#ccffcc";
g.fillRect(
  x * TILE_SIZE,
  y * TILE_SIZE,
  TILE_SIZE,
  TILE_SIZE);
}
}
```

</td></tr>
</table>

As usual, after we PUSH CODE INTO CLASSES, we have a function with only one line: drawTile. So, we use INLINE METHOD.

Listing 4.105 Before

```
function drawMap(
  g: CanvasRenderingContext2D)
{
  for (let y = 0; y < map.length; y++) {
    for (let x = 0; x < map[y].length; x++){
      drawTile(g, x, y);
    }
  }
}
function drawTile(
  g: CanvasRenderingContext2D,
  x: number, y: number)
{
  map[y][x].draw(g);
}
```

Listing 4.106 After

```
function drawMap(
  g: CanvasRenderingContext2D)
{
  for (let y = 0; y < map.length; y++) {
    for (let x = 0; x < map[y].length; x++){
      map[y][x].draw(g, x, y);        ◁─┐
    }                                    │
  }                            **Inlined body** │
}
```

       ◁─┐ **drawTile** is
         │ deleted.

At this point, you may be wondering: What is up with all the code duplication in the classes? Couldn't we use an abstract class instead of the interface and put all the common code there? Let's answer each question in turn.

4.3.1 Couldn't we use an abstract class instead of the interface?

First of all, yes. Yes, we could do that, and it would avoid code duplication. However, that approach also has some significant drawbacks. First, using an interface forces us to actively do something for each new class we introduce. Therefore, we cannot accidentally forget a property or override something we shouldn't. This is especially problematic six months from now when we have forgotten how this works and we return to add a new tile type.

This concept is so strong that it is also formalized in a rule that prevents us from using abstract classes: ONLY INHERIT FROM INTERFACES.

4.3.2 *Rule: ONLY INHERIT FROM INTERFACES*

STATEMENT

Only inherit from interfaces.

EXPLANATION

This rule simply states that we can only inherit from interfaces, as opposed to classes or abstract classes. The most common reason people use abstract classes is to provide a default implementation for some methods while having others be abstract. This reduces duplication and is convenient if we are lazy.

Unfortunately, the disadvantages are much more significant. Shared code causes coupling. In this case, the coupling is the code in the abstract class. Imagine that two methods are implemented in the abstract class: methodA and methodB. We find out that one subclass needs only methodA and another needs only methodB. Our only option, in this case, is to override one of the methods with an empty version.

When we have a method with a default implementation, there are two scenarios: either every possible subclass needs the method, in which case we can easily move the method out of the class; or *some* subclasses need to override the method, but because it has an implementation, the compiler does not remind us of the method when we add a new subclass.

This is another instance of the issues with defaults, discussed earlier. In this case, it is better to leave methods entirely abstract because then we need to explicitly handle these cases.

When multiple classes need to share code, we can put that code in another shared class. We return to this in chapter 5, when we discuss INTRODUCE STRATEGY PATTERN (P5.4.2).

SMELL

I derived this rule from the principle "Favor object composition over inheritance" from the book *Design Patterns* by Erich Gamma, Richard Helm, Ralph Johnson, and John Vlissides (often referred to as the Gang of Four, as mentioned previously). This book also introduced the concept of *design patterns* to object-oriented programming.

INTENT

The smell states plainly that we should share code by referring other objects in favor of inheriting from them. This rule takes it to the extreme, as it is extremely rare for a problem to require inheritance; and when a problem doesn't, composition gives us a more flexible and stable solution.

REFERENCES

As mentioned, the rule comes from the book *Design Patterns*. We explore a better solution to get the desired code sharing in chapter 5 when we discuss the INTRODUCE STRATEGY PATTERN (P5.4.2) refactoring.

4.3.3 *What is up with all this code duplication?*

In many cases, code duplication is bad. Everybody knows this, but let's think about why it is. Code duplication is bad when we need to maintain the code because we have to change something in a way that propagates throughout the program.

If we have duplicated code, and we change it in one place, we now have two different functions. Another way to say this is that code duplication is bad because it encourages divergence.

In most cases, that is not what we want; but in our example case, it would be better. We expect that the graphics for different tiles should change over time and should be different. To make a point of this, consider how easy it would be to make the keys round.

If the code should have converged, how should we have dealt with it, when we cannot use inheritance? We return to this exact situation in the next chapter.

4.4 *Refactoring a pair of complex if statements*

The next two functions that remain in violation of our rules are moveHorizontal and moveVertical. They are almost identical, so I present only the more complicated of the two, leaving the other as an exercise for you. moveHorizontal currently looks complicated; luckily, we can ignore most of it for now.

Listing 4.107 Initial

```
function moveHorizontal(dx: number) {
  if (map[playery][playerx + dx].isFlux()
        || map[playery][playerx + dx].isAir()) {      ← ⎤ ||s that we want
    moveToTile(playerx + dx, playery);                   ⎟ to preserve
  } else if ((map[playery][playerx + dx].isStone()       ⎦
        || map[playery][playerx + dx].isBox())     ←
        && map[playery][playerx + dx + dx].isAir()
        && !map[playery + 1][playerx + dx].isAir()) {
    map[playery][playerx + dx + dx] = map[playery][playerx + dx];
    moveToTile(playerx + dx, playery);
  } else if (map[playery][playerx + dx].isKey1()) {
    removeLock1();
    moveToTile(playerx + dx, playery);
  } else if (map[playery][playerx + dx].isKey2()) {
    removeLock2();
    moveToTile(playerx + dx, playery);
  }
}
```

First, notice that we have two ||s. These express something about the underlying domain. So, we would like to not only preserve this structure but emphasize it. We do so by pushing only that part into the classes.

This approach is a little different from what we have done before, as we are not pushing an entire method; however, the process stays the same. The most difficult part is coming up with a good name. Now is the time to look at what the code is doing and be careful. We want to state that there is a relation between flux and air; it relates to the game and not something general, so we will not dwell on it but will simply say that they are *edible*:

1 Introduce an isEdible method in the Tile interface.

2 In each class, add a method with a slightly wrong name: isEdible2.

3 As the body, put **return this**.isFlux() || **this**.isAir();.

4 Inline the values of isFlux and isAir.

5 Remove the temporary 2 in the name.

6 Replace map[playery][playerx + dx].isFlux() || map[playery][playerx + dx].isAir() *only here*. We cannot replace it everywhere because we do not know if other ||s refer to the same property (i.e., being edible).

The same situation is true for the other ||s. Here, boxes and stones share the property of being pushable in this context. Following the same pattern, we end up with the following code.

Listing 4.108 Before

```
function moveHorizontal(dx: number) {
  if (map[playery][playerx + dx].isFlux()
      || map[playery][playerx + dx].isAir()) {          ||s to be
    moveToTile(playerx + dx, playery);                  extracted
  } else if ((map[playery][playerx + dx].isStone()
      || map[playery][playerx + dx].isBox())
      && map[playery][playerx + dx + dx].isAir()
      && !map[playery + 1][playerx + dx].isAir()) {
    map[playery][playerx + dx + dx] = map[playery][playerx + dx];
    moveToTile(playerx + dx, playery);
  } else if (map[playery][playerx + dx].isKey1()) {
    removeLock1();
    moveToTile(playerx + dx, playery);
  } else if (map[playery][playerx + dx].isKey2()) {
    removeLock2();
    moveToTile(playerx + dx, playery);
  }
}
```

Listing 4.109 After

```
function moveHorizontal(dx: number) {
  if (map[playery][playerx + dx].isEdible()) {          New helper
    moveToTile(playerx + dx, playery);                  methods
  } else if (map[playery][playerx + dx].isPushable()
      && map[playery][playerx + dx + dx].isAir()
      && !map[playery + 1][playerx + dx].isAir()) {
    map[playery][playerx + dx + dx] = map[playery][playerx + dx];
    moveToTile(playerx + dx, playery);
  } else if (map[playery][playerx + dx].isKey1()) {
```

```
        removeLock1();
        moveToTile(playerx + dx, playery);
    } else if (map[playery][playerx + dx].isKey2()) {
        removeLock2();
        moveToTile(playerx + dx, playery);
    }
}
interface Tile {
    // ...
    isEdible(): boolean;
    isPushable(): boolean;
}
class Box implements Tile {
    // ...
    isEdible() { return false; }
    isPushable() { return true; }
}
class Air implements Tile {
    // ...
    isEdible() { return true; }
    isPushable() { return false; }
}
```

Box and Stone
are similar.

Air and Flux
are similar.

Having preserved the behavior of the ||s, we move on as normal and look at the context. The context of this code is map[playery][playerx + dx], as it is used in every **if**. Here we see that PUSH CODE INTO CLASSES applies not only when we start with a series of equality checks but also to anything with a clear context—that is, a lot of method invocations on the same instance ([.]s with the same thing on the left).

So, we push the code into map[playery][playerx + dx]; Tile again. After PUSH CODE INTO CLASSES, the code looks like this.

Listing 4.110 After PUSH CODE INTO CLASSES

```
function moveHorizontal(dx: number) {
    map[playery][playerx + dx].moveHorizontal(dx);
}
interface Tile {
    // ...
    moveHorizontal(dx: number): void;
}
class Box implements Tile {
    // ...
    moveHorizontal(dx: number) {
        if (map[playery][playerx + dx + dx].isAir()
            && !map[playery + 1][playerx + dx].isAir()) {
            map[playery][playerx + dx + dx] = this;
            moveToTile(playerx + dx, playery);
        }
    }
}
class Key1 implements Tile {
    // ...
    moveHorizontal(dx: number) {
```

Box and Stone
are similar.

Key1 and Key2
are similar.

```
      removeLock1();
      moveToTile(playerx + dx, playery);
   }
}
class Lock1 implements Tile {
   // ...
   moveHorizontal(dx: number) { }
}
class Air implements Tile {
   // ...
   moveHorizontal(dx: number) {
      moveToTile(playerx + dx, playery);
   }
}
```

The rest are empty.

Air and Flux are similar.

As usual, the original moveHorizontal method is only a single line, so we inline it. Notice that because this **if** was more complex, there are artifacts from it in Box and Stone. Luckily, they still comply with our rules. Now you can do the same thing for the moveVertical method.

The only method that remains in conflict with our new rule NEVER USE **if** WITH **else** is updateTile. But that method has a hidden structure, which we explore further in the next chapter.

4.5 Removing dead code

We end this chapter with some cleanup. We introduced a lot of new methods, and we deleted some after inlining them, but we can go further.

Many IDEs—including Visual Studio Code—indicate if a function is unused. Whenever we see such an indication and we are not in the middle of something, we should delete the function immediately. Deleting code saves us time because we don't have to deal with it in the future.

Unfortunately, because interfaces are public, no IDE can tell you whether the methods in an interface are unused. We may intend to use them in the future, or they may be used by something outside of our scope. In general, we cannot easily delete methods from interfaces.

But the interfaces we have considered in this chapter were all introduced by us; therefore, we know the entire scope. We are free to do with them as we please: in particular, we can delete unused methods from them. Here is a technique for discovering whether methods are unused:

1 Compile. There should be no errors.
2 Delete a method from the interface.
3 Compile.
   a If the compiler errors, undo, and move on.
   b Otherwise, go through each class and check whether you can delete the same method from it without getting errors.

This is a simple but useful technique. After cleaning our interfaces, they have only 1 method in one interface and 10 methods in the other interface, respectively. I am such a big fan of deleting code that I have made a refactoring pattern out of this process: TRY DELETE THEN COMPILE.

4.5.1 *Refactoring pattern:* TRY DELETE THEN COMPILE

DESCRIPTION

This refactoring pattern's primary use is to remove unused methods from interfaces when we know the interfaces' entire scope. We can also use this pattern to find and remove any unused methods. Performing TRY DELETE THEN COMPILE is as simple as the name describes: try deleting a method, and see if the compiler allows us to do so. This refactoring pattern is interesting not for its sophistication but for its purpose. Note that we should not perform this refactoring while implementing new features, as we might delete methods that are not used *yet*.

Having expired code in a codebase drags it down. The code takes time to read or ignore, and it makes compilation and analyses slower and testing more difficult. The quicker we can remove irrelevant code, the cheaper the process in terms of cost and effort.

To help identify unused methods, lots of editors highlight them in some way. But the analyses in these editors can be cheated. One of the things that can cheat the analyses is an interface. If a method is in an interface, it may be because the method needs to be available for code outside of our scope or because we need the method for code inside our scope. Editors cannot tell the difference. The only safe option is to assume that all interface methods are meant to be used outside our scope.

When we know an interface is used only in our scope, we need to clean it up manually. This is the purpose of this refactoring pattern.

PROCESS

1 Compile. There should be no errors.
2 Delete a method from the interface.
3 Compile.
   a If the compiler errors, undo, and move on.
   b Otherwise, go through each class and check whether you can delete the same method from it without getting errors.

EXAMPLE

There are three unused methods in this artificial piece of code, but they are not all highlighted by the editor. In some editors, none are highlighted.

> Listing 4.111 Initial

```
interface A {
  m1(): void;
  m2(): void;
}
```

```
class B implements A {
  m1() { console.log("m1"); }
  m2() { this.m3(); }
  m3() { console.log("m3"); }
}
let a = new B();
a.m1();
```

Following the process, can you discover and eliminate the three unused methods?

Summary

- The rules NEVER USE **if** WITH **else** (R4.1.1) and NEVER USE **switch** (R4.2.4) state that we should have **else**s or **switch**es only at the edges of our program. Both **else**s and **switch**es are low-level control-flow operators. In the core of our applications, we should use the refactoring patterns REPLACE TYPE CODE WITH CLASSES (P4.1.3) and PUSH CODE INTO CLASSES (P4.1.5) to replace **switch**es and **else if** chains with high-level classes and methods.

- Overly general methods can prevent us from refactoring. In these cases, we can use the refactoring pattern SPECIALIZE METHOD (P4.2.2) to remove unnecessary generality.

- The rule ONLY INHERIT FROM INTERFACES (P4.3.2) prevents us from reusing code by using abstract classes and class inheritance because these types of inheritance impose unnecessarily tight coupling.

- We added two refactoring patterns for cleaning up after refactoring. INLINE METHOD (P4.1.7) and TRY DELETE THEN COMPILE (P4.5.1) can both remove methods that no longer add readability.

Fuse similar code together

This chapter covers

- Unifying similar classes with UNIFY SIMILAR CLASSES
- Exposing structure with conditional arithmetic
- Understanding simple UML class diagrams
- Unifying similar code with INTRODUCE STRATEGY-PATTERN (P5.4.2)
- Removing clutter with NO INTERFACE WITH ONLY ONE IMPLEMENTATION (R5.4.3)

In the previous chapter, I mentioned that we are not finished with updateTile. It violates several rules, most notably NEVER USE **if** WITH **else** (R4.1.1). We also worked to preserve the ||s in the code because they expressed structure. In this chapter, we explore how to expose more such structures in the code.

This is updateTile at the moment.

Listing 5.1 Initial

```
function updateTile(x: number, y: number) {
  if ((map[y][x].isStone() || map[y][x].isFallingStone())
      && map[y + 1][x].isAir()) {
    map[y + 1][x] = new FallingStone();
```

```
    map[y][x] = new Air();
  } else if ((map[y][x].isBox() || map[y][x].isFallingBox())
        && map[y + 1][x].isAir()) {
    map[y + 1][x] = new FallingBox();
    map[y][x] = new Air();
  } else if (map[y][x].isFallingStone()) {
    map[y][x] = new Stone();
  } else if (map[y][x].isFallingBox()) {
    map[y][x] = new Box();
  }
}
```

5.1 Unifying similar classes

The first thing we spot is that, as was the case earlier, we have parenthesized expressions (that is, `(map[y][x].isStone() || map[y][x].isFallingStone())`) that express a relation we want to not only preserve but also emphasize. Therefore, our first step is to introduce one function for each of the two parenthesized ||s. We say that `stony` and `boxy` should be understood as "behaves like a stone" and "behaves like a box," respectively.

Listing 5.2 Before

```
function updateTile(x: number, y: number) {
  if ((map[y][x].isStone()
        || map[y][x].isFallingStone())
        && map[y + 1][x].isAir()) {
    map[y + 1][x] = new FallingStone();
    map[y][x] = new Air();
  } else if ((map[y][x].isBox()
        || map[y][x].isFallingBox())
        && map[y + 1][x].isAir()) {
    map[y + 1][x] = new FallingBox();
    map[y][x] = new Air();
  } else if (map[y][x].isFallingStone()) {
    map[y][x] = new Stone();
  } else if (map[y][x].isFallingBox()) {
    map[y][x] = new Box();
  }
}
```

Listing 5.3 After

```
function updateTile(x: number, y: number) {
  if (map[y][x].isStony()

        && map[y + 1][x].isAir()) {
    map[y + 1][x] = new FallingStone();
    map[y][x] = new Air();
  } else if (map[y][x].isBoxy()

        && map[y + 1][x].isAir()) {
    map[y + 1][x] = new FallingBox();
    map[y][x] = new Air();
  } else if (map[y][x].isFallingStone()) {
    map[y][x] = new Stone();
  } else if (map[y][x].isFallingBox()) {
    map[y][x] = new Box();
  }
}
```

New helper methods

```
interface Tile {
  // ...
  isStony(): boolean;
  isBoxy(): boolean;
}
class Air implements Tile {
  // ...
  isStony() { return false; }
  isBoxy() { return false; }
}
```

Having dealt with the ||s, we can push the code into classes, but we can also wait and first take a look at the classes and the many methods we introduced in the last chapter. At this point, TRY DELETE THEN COMPILE (P4.5.1) lets us delete isStone and isBox.

We notice that the only difference between Stone and FallingStone is the result of the isFallingStone and moveHorizontal methods.

Listing 5.4 Stone	Listing 5.5 FallingStone

```
class Stone implements Tile {
  isAir() { return false; }
  isFallingStone() { return false; }
  isFallingBox() { return false; }
  isLock1() { return false; }
  isLock2() { return false; }
  draw(g: CanvasRenderingContext2D,
    x: number, y: number)
  {
    // ...
  }
  moveVertical(dy: number) { }
  isStony() { return true; }
  isBoxy() { return false; }
  moveHorizontal(dx: number) {
    // ...
  }
}
```

```
class FallingStone implements Tile {
  isAir() { return false; }
  isFallingStone() { return true; }
  isFallingBox() { return false; }
  isLock1() { return false; }
  isLock2() { return false; }
  draw(g: CanvasRenderingContext2D,
    x: number, y: number)
  {
    // ...
  }
  moveVertical(dy: number) { }
  isStony() { return true; }
  isBoxy() { return false; }
  moveHorizontal(dx: number) {
  }
}
```

Only differences

When a method returns a constant, we call it a *constant method*. We can join these two classes because they share a constant method that returns a different value in each case. Joining two classes like this happens in two phases, and the process is reminiscent of the algorithm for adding fractions. The first step in adding fractions is making the denominators equal, and in the same way, the first phase in joining classes is to make the classes equal in all but the constant methods. The second phase for fractions is the actual addition; for classes, it's the actual joining. Let's see how it looks in practice:

1. The first phase makes the two moveHorizontals equal:
   a. In the body of each moveHorizontal, add an enclosing if (true) { } around the existing code.

Listing 5.6 Before

```
class Stone implements Tile {
  // ...
  moveHorizontal(dx: number) {

    if (map[playery][playerx+dx+dx].isAir()
    && !map[playery+1][playerx+dx].isAir())
    {
      map[playery][playerx+dx + dx] = this;
      moveToTile(playerx+dx, playery);
    }

  }
}
class FallingStone implements Tile {
  // ...
  moveHorizontal(dx: number) {

  }
}
```

Listing 5.7 After (1/8)

```
class Stone implements Tile {
  // ...
  moveHorizontal(dx: number) {
    if (true) {
      if (map[playery][playerx+dx+dx].isAir()
      && !map[playery+1][playerx+dx].isAir())
      {
        map[playery][playerx+dx + dx] = this;
        moveToTile(playerx+dx, playery);
      }
    }
  }
}
class FallingStone implements Tile {
  // ...
  moveHorizontal(dx: number) {
    if (true) { }
  }
}
```

New if (true)s

b Replace **true** with isFallingStone() === **true** and isFallingStone() === **false**, respectively.

Listing 5.8 Before

```
class Stone implements Tile {
  // ...
  moveHorizontal(dx: number) {
    if (true) {
      if (map[playery][playerx+dx+dx].isAir()
      && !map[playery+1][playerx+dx].isAir())
      {
        map[playery][playerx+dx + dx] = this;
        moveToTile(playerx+dx, playery);
      }
    }
  }
}
class FallingStone implements Tile {
  // ...
  moveHorizontal(dx: number) {
    if (true) { }
  }
}
```

Listing 5.9 After (2/8)

```
class Stone implements Tile {
  // ...
  moveHorizontal(dx: number) {
    if (this.isFallingStone() === false) {
      if (map[playery][playerx+dx+dx].isAir()
      && !map[playery+1][playerx+dx].isAir())
      {
        map[playery][playerx+dx + dx] = this;
        moveToTile(playerx+dx, playery);
      }
    }
  }
}
class FallingStone implements Tile {
  // ...
  moveHorizontal(dx: number) {
    if (this.isFallingStone() === true) { }
  }
}
```

Specialized conditions

c Copy the body of each moveHorizontal, and paste it with an **else** into the other moveHorizontal.

Listing 5.10 Before	Listing 5.11 After (3/8)

```
class Stone implements Tile {
// ...
moveHorizontal(dx: number) {
  if (this.isFallingStone() === false) {
    if (map[playery] [playerx+dx+dx].isAir()
    && !map[playery+1] [playerx+dx].isAir())
    {
      map[playery] [playerx+dx + dx] = this;
      moveToTile(playerx+dx, playery);
    }
  }



}
}
class FallingStone implements Tile {
  // ...
  moveHorizontal(dx: number) {









    if (this.isFallingStone() === true)
    {
    }
  }
}
```

Body from the other method

```
class Stone implements Tile {
// ...
moveHorizontal(dx: number) {
  if (this.isFallingStone() === false) {
    if (map[playery] [playerx+dx+dx].isAir()
    && !map[playery+1] [playerx+dx].isAir())
    {
      map[playery] [playerx+dx + dx] = this;
      moveToTile(playerx+dx, playery);
    }
  }
  else if (this.isFallingStone() === true)
  {
  }
}
}
class FallingStone implements Tile {
  // ...
  moveHorizontal(dx: number) {
  if (this.isFallingStone() === false) {
    if (map[playery] [playerx+dx+dx].isAir()
    && !map[playery+1] [playerx+dx].isAir())
    {
      map[playery] [playerx+dx + dx] = this;
      moveToTile(playerx+dx, playery);
    }
  }
  else if (this.isFallingStone() === true)
  {
  }
}
}
```

2 Now that only the isFallingStone constant methods are different, the second phase begins by introducing a falling field and assigning its value in the constructor.

| Listing 5.12 Before | Listing 5.13 After (4/8) |

```
class Stone implements Tile {




  // ...
  isFallingStone() { return false; }
}
class FallingStone implements Tile {




  // ...
  isFallingStone() { return true; }
}
```

```
class Stone implements Tile {
  private falling: boolean;          ◁─┐
  constructor() {
    this.falling = false;
  }
  // ...
  isFallingStone() { return false; }
}
class FallingStone implements Tile {
  private falling: boolean;          ◁─┘
  constructor() {
    this.falling = true;
  }
  // ...
  isFallingStone() { return true; }
}
```

New field

Assigns a default value to the new field

3 Change isFallingStone to return the new falling field.

| Listing 5.14 Before | Listing 5.15 After (5/8) |

```
class Stone implements Tile {
  // ...
  isFallingStone() { return false; }
}
class FallingStone implements Tile {
  // ...
  isFallingStone() { return true; }
}
```

```
class Stone implements Tile {
  // ...
  isFallingStone() { return this.falling; } ◁─┐
}
class FallingStone implements Tile {
  // ...
  isFallingStone() { return this.falling; } ◁─┘
}
```

Returns a field instead of a constant

4 Compile to ensure that we have not broken anything yet.

5 For each of the classes:

a Copy the default value of falling, and then make the default value a parameter.

| Listing 5.16 Before | Listing 5.17 After (6/8) |

```
class Stone implements Tile {
  private falling: boolean;
  constructor() {
    this.falling = false;
  }
  // ...
}
```

```
class Stone implements Tile {
  private falling: boolean;
  constructor(falling: boolean) {
    this.falling = falling;
  }
  // ...
}
```

Makes falling a parameter

b Go through the compiler errors, and insert the default value as an argument.

Listing 5.18   Before

```
/// ...
  new Stone();
/// ...
```

Listing 5.19   After (7/8)

```
/// ...
  new Stone(false);        ◁──┐  Calls with the
/// ...                         │  default value
```

6   Delete all but one of the classes we are unifying, and fix all of the compile errors by switching to the class that is still there.

Listing 5.20   Before

```
/// ...
  new FallingStone(true);
/// ...
```

Listing 5.21   After (8/8)

```
/// ...                          Replaces the
  new Stone(true);    ◁──┤       deleted class with
/// ...                          the unified one
```

This unification amounts to the following transformation.

Listing 5.22   Before

```
function updateTile(x: number, y: number) {
  if (map[y][x].isStony()
          && map[y + 1][x].isAir()) {
    map[y + 1][x] = new FallingStone();
    map[y][x] = new Air();
  } else if (map[y][x].isBoxy()
          && map[y + 1][x].isAir()) {
    map[y + 1][x] = new FallingBox();
    map[y][x] = new Air();
  } else if (map[y][x].isFallingStone()) {
    map[y][x] = new Stone();
  } else if (map[y][x].isFallingBox()) {
    map[y][x] = new Box();
  }
}
class Stone implements Tile {
  // ...
  isFallingStone() { return false; }
  moveHorizontal(dx: number) {
    if (map[playery][playerx+dx+dx].isAir()
    && !map[playery+1][playerx+dx].isAir())
    {
      map[playery][playerx+dx + dx] = this;
      moveToTile(playerx+dx, playery);
    }
  }
}                              isFallingStone
                               returns this field.
class FallingStone implements Tile {
  // ...
  isFallingStone() { return true; }
  moveHorizontal(dx: number) { }
}
```

Listing 5.23   After

```
function updateTile(x: number, y: number) {
  if (map[y][x].isStony()
          && map[y + 1][x].isAir()) {
    map[y + 1][x] = new Stone(true);    ◁──
    map[y][x] = new Air();
  } else if (map[y][x].isBoxy()
          && map[y + 1][x].isAir()) {
    map[y + 1][x] = new FallingBox();
    map[y][x] = new Air();
  } else if (map[y][x].isFallingStone()) {
    map[y][x] = new Stone(false);    ◁──
  } else if (map[y][x].isFallingBox()) {
    map[y][x] = new Box();
  }                        Private field, set
}                          in the constructor
class Stone implements Tile {
  constructor(private falling: boolean) { }  ◁──
  // ...
  isFallingStone() { return this.falling; }  ◁──
  moveHorizontal(dx: number) {
    if (this.isFallingStone() === false) {
      if (map[playery][playerx+dx+dx].isAir()
      && !map[playery+1][playerx+dx].isAir())
      {
        map[playery][playerx+dx + dx] = this;
        moveToTile(playerx+dx, playery);
      }
    } else if(this.isFallingStone() === true)
    {
                              moveHorizontal
    }                         has the combined
  }                           bodies.
}            FallingStone
  ◁──        is removed.
```

In TypeScript ...

Constructors behave a little differently than in most languages. First, we can have only one constructor, and it is always called `constructor`.

Second, putting `public` or `private` in front of a parameter to the constructor automatically makes an instance variable and assigns it the value of the argument. So the following are equivalent.

Before

```
class Stone implements Tile {
  private falling: boolean;
  constructor(falling: boolean) {
    this.falling = falling;
  }
}
```

After

```
class Stone implements Tile {

  constructor(
    private falling: boolean) { }
}
```

We generally prefer the version on the right in this book.

Looking at the resulting `moveHorizontal`, we spot multiple interesting points. The most obvious is that it contains an empty `if`. Even more significant, it now contains an `else`, which means it violates NEVER USE `if` WITH `else`. A common effect of joining classes the way we just did is that it exposes potentially hidden type codes. In this case, the Boolean `falling` is a type code. We can expose this type code by making it into an enum.

Listing 5.24 Before

```
/// ...
  new Stone(true);
/// ...
  new Stone(false);
/// ...
class Stone implements Tile {
  constructor(private falling: boolean)
  { }
  // ...
  isFallingStone() {
    return this.falling;

  }
}
```

Listing 5.25 After

```
enum FallingState {
  FALLING, RESTING
}
/// ...
  new Stone(FallingState.FALLING);
/// ...
  new Stone(FallingState.RESTING);
/// ...
class Stone implements Tile {
  constructor(private falling: FallingState)
  { }
  // ...
  isFallingStone() {
    return this.falling
      === FallingState.FALLING;
  }
}
```

This change has already made the code more readable because we get away with the unnamed Boolean arguments to Stone. But even better, we know how to deal with enums: REPLACE TYPE CODE WITH CLASSES (P4.1.3).

Listing 5.26 Before	Listing 5.27 After

```
enum FallingState {
  FALLING, RESTING

}
```

```
interface FallingState {
  isFalling(): boolean;
  isResting(): boolean;
}
class Falling implements FallingState {
  isFalling() { return true; }
  isResting() { return false; }
}
class Resting implements FallingState {
  isFalling() { return false; }
  isResting() { return true; }
}
```

```
  new Stone(FallingState.FALLING);
  new Stone(FallingState.RESTING);
class Stone implements Tile {
  constructor(private falling:
FallingState)
  { }
  // ...
  isFallingStone() {
    return this.falling
      === FallingState.FALLING;
  }
}
```

```
  new Stone(new Falling());
  new Stone(new Resting());
class Stone implements Tile {
  constructor(private falling:
FallingState)
  { }
  // ...
  isFallingStone() {
    return this.falling.isFalling();
  }
}
```

If we are bothered that the **news** are slightly slower, we can extract them to constants; but remember, performance optimization should be guided by profiling tools. If we inline isFallingStone in the method moveHorizontal, we see that we should probably use PUSH CODE INTO CLASSES (P4.1.5).

Listing 5.28 Before	Listing 5.29 After

```
interface FallingState {
  // ...



}
class Falling implements FallingState {
  // ...



}
```

```
interface FallingState {
  // ...
  moveHorizontal(
    tile: Tile, dx: number): void;
}
class Falling implements FallingState {
  // ...
  moveHorizontal(tile: Tile, dx: number) {
  }
}
```

```
class Resting implements FallingState {        class Resting implements FallingState {
  // ...                                          // ...
}                                                  moveHorizontal(tile: Tile, dx: number) {
class Stone implements Tile {                        if (map[playery][playerx+dx+dx].isAir()
  // ...                                             && !map[playery+1][playerx+dx].isAir())
  moveHorizontal(dx: number) {                       {
    if (!this.falling.isFalling()) {                   map[playery][playerx+dx + dx] = tile;
      if (map[playery][playerx+dx+dx].isAir()          moveToTile(playerx+dx, playery);
      && !map[playery+1][playerx+dx].isAir())        }
      {                                            }
        map[playery][playerx+dx + dx] = this;    }
        moveToTile(playerx+dx, playery);         class Stone implements Tile {
      }                                            // ...
    } else if (this.falling.isFalling()) {         moveHorizontal(dx: number) {
    }                                                this.falling.moveHorizontal(this, dx);
  }                                                }
}                                                }
```

Finally, since we introduced a new interface, we can use TRY DELETE THEN COMPILE to remove isResting. I leave it to you to do the same for Box and FallingBox; notice that you can reuse FallingState. We call unifying two similar classes like this UNIFY SIMILAR CLASSES.

5.1.1 Refactoring pattern: UNIFY SIMILAR CLASSES

DESCRIPTION

Whenever we have two or more classes that differ from each other in a set of constant methods, we can use this refactoring pattern to unify them. A set of constant methods is called a *basis*. A basis with two methods is called a *two-point basis*. We want our basis to have as few methods as possible. When we want to unify X classes, we need at most an $(X - 1)$–point basis. Unifying classes is great because having fewer classes usually means we uncover more structure.

PROCESS

1 The first phase is to make all the non-basis methods equal. For each of these methods, perform these steps:

   a In the body of each version of the method, add an enclosing if (**true**) { } around the existing code.

   b Replace **true** with an expression calling all the basis methods and comparing their result to their constant values.

   c Copy the body of each version, and paste it with an **else** into all the other versions.

2 Now that only the basis methods are different, the second phase begins by introducing a field for each method in the basis and assigning its constant in the constructor.

3 Change the methods to return the new fields instead of the constants.

4 Compile to ensure that we have not broken anything yet.

5 For each class, one field at a time:

a Copy the default value of the field, and then make the default value a parameter.

b Go through the compiler errors, and insert the default value as an argument.

6 After all the classes are identical, delete all but one of the unified classes, and fix all the compile errors by switching to the remaining class.

EXAMPLE

In this example, we have a traffic light with three classes that are pretty similar, so we have decided to unify them.

Listing 5.30   Initial

```
function nextColor(t: TrafficColor) {
  if (t.color() === "red") return new Green();
  else if (t.color() === "green") return new Yellow();
  else if (t.color() === "yellow") return new Red();
}
interface TrafficColor {
  color(): string;
  check(car: Car): void;
}
class Red implements TrafficColor {
  color() { return "red"; }
  check(car: Car) { car.stop(); }
}
class Yellow implements TrafficColor {
  color() { return "yellow"; }
  check(car: Car) { car.stop(); }
}
class Green implements TrafficColor {
  color() { return "green"; }
  check(car: Car) { car.drive(); }
}
```

We follow the process:

1 The basis method is `color` as it returns a different constant in each class, so we need to make the `check` methods equal. For each of these methods, perform these steps:

a In the body of each version of `check`, add an enclosing if (**true**) { } around the existing code.

Listing 5.31 Before

```
class Red implements TrafficColor {
  // ...
  check(car: Car) {

    car.stop();

  }
}
class Yellow implements TrafficColor {
  // ...
  check(car: Car) {

    car.stop();

  }
}
class Green implements TrafficColor {
  // ...
  check(car: Car) {

    car.drive();

  }
}
```

Listing 5.32 After (1/8)

```
class Red implements TrafficColor {
  // ...
  check(car: Car) {
    if (true) {                    ◄─────────┐
      car.stop();                            │
    }                                        │
  }                                          │
}                                            │
class Yellow implements TrafficColor {       │
  // ...                                      │
  check(car: Car) {                          │
    if (true) {           ◄──────            │
      car.stop();                            │
    }                     Added if           │
  }                       (true) { }         │
}                                            │
class Green implements TrafficColor {        │
  // ...                                      │
  check(car: Car) {                          │
    if (true) {           ◄──────────────────┘
      car.drive();
    }
  }
}
```

ᵇ Replace **true** with an expression calling the basis method and comparing the result to the constant values.

Listing 5.33 Before

```
class Red implements TrafficColor {
  color() { return "red"; }
  check(car: Car) {
    if (true) {
      car.stop();
    }
  }
}
class Yellow implements TrafficColor {
  color() { return "yellow"; }
  check(car: Car) {
    if (true) {
      car.stop();
    }
  }
}
class Green implements TrafficColor {
  color() { return "green"; }
  check(car: Car) {
    if (true) {
      car.drive();
    }
  }
}
```

Listing 5.34 After (2/8)

```
class Red implements TrafficColor {
  color() { return "red"; }
  check(car: Car) {
    if (this.color() === "red") {      ◄─────────┐
      car.stop();                                │
    }                                            │
  }                                              │
}                                                │
class Yellow implements TrafficColor {           │
  color() { return "yellow"; }                   │
  check(car: Car) {                              │
    if (this.color() === "yellow") {  ◄──┐       │
      car.stop();                        │       │
    }                     Checking the   │       │
  }                       basis method   │       │
}                                        │       │
class Green implements TrafficColor {    │       │
  color() { return "green"; }            │       │
  check(car: Car) {                      │       │
    if (this.color() === "green") {   ◄──────────┘
      car.drive();
    }
  }
}
```

c Now we copy the body of each version and paste it with an `else` into all the other versions.

Listing 5.35 Before	Listing 5.36 After (3/8)

```
class Red implements TrafficColor {
  // ...
  check(car: Car) {
    if (this.color() === "red") {
      car.stop();
    }



  }
}
class Yellow implements TrafficColor {
  // ...
  check(car: Car) {

    if (this.color() === "yellow") {
      car.stop();
    }



  }
}
class Green implements TrafficColor {
  // ...
  check(car: Car) {



    if (this.color() === "green") {
      car.drive();
    }
  }
}
```

```
class Red implements TrafficColor {
  // ...
  check(car: Car) {
    if (this.color() === "red") {
      car.stop();
    } else if (this.color() === "yellow") {
      car.stop();
    } else if (this.color() === "green") {
      car.drive();
    }
  }
}
class Yellow implements TrafficColor {
  // ...
  check(car: Car) {
    if (this.color() === "red") {
      car.stop();
    } else if (this.color() === "yellow") {
      car.stop();
    } else if (this.color() === "green") {
      car.drive();
    }
  }
}
class Green implements TrafficColor {
  // ...
  check(car: Car) {
    if (this.color() === "red") {
      car.stop();
    } else if (this.color() === "yellow") {
      car.stop();
    } else if (this.color() === "green") {
      car.drive();
    }
  }
}
```

Copying the methods into each other

2 Now the `check` methods are equal, and only the basis methods are different. The second phase begins by introducing a field for the `color` method and assigning its constant in the constructor.

Listing 5.37 Before	Listing 5.38 After (4/8)

```
class Red implements TrafficColor {


  color() { return "red"; }
  // ...
}
class Yellow implements TrafficColor {


  color() { return "yellow"; }
  // ...
}
class Green implements TrafficColor {


  color() { return "green"; }
  // ...
}
```

```
class Red implements TrafficColor {
  constructor(
    private col: string = "red") { }    ◄──┐
  color() { return "red"; }
  // ...
}
class Yellow implements TrafficColor {
  constructor(
    private col: string = "yellow") { }  ◄──┤
  color() { return "yellow"; }
  // ...
}
class Green implements TrafficColor {
  constructor(
    private col: string = "green") { }   ◄──┤
  color() { return "green"; }
  // ...                           Added
}                               constructors
```

3 Change the methods to return the new fields instead of the constants.

Listing 5.39 Before	Listing 5.40 After (5/8)

```
class Red implements TrafficColor {
  // ...
  color() { return "red"; }
}
class Yellow implements TrafficColor {
  // ...
  color() { return "yellow"; }
}
class Green implements TrafficColor {
  // ...
  color() { return "green"; }
}
```

```
class Red implements TrafficColor {
  // ...
  color() { return this.col; }      ◄──┐
}
class Yellow implements TrafficColor {
  // ...
  color() { return this.col; }      ◄──┤
}
class Green implements TrafficColor {
  // ...
  color() { return this.col; }      ◄──┤
}                          Returns a field
                        instead of a constant
```

4 Compile to ensure that we have not broken anything yet.
5 For each class, one field at a time:
   a Copy the default value of the field, and then make the default value a
     parameter.

Listing 5.41 Before	Listing 5.42 After (6/8)

```
class Red implements TrafficColor {
  constructor(
    private col: string = "red") { }
  // ...
}
```

```
class Red implements TrafficColor {
  constructor(
    private col: string) { }    ◄──  Cut
  // ...                              default
}                                     value
```

b Go through the compiler errors, and insert the default value as an argument.

Listing 5.43 Before

```
function nextColor(t: TrafficColor) {
  if (t.color() === "red")
    return new Green();
  else if (t.color() === "green")
    return new Yellow();
  else if (t.color() === "yellow")
    return new Red();
}
```

Listing 5.44 After (7/8)

```
function nextColor(t: TrafficColor) {
  if (t.color() === "red")
    return new Green();
  else if (t.color() === "green")
    return new Yellow();
  else if (t.color() === "yellow")
    return new Red("red");
}
```
◁—— **Fix error by pasting**

6 After all the classes are identical, delete all but one of the unified classes, and fix all the compile errors by switching to the remaining class.

Listing 5.45 Before

```
function nextColor(t: TrafficColor) {
  if (t.color() === "red")
    return new Green();
  else if (t.color() === "green")
    return new Yellow();
  else if (t.color() === "yellow")
    return new Red();
}
class Yellow implements TrafficColor { ... }
class Green implements TrafficColor { ... }
```

Listing 5.46 After (8/8)

```
function nextColor(t: TrafficColor) {
  if (t.color() === "red")
    return new Red("green");
  else if (t.color() === "green")
    return new Red("yellow");
  else if (t.color() === "yellow")
    return new Red("red");
}
```
◁——
◁——

Deleting the classes Yellow and Green

At this point, we don't need the interface, and we should rename Red. We should also work toward removing the **if** with the **elses**—maybe using an upcoming refactoring pattern. However, we have successfully unified the three classes.

Listing 5.47 Before

```
function nextColor(t: TrafficColor) {
  if (t.color() === "red")
    return new Green();
  else if (t.color() === "green")
    return new Yellow();
  else if (t.color() === "yellow")
    return new Red();
}
interface TrafficColor {
  color(): string;
  check(car: Car): void;
}
```

Listing 5.48 After

```
function nextColor(t: TrafficColor) {
  if (t.color() === "red")
    return new Red("green");
  else if (t.color() === "green")
    return new Red("yellow");
  else if (t.color() === "yellow")
    return new Red("red");
}
interface TrafficColor {
  color(): string;
  check(car: Car): void;
}
```

```
class Red implements TrafficColor {          class Red implements TrafficColor {
  color() { return "red"; }                    constructor(private col: string) { }
  check(car: Car) { car.stop(); }              color() { return this.col; }
}                                              check(car: Car) {
class Yellow implements TrafficColor {           if (this.color() === "red") {
  color() { return "yellow"; }                     car.stop();
  check(car: Car) { car.stop(); }                } else if (this.color() === "yellow") {
}                                                  car.stop();
class Green implements TrafficColor {            } else if (this.color() === "green") {
  color() { return "green"; }                      car.drive();
  check(car: Car) { car.drive(); }               }
}                                              }
                                             }
```

At this point, it might make sense to extract the three colors into constants to avoid having to instantiate them over and over again. Luckily, this is trivial to do.

FURTHER READING

To my knowledge, this is the first description of this process as a refactoring pattern.

5.2 Unifying simple conditions

To proceed with updateTile, we would like to make the bodies of some of the **ifs** more similar. Let's look at the code.

Listing 5.49 Initial

```
function updateTile(x: number, y: number) {
  if (map[y][x].isStony()
          && map[y + 1][x].isAir()) {
    map[y + 1][x] = new Stone(new Falling());
    map[y][x] = new Air();
  } else if (map[y][x].isBoxy()
          && map[y + 1][x].isAir()) {
    map[y + 1][x] = new Box(new Falling());
    map[y][x] = new Air();
  } else if (map[y][x].isFallingStone()) {
    map[y][x] = new Stone(new Resting());
  } else if (map[y][x].isFallingBox()) {
    map[y][x] = new Box(new Resting());
  }
}
```

We decide to introduce methods for setting and unsetting the new falling field.

Listing 5.50 After introducing drop and rest

```
interface Tile {              New method for
  // ...                      setting the new field;
  drop(): void;               empty in most classes
  rest(): void;
}                             New method for unsetting the
                              new field; empty in most classes
```

```
class Stone implements Tile {
    // ...
    drop() { this.falling = new Falling(); }
    rest() { this.falling = new Resting(); }
}
class Flux implements Tile {
    // ...
    drop() { }
    rest() { }
}
```

New method for unsetting the new field; empty in most classes →

New method for setting the new field; empty in most classes ←

Doing one thing at a time, we deal with rest first and drop soon. We can use rest directly in updateTile.

Listing 5.51   Before

```
function updateTile(x: number, y: number) {
    if (map[y][x].isStony()
            && map[y + 1][x].isAir()) {
        map[y+1][x] = new Stone(new Falling());
        map[y][x] = new Air();
    } else if (map[y][x].isBoxy()
            && map[y + 1][x].isAir()) {
        map[y + 1][x] = new Box(new Falling());
        map[y][x] = new Air();
    } else if (map[y][x].isFallingStone()) {
        map[y][x] = new Stone(new Resting());
    } else if (map[y][x].isFallingBox()) {
        map[y][x] = new Box(new Resting());
    }
}
```

Listing 5.52   After

```
function updateTile(x: number, y: number) {
    if (map[y][x].isStony()
            && map[y + 1][x].isAir()) {
        map[y+1][x] = new Stone(new Falling());
        map[y][x] = new Air();
    } else if (map[y][x].isBoxy()
            && map[y + 1][x].isAir()) {
        map[y + 1][x] = new Box(new Falling());
        map[y][x] = new Air();
    } else if (map[y][x].isFallingStone()) {
        map[y][x].rest();
    } else if (map[y][x].isFallingBox()) {
        map[y][x].rest();
    }
}
```

Uses the new helper method

We see that the body of the last two ifs is the same. When two if statements that are next to each other have the same body, we can join them by simply putting an || between the two conditions.

Listing 5.53   Before

```
function updateTile(x: number, y: number) {
    if (map[y][x].isStony()
            && map[y + 1][x].isAir()) {
        map[y+1][x] = new Stone(new Falling());
        map[y][x] = new Air();
    } else if (map[y][x].isBoxy()
            && map[y + 1][x].isAir()) {
        map[y + 1][x] = new Box(new Falling());
        map[y][x] = new Air();
    } else if (map[y][x].isFallingStone()) {
        map[y][x].rest();
    } else if (map[y][x].isFallingBox()) {
        map[y][x].rest();
    }
}
```

Listing 5.54   After

```
function updateTile(x: number, y: number) {
    if (map[y][x].isStony()
            && map[y + 1][x].isAir()) {
        map[y+1][x] = new Stone(new Falling());
        map[y][x] = new Air();
    } else if (map[y][x].isBoxy()
            && map[y + 1][x].isAir()) {
        map[y + 1][x] = new Box(new Falling());
        map[y][x] = new Air();
    } else if (map[y][x].isFallingStone()
            || map[y][x].isFallingBox()) {
        map[y][x].rest();
    }
}
```

Combined condition

We're used to ||s by now, so it should come as no surprise that we immediately push the || expression into the classes, naming them after what the two method names have in common: isFalling.

I want to repeat an important point from chapter 2. Throughout this process, we are not making any judgments: we are simply following the code's existing structure. We are doing these refactorings without really knowing what the code does. This is important because refactoring can be expensive if you have to first understand all of the code. The fact that some refactoring patterns are possible without studying the code can save you considerable time.

The resulting code looks like this.

Listing 5.55   Before

```
function updateTile(x: number, y:
number) {
  if (map[y][x].isStony()
        && map[y + 1][x].isAir()) {
    map[y+1][x] = new Stone(new
Falling());
    map[y][x] = new Air();
  } else if (map[y][x].isBoxy()
        && map[y + 1][x].isAir()) {
    map[y + 1][x] = new Box(new
Falling());
    map[y][x] = new Air();
  } else if (map[y][x].isFallingStone()
        || map[y][x].isFallingBox()) {
    map[y][x].rest();
  }
}
```

Listing 5.56   After

```
function updateTile(x: number, y:
number) {
  if (map[y][x].isStony()
        && map[y + 1][x].isAir()) {
    map[y+1][x] = new Stone(new
Falling());
    map[y][x] = new Air();
  } else if (map[y][x].isBoxy()
        && map[y + 1][x].isAir()) {
    map[y + 1][x] = new Box(new
Falling());
    map[y][x] = new Air();
  } else if (map[y][x].isFalling()) {    ◄─┐

    map[y][x].rest();            **Uses the new**
  }                              **helper method**
}
```

Even though this refactoring pattern is one of the simplest in the book, its power enables more powerful ones. Without further ado, here is COMBINE ifs.

5.2.1   Refactoring pattern: COMBINE IFS

DESCRIPTION

This refactoring pattern reduces duplication by joining consecutive ifs that have identical bodies. We usually encounter this condition only during targeted refactoring, where we deliberately try to make it happen—it is unnatural to write ifs with identical bodies next to each other. This pattern is useful because it exposes a relation in the two expressions by adding an ||, which—as we have seen—we like to take advantage of.

PROCESS

1 Verify that the bodies are indeed the same.
2 Select the code between the closing parenthesis of the first if and the opening parenthesis of the **else if**, press Delete, and insert an ||. Insert an opening

parenthesis after the `if` and a closing parenthesis before {. We always keep the parentheses around the expressions to make sure we do not change the behavior.

Listing 5.57   Before

```
if (expression1) {
  // body
} else if (expression2) {
  // same body
}
```

Listing 5.58   After

```
if ((expression1) || (expression2)) {
  // body
}
```

3 If the expressions are simple, we can remove the superfluous parentheses or configure our editor to do it.

EXAMPLE

In this example, we have some logic to determine what to do with an invoice.

Listing 5.59   Initial

```
if (today.getDate() === 1 && account.getBalance() > invoice.getAmount()) {
  account.pay(bill);
} else if (invoice.isLastDayOfPayment() && invoice.isApproved()) {
  account.pay(bill);
}
```

We follow the process:

1 Verify that the bodies are indeed the same.
2 Select the code between the closing parenthesis of the first `if` and the opening parenthesis of the `else if`, press Delete, and insert an ||. Insert an opening parenthesis after the `if` and a closing parenthesis before {. We always keep the parentheses around the expressions to make sure we do not change the behavior.

Listing 5.60   Before

```
if (today.getDate() === 1
  && account.getBalance()
  > invoice.getAmount())
{
  account.pay(bill);
} else if (invoice.isLastDayOfPayment()
  && invoice.isApproved())
{
  account.pay(bill);
}
```

Listing 5.61   After

```
if ((today.getDate() === 1
  && account.getBalance()
  > invoice.getAmount())
  || (invoice.isLastDayOfPayment()
  && invoice.isApproved()))
{
  account.pay(bill);
}
```

Condition of the first if (parenthesized)

Condition of the second if (parenthesized)

3 If the expressions are simple, we can remove the superfluous parentheses or configure our editor to do it.

Many people in the industry consider this common knowledge. So, I think this is the first description of it as an official refactoring pattern.

5.3 Unifying complex conditions

Looking at the first `if` of `updateTile`, we realize that it simply replaces one stone with air and one air with stone. This is the same as moving the stone tile and setting it to falling using the `drop` function. The same is true for the box case.

Listing 5.62 Before

```
function updateTile(x: number, y: number) {
  if (map[y][x].isStony()
        && map[y + 1][x].isAir()) {
    map[y+1][x] = new Stone(new Falling());

    map[y][x] = new Air();
  } else if (map[y][x].isBoxy()
        && map[y + 1][x].isAir()) {
    map[y + 1][x] = new Box(new Falling());

    map[y][x] = new Air();
  } else if (map[y][x].isFalling()) {
    map[y][x].rest();
  }
}
```

Listing 5.63 After

```
function updateTile(x: number, y:
number) {
  if (map[y][x].isStony()
        && map[y + 1][x].isAir()) {
    map[y][x].drop();
    map[y + 1][x] = map[y][x];
    map[y][x] = new Air();
  } else if (map[y][x].isBoxy()
        && map[y + 1][x].isAir()) {
    map[y][x].drop();
    map[y + 1][x] = map[y][x];
    map[y][x] = new Air();
  } else if (map[y][x].isFalling()) {
    map[y][x].rest();
  }
}
```
Sets the stone or box to fall, swaps the tiles, and puts in new air

Now the bodies of the two first `if`s are the same. We can again use COMBINE `if`s to join the two `if`s into a single `if` by putting an `||` between the conditions.

Listing 5.64 Before

```
function updateTile(x: number, y:
number) {
  if (map[y][x].isStony()
        && map[y + 1][x].isAir()) {
    map[y][x].drop();
    map[y + 1][x] = map[y][x];
    map[y][x] = new Air();
  } else if (map[y][x].isBoxy()
        && map[y + 1][x].isAir()) {
    map[y][x].drop();
    map[y + 1][x] = map[y][x];
    map[y][x] = new Air();
  } else if (map[y][x].isFalling()) {
    map[y][x].rest();
  }
}
```

Listing 5.65 After

```
function updateTile(x: number, y:
number) {
  if (map[y][x].isStony()
        && map[y + 1][x].isAir()
        || map[y][x].isBoxy()
        && map[y + 1][x].isAir()) {
```
Combined conditions
```
    map[y][x].drop();
    map[y + 1][x] = map[y][x];
    map[y][x] = new Air();
  } else if (map[y][x].isFalling()) {
    map[y][x].rest();
  }
}
```

The resulting condition is slightly more complex than last time. Therefore, this is a good time to discuss how to work with such conditions.

5.3.1 *Using arithmetic rules for conditions*

We can manipulate a conditional expression the same way we do most of the code in this book: without knowing what it does. Without going into the theoretical background, it turns out that || (and |) behave like + (addition), and && (and &) behave like × (multiplication). A mnemonic trick to help remember this is that the two lines of || can form a +, and there is a × hidden inside the &, as shown in figure 5.1. This helps us remember when we need parentheses around ||, and all our regular arithmetic rules apply.

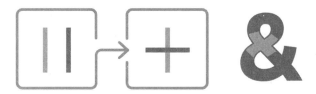

Figure 5.1   Mnemonic to help remember precedence

The rules in figure 5.2 apply in all cases except when the conditions have side effects. To be able to use these rules as we expect, we should always avoid using side effects in conditions: USE PURE CONDITIONS.

$$a + b + c = (a + b) + c = a + (b + c) \qquad (\text{+ is associative})$$
$$a \cdot b \cdot c = (a \cdot b) \cdot c = a \cdot (b \cdot c) \qquad (\cdot \text{ is associative})$$
$$a + b = b + a \qquad (\text{+ is commutative})$$
$$a \cdot b = b \cdot a \qquad (\cdot \text{ is commutative})$$
$$a \cdot (b + c) = a \cdot b + a \cdot c \qquad (\cdot \text{ distributes over + on the left})$$
$$(a + b) \cdot c = a \cdot c + b \cdot c \qquad (\cdot \text{ distributes over + on the right})$$

Figure 5.2   Arithmetic rules

5.3.2 *Rule:* USE PURE CONDITIONS

STATEMENT
Conditions should always be pure.

EXPLANATION
Conditions are what comes after **if** or **while** and what is in the middle part of **for** loops. *Pure* means the conditions do not have side effects. *Side effects* mean the conditions

assign values to variables, throw exceptions, or interact with I/O, such as printing something, writing to files, etc.

Having pure conditions is important for multiple reasons. First, as mentioned, conditions with side effects prevent us from using the earlier rules. Second, side effects are uncommon in conditions, so we do not expect conditions to have side effects; this means they are something we need to discover, implying that we should spend more time investigating and more cognitive capacity keeping track of which conditions have which side effects.

Code like the following is common, where `readLine` both returns the next line and advances the pointer. Advancing the pointer is a side effect, so our condition is not pure. A better implementation, on the right, separates the responsibility of getting the line and moving the pointer. It would be even better to also introduce a method that checks whether there is more to read instead of returning `null`, but that is a discussion for another time.

Listing 5.66 Before

```
class Reader {
  private data: string[];
  private current: number;



  readLine() {
    this.current++;
    return this.data[this.current] || null;
  }
}
/// ...
let br = new Reader();
let line: string | null;
while ((line = br.readLine()) !== null) {
  console.log(line);
}
```

Listing 5.67 After

```
class Reader {
  private data: string[];         New method
  private current: number;        with a side effect
  nextLine() {
    this.current++;               Side effect removed
  }                               from the existing method
  readLine() {
    return this.data[this.current] || null;
  }
}
                                  Changed to a for loop to
/// ...                           ensure that we remember
let br = new Reader();            to call nextLine
for (;br.readLine() !== null;br.nextLine()){
  let line = br.readLine();       Second call
  console.log(line);             to get the
}                                current line
```

Notice that we can call `readLine` as many times as we want to, with no side effects.

In cases where we do not have control over the implementation and therefore cannot split the return from the side effects, we can use a cache. There are many ways to implement caches; so, without going into detail about the implementation, here is a general-purpose cache that can take any method and split the side effect part from the return part.

Listing 5.68 Cache

```
class Cacher<T> {
  private data: T;
  constructor(private mutator: () => T) {
    this.data = this.mutator();
  }
```

```
get() {
  return this.data;
}
next() {
  this.data = this.mutator();
}
}

let tmpBr = new Reader();              ⊲┐
let br = new Cacher(() => tmpBr.readLine());   ⊲┐
for (; br.get() !== null; br.next()) {
  let line = br.get();
  console.log(line);
}
```

Instantiating the Reader as usual, but with a temporary name

Wraps the specific call in the cache

SMELL

This rule originates from a general smell that states, "Separate queries from commands"; you can find it in the book *Design by Contract, by Example* by Richard Mitchell and Jim McKim (Addison-Wesley, 2001). For once, this smell is not difficult to get a feel for. In the smell, "commands" refers to anything with side effects, and "queries" means anything pure. An easy way to follow this smell is to only allow side effects in void methods: they either have side effects or return something, but not both.

The only difference between the general smell and this rule, then, is that we focus on the call site instead of the definition site. In the original work, Mitchell and McKim build more principles on top that rely on strict separation in all cases. We have loosened the smell to focus on conditions because mixing queries and commands outside conditions does not affect our ability to refactor; adhering to the smell is perhaps more a matter of style. It is also more common to have methods both return and mutate something, so we are practiced at spotting it. Indeed, one of the most common operators in programming, ++, both increments and returns a value.

It is also easy to argue that this rule also has roots in "Methods should do one thing," from Robert C. Martin's *Clean Code* (Pearson, 2008). Having a side effect is one thing, and returning something is another.

INTENT

The intent is to separate getting data and changing data. This makes our code cleaner and more predictable. It usually also enables better naming because the methods are simpler. Side effects fall under the category of mutating global state, which is dangerous, as described in chapter 2. Therefore, isolating the mutating makes it easier to manage.

REFERENCES

You can read about queries and commands and how to use them to make assertions—sometimes called *contracts*—in *Design by Contract, by Example* by Richard Mitchell and Jim McKim.

5.3.3 *Applying condition arithmetic*

Working with conditions according to the rules in figure 5.2 is powerful. Consider our condition from `updateTile`: we first transform it into a math equation, after which we can easily use familiar arithmetic rules to simplify it and then transform it back into code. This transformation is illustrated in figure 5.3.

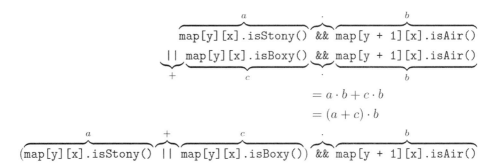

Figure 5.3   Applying arithmetic rules

Practicing the process of transforming a condition into a math equation, simplifying it, and changing it back to code in your head can be invaluable when you have to simplify more complex conditions in the real world. This technique can also help you spot tricky parenthesis errors in conditions.

> **A story from real life**
>
> I have spent so much time practicing this process that it is automatic to me. Several times in my career as a consultant, I have been brought onto a project for the sole purpose of tracking down errors with parentheses in conditions. If you haven't learned this trick, then these bugs are extremely difficult to spot, and their effects can seem unpredictable.

Putting our earlier simplification into the code, we get the following.

Listing 5.69   Before

```
function updateTile(x: number, y: number) {
  if (map[y][x].isStony()
        && map[y + 1][x].isAir()
        || map[y][x].isBoxy()
        && map[y + 1][x].isAir()) {
    map[y][x].drop();
    map[y + 1][x] = map[y][x];
    map[y][x] = new Air();
  } else if (map[y][x].isFalling()) {
    map[y][x].rest();
  }
}
```

Listing 5.70   After

```
function updateTile(x: number, y: number) {
  if ((map[y][x].isStony()          ◁────────┐
        || map[y][x].isBoxy())       ◁──┐    │
        && map[y + 1][x].isAir()) {      │    │
    map[y][x].drop();                    │    │
    map[y + 1][x] = map[y][x];           │    │
    map[y][x] = new Air();               │    │
  } else if (map[y][x].isFalling()) {    │    │
    map[y][x].rest();                    │    │
  }                                      │    │
}              Condition simplified, ────┴────┘
                with a parenthesis
```

Now we are in a situation similar to earlier: we have an || that we want to push into the classes. In chapter 4, we had a relation between stones and boxes and called the method pushable. However, that name does not make sense in this situation. It is important not to blindly reuse a name just because it addresses the same relation: it should also include the context. So, in this case, we write a new method called canFall.

After PUSH CODE INTO CLASSES, we have another nice simplification.

Listing 5.71   Before

```
function updateTile(x: number, y: number) {
  if ((map[y][x].isStony()
        || map[y][x].isBoxy())
        && map[y + 1][x].isAir()) {
    map[y][x].drop();
    map[y + 1][x] = map[y][x];
    map[y][x] = new Air();
  } else if (map[y][x].isFalling()) {
    map[y][x].rest();
  }
}
```

Listing 5.72   After

```
function updateTile(x: number, y: number) {
  if (map[y][x].canFall()        ◁──────────┐
                                            │
        && map[y + 1][x].isAir()) {         │
    map[y][x].drop();                       │
    map[y + 1][x] = map[y][x];              │
    map[y][x] = new Air();                  │
  } else if (map[y][x].isFalling()) {       │
    map[y][x].rest();                       │
  }                                         │
}                            Uses the new ──┘
                             helper method
```

5.4   *Unifying code across classes*

Continuing with updateTile, there is nothing more to postpone pushing it into classes.

Listing 5.73   Before

```
function updateTile(x: number, y: number) {
  if (map[y][x].canFall()
        && map[y + 1][x].isAir()) {
    map[y][x].drop();
    map[y + 1][x] = map[y][x];
    map[y][x] = new Air();
  } else if (map[y][x].isFalling()) {
    map[y][x].rest();
  }
}
```

Listing 5.74   After

```
function updateTile(x: number, y: number) {
  map[y][x].update(x, y);
}
interface Tile {
  // ...
  update(x: number, y: number): void;
}
class Air implements Tile {
  // ...
  update(x: number, y: number) { }
}
class Stone implements Tile {
  // ...
  update(x: number, y: number) {
    if (map[y + 1][x].isAir()) {
      this.falling = new Falling();
      map[y + 1][x] = this;
      map[y][x] = new Air();
    } else if (this.falling.isFalling()) {
      this.falling = new Resting();
    }
  }
}
```

We inline updateTile to clean up. Having pushed many methods into our classes, we have introduced many methods in our interface. This is a good time to do some midway cleaning with TRY DELETE THEN COMPILE. Notice that this removes almost all the isX methods we have introduced. The ones we are left with all have some sort of special meaning, like isLockX and isAir, which affect the behavior of other tiles.

Currently, we have this exact code in both Stone and Box. Contrary to our earlier situation (section 4.6), this is not a place where we want divergence. The falling behavior should stay in sync, and it also seems like something that we might use again later if we introduce more tiles.

1 We first make a new FallStrategy class.

Listing 5.75 New class

```
class FallStrategy {
}
```

2 Instantiate FallStrategy in the constructor of Stone and Box.

Listing 5.76 Before

```
class Stone implements Tile {

  constructor(
    private falling: FallingState)
  {

  }
  // ...
}
```

Listing 5.77 After (1/5)

```
class Stone implements Tile {
  private fallStrategy: FallStrategy;   ◁──
  constructor(
    private falling: FallingState)   New field
  {
    this.fallStrategy = new FallStrategy(); ◁──
  }
  // ...                           Initializes
}                                  the new field
```

3 We move update the same way we do with PUSH CODE INTO CLASSES.

Listing 5.78 Before

```
class Stone implements Tile {
  // ...
  update(x: number, y: number) {
    if (map[y + 1][x].isAir()) {
      this.falling = new Falling();
      map[y + 1][x] = this;
      map[y][x] = new Air();
    } else if (this.falling.isFalling()) {
      this.falling = new Resting();
    }
  }
}
class FallStrategy {
}
```

Listing 5.79 After (2/5)

```
class Stone implements Tile {
  update(x: number, y: number) {
    this.fallStrategy.update(x, y);
  }
}
class FallStrategy {
  update(x: number, y: number) {
    if (map[y + 1][x].isAir()) {
      this.falling = new Falling();
      map[y + 1][x] = this;
      map[y][x] = new Air();
    } else if (this.falling.isFalling()) {
      this.falling = new Resting();
    }
  }
}
```

4 We are dependent on the `falling` field, so we do the following:

  a Move the `falling` field, and make an accessor for it in `FallStrategy`.

Listing 5.80 Before	Listing 5.81 After (3/5)

```
class Stone implements Tile {
  private fallStrategy: FallStrategy;
  constructor(
    private falling: FallingState)
  {
    this.fallStrategy = new
FallStrategy();

  }
  // ...
}
class FallStrategy {
  // ...
}
```

Adds a
constructor with
a parameter

```
class Stone implements Tile {
  private fallStrategy: FallStrategy;
  constructor(
    falling: FallingState)        ◁──┤ Removes
  {                                      private
    this.fallStrategy =
      new FallStrategy(falling);  ◁──
  }
  // ...                            Adds an
}                                   argument
class FallStrategy {
  constructor(
    private falling: FallingState)
  {

  }
  getFalling() { return this.falling; }  ◁──
  // ...
}                                    New accessor
                                     for the field
```

  b Fix errors in the original class by using the new accessors.

Listing 5.82 Before	Listing 5.83 After (4/5)

```
class Stone implements Tile {
  // ...
  moveHorizontal(dx: number) {
    this.falling

      .moveHorizontal(this, dx);
  }
}
```

```
class Stone implements Tile {
  // ...
  moveHorizontal(dx: number) {        Using
    this.fallStrategy                 the new
      .getFalling()                   accessor
      .moveHorizontal(this, dx);  ◁──
  }
}
```

5 Add a `tile` parameter to replace **this** for the remaining errors in `FallStrategy`.

Listing 5.84 Before	Listing 5.85 After (5/5)

```
class Stone implements Tile {
  // ...
  update(x: number, y: number) {
    this.fallStrategy.update(x, y);
  }
}
class FallStrategy {
  update(x: number, y: number) {
```

```
class Stone implements Tile {
  // ...
  update(x: number, y: number) {
    this.fallStrategy.update(this, x, y);  ◁──┐
  }
}
class FallStrategy {
  update(tile: Tile, x: number, y: number){  ◁──
```

Adding a parameter
to replace "this"

```
    if (map[y + 1][x].isAir()) {           if (map[y + 1][x].isAir()) {
      this.falling = new Falling();           this.falling = new Falling();
      map[y + 1][x] = this;                   map[y + 1][x] = tile;        ⟵──────────┐
      map[y][x] = new Air();                   map[y][x] = new Air();                  │
    } else if (this.falling.isFalling())    } else if (this.falling.isFalling()) {
{                                              this.falling = new Resting();
      this.falling = new Resting();         }
    }                                     }                                Adding a parameter
  }                                                                        to replace "this"
}                                       }
```

This results in the following transformation.

Listing 5.86   Before

```
class Stone implements Tile {

  constructor(private falling: FallingState)
  {

  }
  // ...
  update(x: number, y: number) {
    if (map[y + 1][x].isAir()) {
      this.falling = new Falling();
      map[y + 1][x] = this;
      map[y][x] = new Air();
    } else if (this.falling.isFalling()) {
      this.falling = new Resting();
    }
  }
}
```

Listing 5.87   After

```
class Stone implements Tile {
  private fallStrategy: FallStrategy;
  constructor(falling: FallingState)
  {
    this.fallStrategy =
      new FallStrategy(falling);
  }
  // ...
  update(x: number, y: number) {
    this.fallStrategy.update(this, x, y);
  }
}
class FallStrategy {
  constructor(private falling: FallingState)
  { }
  isFalling() { return this.falling; }
  update(tile: Tile, x: number, y: number) {
    if (map[y + 1][x].isAir()) {
      this.falling = new Falling();
      map[y + 1][x] = tile;
      map[y][x] = new Air();
    } else if (this.falling.isFalling()) {
      this.falling = new Resting();
    }
  }
}
```

In FallStrategy.update, if we look closely at the **else if**, we see that if falling is **true**, it is set to **false**; otherwise, it is already **false**. So we can remove the condition.

Listing 5.88   Before

```
class FallStrategy {
  // ...
  update(tile: Tile, x: number, y: number) {
    if (map[y + 1][x].isAir()) {
      this.falling = new Falling();
      map[y + 1][x] = tile;
      map[y][x] = new Air();
    } else if (this.falling.isFalling()) {
      this.falling = new Resting();
    }
  }
}
```

Listing 5.89   After

```
class FallStrategy {
  // ...
  update(tile: Tile, x: number, y: number) {
    if (map[y + 1][x].isAir()) {
      this.falling = new Falling();
      map[y + 1][x] = tile;
      map[y][x] = new Air();
    } else {                        ◁——┐ Removed
      this.falling = new Resting();      │ condition
    }
  }
}
```

Now the code assigns `falling` in all paths, so we can factor it out. We also remove the empty `else`. We then have an `if` that checks the same value as the variable; in such cases, we like to use the variable directly, instead.

Listing 5.90   Before

```
class FallStrategy {
  // ...
  update(tile: Tile, x: number, y: number) {
    if (map[y + 1][x].isAir()) {
      this.falling = new Falling();
      map[y + 1][x] = tile;
      map[y][x] = new Air();
    } else {
      this.falling = new Resting();
    }
  }
}
```

Listing 5.91   After

```
class FallStrategy {
  // ...
  update(tile: Tile, x: number, y: number) {
    this.falling = map[y + 1][x].isAir()
      ? new Falling()
      : new Resting();              ◁——┐
    if (this.falling.isFalling()) {     │
      map[y + 1][x] = tile;             │
      map[y][x] = new Air();            │
    }                                   │
  }                          Factoring  │
}                       this.falling out of if
```

We are within five lines! But we are not done yet. Remember that we have a rule stating `if` ONLY AT THE START (R3.5.1). We still need to follow this rule, so we do a simple EXTRACT METHOD (P3.2.1).

Listing 5.92   Before

```
class FallStrategy {
  // ...
  update(tile: Tile, x: number, y: number) {
    this.falling = map[y + 1][x].isAir()
      ? new Falling()
      : new Resting();
    if (this.falling.isFalling()) {
      map[y + 1][x] = tile;
      map[y][x] = new Air();
    }
  }
}
```

Listing 5.93   After

```
class FallStrategy {
  // ...
  update(tile: Tile, x: number, y: number) {
    this.falling = map[y + 1][x].isAir()
      ? new Falling()
      : new Resting();
    this.drop(tile, x, y);          ◁——┐ Extracted
  }                                      │ method
  private drop(tile: Tile,        ◁——────┘
    x: number, y: number)
  {
```

```
                                 if (this.falling.isFalling()) {
                                   map[y + 1][x] = tile;
                                   map[y][x] = new Air();
                                 }
                               }
                             }
```

Inline `updateTile`, compile, test, commit, and take a break.

The refactoring pattern we went through to unify the "fall code" is called INTRODUCE STRATEGY PATTERN. It is the most sophisticated refactoring pattern in this book. It is also referenced in many other places, all of which use diagrams to demonstrate its effect. We don't want to go against tradition, so we first need to take a detour for a primer in UML class diagrams.

5.4.1 *Introducing UML class diagrams to depict class relations*

Sometimes we need to communicate properties about code like its architecture or the order in which things happen. Some of these properties are easier to convey with diagrams; therefore, we have a framework called Unified Modeling Language (UML).

UML comprises many types of standard diagrams to convey specific properties about code. A few examples include sequence diagrams, class diagrams, and activity diagrams. Explaining all of these is out of the scope of this book. The strategy pattern—and some other patterns—are most commonly demonstrated with a specific type of UML diagram called a *class diagram*. It is my goal that after you read this book, you will be able to pick up any other book about clean code or refactoring and understand it. So, this section explains how class diagrams work.

Class diagrams illustrate the structures of interfaces and classes and how they relate to each other. We represent classes with boxes, a title, and sometimes methods, but rarely fields. Interfaces are represented like classes but with **interface** above the title. We can also denote whether methods and fields are **private** (-) or **public** (+). Here is how a small class with fields and methods is depicted in a class diagram.

Listing 5.94 A complete class	Figure 5.4 Class diagram

```
class Cls {
  private text: string = "Hello";
  public name: string;
  private getText() { return this.text;
}
  printText() {
console.log(this.getText()); }
}
```

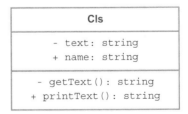

In most cases, it is only interesting to talk about the public interface of a class. Thus we usually don't include anything private. Most fields are private—for good reason, as we discuss in the next chapter. Since we often depict only public methods, we don't need to include visibility.

The most important part of a class diagram is the relations between the classes and interfaces. They fall into three categories: "X uses a Y," "X is a Y," and "X has a Y" or "X has Ys." Within each of these categories, two specific arrow types communicate slightly different things. The types of relations depicted in a class diagram are shown in figure 5.5.

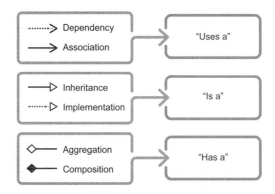

Figure 5.5   UML relations

We can simplify this a bit. The rule ONLY INHERIT FROM INTERFACES (R4.3.2) prevents us from using the inheritance arrow. The "uses" arrows are generally used when we don't know or don't care what the relation is. The difference between composition and aggregation is mostly aesthetic. So, most of the time, we can get away with two of the relation types: composition and implementation. Here are two simple uses of classes and diagrams.

Listing 5.95   Implements

```
interface A {
  m(): void;
}
class B implements A {
  m() { console.log("Hello"); }
}
```

Figure 5.6   Implementation

«interface»
A
m(): void

B

Notice that we do not need to show that B also has an m method because the interface already tells us that.

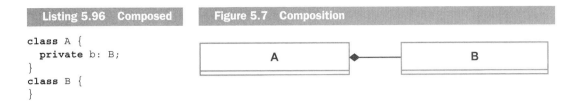

Listing 5.96   Composed

```
class A {
  private b: B;
}
class B {
}
```

Figure 5.7   Composition

A ◆— B

Making class diagrams for an entire program quickly becomes overwhelming and thus is not helpful. We use them mostly to illustrate design patterns or small parts of the software architecture, so we only include important methods. Figure 5.8 shows a class diagram focusing on FallStrategy. Armed with the knowledge of how to use class diagrams, we can illustrate the effect of INTRODUCE STRATEGY PATTERN.

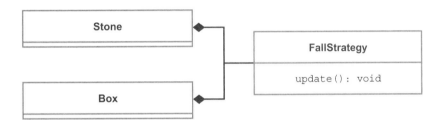

Figure 5.8   Class diagram with a focus on FallStrategy

5.4.2   Refactoring pattern: INTRODUCE STRATEGY PATTERN

DESCRIPTION

We have already discussed how an **if** statement is a low-level control flow operator. We have also mentioned how using objects is advantageous. The concept of introducing variance by instantiating another class is called the *strategy* pattern. It is commonly illustrated with a class diagram similar to the ones previous; see figure 5.9.

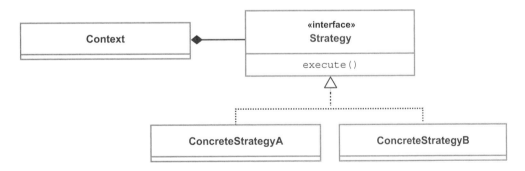

Figure 5.9   Strategy pattern as a class diagram

Many patterns are variations of the strategy pattern; if our strategy has fields, we call it a *state pattern*, instead. These distinctions are mostly academic—they make us sound smart, but in practice, knowing the correct names does not add much to our communication. The fundamental idea is the same: enable change by adding classes (we discussed the advantages of doing this in chapter 2). For this reason, we use the term *strategy pattern* to describe moving any code into its own class. When we do not use the new variation option, we have still added the possibility.

Notice that this is different from transforming type codes into classes. Those classes represent data, and as such, we tend to push lots of methods into them. We rarely add methods to strategy classes after they are finished; instead, we prefer to create a new class if we need to change functionality.

Because variance is the purpose of the strategy pattern, it is always depicted with inheritance: usually from an interface, but sometimes from an abstract class. We have already discussed the disadvantages of that, but we did not use inheritance.

The variance of the strategy pattern is the ultimate form of late binding. At runtime, the strategy pattern allows us to load classes that are completely unknown to our code and seamlessly integrate them into our control flow—no need to even recompile the code. If you take only one thing away from this book, let it be how powerful and useful the strategy pattern is.

There are two situations for introducing a strategy pattern. First, we can refactor because we want to introduce variation in the code. In this case, we should have an interface in the end. However, to make this refactoring as quick as possible, we recommend postponing the interface. Second, in the situation with the fall code, we do not expect to add variance any time soon; we merely wish to unify behavior across classes. We have a rule stating NO INTERFACE WITH ONLY ONE IMPLEMENTATION (R5.4.3). When we need the interface—whether immediately or later—we use a refactoring pattern called EXTRACT INTERFACE FROM IMPLEMENTATION (P5.4.4). Both the rule and the refactoring are explained next.

PROCESS

1 Perform EXTRACT METHOD on the code we want to isolate. If we want to unify it with something else, make sure the methods are identical.

2 Make a new class.

3 Instantiate the new class in the constructor.

4 Move the method into the new class.

5 If there are dependencies on any fields:

   a Move along any fields to the new class, making accessors for the fields.

   b Fix errors in the original class by using the new accessors.

6 Add a parameter to replace **this** for the remaining errors in the new class.

7 INLINE METHOD (P4.1.7) to reverse the extraction from step 1.

EXAMPLE

In this scenario, we imagine having two classes that can process an array in batches, meaning we can pass the classes small arrays that are slices—or batches—of a bigger array. This is common when working with more data than our RAM can fit or when streaming data. In this case, we have a batch processor for finding the minimum element and one for finding the sum.

Listing 5.97   Initial

```
class ArrayMinimum {
  constructor(private accumulator: number) {
  }
  process(arr: number[]) {
    for (let i = 0; i < arr.length; i++)
      if (this.accumulator > arr[i])
        this.accumulator = arr[i];
    return this.accumulator;
  }
}
class ArraySum {
  constructor(private accumulator: number) {
  }
  process(arr: number[]) {
    for (let i = 0; i < arr.length; i++)
      this.accumulator += arr[i];
    return this.accumulator;
  }
}
```

These batch processors are similar but not identical. We will demonstrate how to extract the strategy from both at the same time so the classes are ready to be unified afterward:

1   We perform EXTRACT METHOD on the code we want to isolate. Because we eventually want to unify the two classes, we make sure the methods are identical.

Listing 5.98   Before

```
class ArrayMinimum {
  constructor(private accumulator: number) {
  }
  process(arr: number[]) {
    for (let i = 0; i < arr.length; i++)
      if (this.accumulator > arr[i])
        this.accumulator = arr[i];
    return this.accumulator;
  }



}
```

Listing 5.99   After (1/7)

```
class ArrayMinimum {
  constructor(private accumulator: number) {
  }
  process(arr: number[]) {
    for (let i = 0; i < arr.length; i++)
      this.processElement(arr[i]);      ⟵┐

    return this.accumulator;            Extracted
  }                                     method
  processElement(e: number) {        ⟵ and call
    if (this.accumulator > e)
      this.accumulator = e;
  }
}
```

```
class ArraySum {                          class ArraySum {
  constructor(private accumulator: number) {   constructor(private accumulator: number) {
  }                                         }
  process(arr: number[]) {                 process(arr: number[]) {
    for (let i = 0; i < arr.length; i++)     for (let i = 0; i < arr.length; i++)
      this.accumulator += arr[i];             this.processElement(arr[i]);   ◁──
    return this.accumulator;                 return this.accumulator;
  }                                         }
}                                         processElement(e: number) {
                                            this.accumulator += e;
                                          }
                                        }
```

Extracted
method
and call

2 Make new classes.

Listing 5.100   After (2/7)

```
class MinimumProcessor {
}
class SumProcessor {
}
```

3 Instantiate the new classes in the constructors.

Listing 5.101   Before

```
class ArrayMinimum {

  constructor(private accumulator: number) {

  }
  // ...
}
class ArraySum {

  constructor(private accumulator: number) {

  }
  // ...
}
```

Listing 5.102   After (3/7)

```
class ArrayMinimum {
  private processor: MinimumProcessor;        ◁──
  constructor(private accumulator: number) {
    this.processor = new MinimumProcessor();  ◁──
  }
  // ...
}
class ArraySum {
  private processor: SumProcessor;            ◁──
  constructor(private accumulator: number) {
    this.processor = new SumProcessor();      ◁──
  }
  // ...                     Adding a field and initializing
}                                  it in the constructor
```

4 Move the methods into MinimumProcessor and SumProcessor, respectively.

Listing 5.103 Before	Listing 5.104 After (4/7)

```
class ArrayMinimum {
  // ...
  processElement(e: number) {
    if (this.accumulator > e)
      this.accumulator = e;
  }
}
class ArraySum {
  // ...
  processElement(e: number) {
    this.accumulator += e;
  }
}
class MinimumProcessor {
}
class SumProcessor {
}
```

```
class ArrayMinimum {
  // ...
  processElement(e: number) {
    this.processor.processElement(e);    ◁
  }
}
class ArraySum {
  // ...
  processElement(e: number) {
    this.processor.processElement(e);
  }
}
class MinimumProcessor {
  processElement(e: number) {           ◁
    if (this.accumulator > e)
      this.accumulator = e;
  }
}
class SumProcessor {
  processElement(e: number) {           ◁
    this.accumulator += e;
  }
}
```

Calling the method in the class

New method

5 As we depend on the accumulator field in both cases, we perform these steps:

   a Move along the accumulator field to the MinimumProcessor and SumProcessor classes, making accessors for them.

Listing 5.105 Before	Listing 5.106 After (5/7)

```
class ArrayMinimum {
  private processor: MinimumProcessor;
  constructor(private accumulator: number) {
    this.processor =
      new MinimumProcessor();
  }
  // ...
}
class ArraySum {
  private processor: SumProcessor;
  constructor(private accumulator: number) {
    this.processor =
      new SumProcessor();
  }
  // ...
}
```

```
class ArrayMinimum {
  private processor: MinimumProcessor;
  constructor(accumulator: number) {       ◁
    this.processor =
      new MinimumProcessor(accumulator);   ◁
  }
  // ...
}
class ArraySum {
  private processor: SumProcessor;
  constructor(accumulator: number) {       ◁
    this.processor =
      new SumProcessor(accumulator);       ◁
  }
  // ...
}
```

Moves the field

```
class MinimumProcessor {                    class MinimumProcessor {
  // ...                                      constructor(private accumulator: number) {  ◄─┐
}                                             }
class SumProcessor {                          getAccumulator() {
  // ...                                        return this.accumulator;
}                                             }
                                              // ...
                                            }
                    Accessor to             class SumProcessor {
                    get the field             constructor(private accumulator: number) {  ◄─┤
                                              }
                                              getAccumulator() {                  Moves
                                                return this.accumulator;          the field
                                              }
                                              // ...
                                            }
```

b Fix errors in the original classes by using the new accessors.

Listing 5.107 Before	Listing 5.108 After (6/7)

```
class ArrayMinimum {                        class ArrayMinimum {
  // ...                                       // ...
  process(arr: number[]) {                     process(arr: number[]) {
    for (let i = 0; i < arr.length; i++)         for (let i = 0; i < arr.length; i++)
      this.processElement(arr[i]);                 this.processElement(arr[i]);
    return this.accumulator;                     return
  }                                         this.processor.getAccumulator(); }   ◄─┐
}                                             }
class ArraySum {                            class ArraySum {
  // ...                                       // ...
  process(arr: number[]) {                     process(arr: number[]) {
    for (let i = 0; i < arr.length; i++)         for (let i = 0; i < arr.length; i++)
      this.processElement(arr[i]);                 this.processElement(arr[i]);
    return this.accumulator;                     return
  }                                         this.processor.getAccumulator(); }   ◄─┘
}                                             }
                                                          Using accessor
                                                          to get the field
```

6 Add a parameter to replace **this** for the remaining errors in the new classes. This is unnecessary in this case since there are no errors in the new classes.

7 INLINE METHOD to reverse the extraction from step 1.

Listing 5.109 Before

```
class ArrayMinimum {
  // ...
  process(arr: number[]) {
    for (let i = 0; i < arr.length; i++)
      this.processElement(arr[i]);
    return this.processor.getAccumulator();
  }
  processElement(e: number) {
    this.processor.processElement(e);
  }
}
class ArraySum {
  // ...
  process(arr: number[]) {
    for (let i = 0; i < arr.length; i++)
      this.processElement(arr[i]);
    return this.processor.getAccumulator();
  }
  processElement(e: number) {
    this.processor.processElement(e);
  }
}
```

processElement removed

Listing 5.110 After (7/7)

```
class ArrayMinimum {
  // ...
  process(arr: number[]) {
    for (let i = 0; i < arr.length; i++)
      this.processor.processElement(arr[i]);
    return this.processor.getAccumulator();
  }
}
class ArraySum {
  // ...
  process(arr: number[]) {
    for (let i = 0; i < arr.length; i++)
      this.processor.processElement(arr[i]);
    return this.processor.getAccumulator();
  }
}
```

processElement method inlined

At this point, the two original classes ArrayMinimum and ArraySum are identical except for the instantiation in the construction. This can be solved by using EXTRACT INTERFACE FROM IMPLEMENTATION, which we will see very soon, and passing it as a parameter.

Listing 5.111 Before

```
class ArrayMinimum {

  constructor(private accumulator: number) {

  }
  process(arr: number[]) {
    for (let i = 0; i < arr.length; i++)
      if (this.accumulator > arr[i])
        this.accumulator = arr[i];
    return this.accumulator;
  }
}
class ArraySum {

  constructor(private accumulator: number) {

  }
  process(arr: number[]) {
    for (let i = 0; i < arr.length; i++)
```

Listing 5.112 After

```
class ArrayMinimum {
  private processor: MinimumProcessor;
  constructor(accumulator: number) {
    processor =
      new MinimumProcessor(accumulator);
  }
  process(arr: number[]) {
    for (let i = 0; i < arr.length; i++)

      this.processor.processElement(arr[i]);
    return this.processor.getAccumulator();
  }
}
class ArraySum {
  private processor: SumProcessor;
  constructor(accumulator: number) {
    processor =
      new SumProcessor(accumulator);
  }
  process(arr: number[]) {
    for (let i = 0; i < arr.length; i++)
```

```
        this.accumulator += arr[i];                this.processor.processElement(arr[i]);
    return this.accumulator;                    return this.processor.getAccumulator();
    }                                        }
}                                        }
                                         class MinimumProcessor {
                                             constructor(private accumulator: number) {
                                             }
                                             getAccumulator() {
                                                 return this.accumulator;
                                             }
                                             processElement(e: number) {
                                                 if (this.accumulator > e)
                                                     this.accumulator = e;
                                             }
                                         }
                                         class SumProcessor {
                                             constructor(private accumulator: number) {
                                             }
                                             getAccumulator() {
                                                 return this.accumulator;
                                             }
                                             processElement(e: number) {
                                                 this.accumulator += e;
                                             }
                                         }
```

FURTHER READING

The strategy pattern was first introduced in *Design Patterns* by the Gang of Four: Erich Gamma, Richard Helm, Ralph Johnson, and John Vlissides (Addison-Wesley, 1994). Because it is so powerful, it can be found in many places. However, the idea of post-imposing the strategy pattern into code comes from Martin Fowler's book *Refactoring* (Addison-Wesley Professional, 1999).

5.4.3   *Rule: NO INTERFACE WITH ONLY ONE IMPLEMENTATION*

STATEMENT

Never have interfaces with only one implementation.

EXPLANATION

This rule states that we should not have interfaces with a single implementation. These lonesome interfaces often come from learning advice such as "Always code up against an interface." However, this approach is not always beneficial.

A simple argument is that an interface with only one implementation does not add readability. Even worse, an interface signals variation; and if there is none, it adds overhead to our mental model. It may also slow us down if we want to modify the implementing class, as we also need to update the interface, which we have to be more careful with. The argument is similar to that of SPECIALIZE METHOD (P4.2.2); interfaces with only one implementing class are a form of generalization that is not helpful.

In many languages, we place interfaces in their own file. In such languages, having an interface with one implementing class uses two files, whereas having only the implementing class uses only one file. A difference of one file is not a significant issue; but if our codebase has an affinity for interfaces with only one descendant, we may have twice as many files as we should, which incurs a major mental overhead.

There are cases where it makes sense to have interfaces with zero implementations. These are useful when we want to make anonymous classes, most commonly for things such as comparators, or to enforce stricter encapsulation through anonymous inner classes. We discuss encapsulation in the next chapter; however, since anonymous inner classes are rarely used in practice, they are out of the scope of this book.

SMELL

A famous saying states, "Every problem in computer science can be solved by introducing another layer of indirection." This is exactly what interfaces are. We hide details under an abstraction. John Carmack was the brilliant lead programmer of *Doom*, *Quake*, and several other games. This rule originates from a smell he explicated in one of his tweets: "Abstraction trades an increase in real complexity for a decrease in perceived complexity"—implying that we should be careful with our abstractions.

INTENT

The intention is to limit unnecessary boilerplate code. Interfaces are a common source of boilerplate; they are especially dangerous because lots of people have been taught that interfaces are always preferable, so they tend to bloat their applications.

REFERENCES

Fred George presented a similar rule in his 2015 GOTO talk "The Secret Assumption of Agile."

5.4.4 *Refactoring pattern:* EXTRACT INTERFACE FROM IMPLEMENTATION

DESCRIPTION

This is another rather simple refactoring. It is useful since it allows us to postpone making interfaces until they are needed (when we want to introduce variance).

PROCESS

1 Create a new interface with the same name as the class we are extracting from.
2 Rename the class from which we want to extract the interface, and make it implement the new interface.
3 Compile, and go through the errors:
   a If the error is caused by a **new**, change the instantiation to the new class name.
   b Otherwise, add the method that is causing the error to the interface.

EXAMPLE

Let's continue with the earlier example, focusing on the SumProcessor.

Listing 5.113   Initial

```
class ArraySum {
  private processor: SumProcessor;
  constructor(accumulator: number) {
    processor = new SumProcessor(accumulator);
  }
  process(arr: number[]) {
    for (let i = 0; i < arr.length; i++)
      this.processor.processElement(arr[i]);
    return this.processor.getAccumulator();
  }
}
class SumProcessor {
  constructor(private accumulator: number) { }
  getAccumulator() { return this.accumulator; }
  processElement(e: number) {
    this.accumulator += e;
  }
}
```

We follow the process:

1   Create a new interface with the same name as the class we are extracting from.

Listing 5.114   Adding a new interface

```
interface SumProcessor {
}
```

2   Rename the class from which we want to extract the interface, and make it implement the new interface.

Listing 5.115   Before

```
class SumProcessor {
 // ...
}
```

Listing 5.116   After (1/3)

```
class TmpName implements SumProcessor {
 // ...
}
```

3   Compile, and go through the errors:

   a   If it is a **new**, change the instantiation to the new class name.

Listing 5.117 Before

```
class ArraySum {
  private processor: SumProcessor;
  constructor(accumulator: number) {
    processor =
      new SumProcessor(accumulator);
  }
  // ...
}
```

Listing 5.118 After (2/3)

```
class ArraySum {
  private processor: SumProcessor;
  constructor(accumulator: number) {
    processor =
      new TmpName(accumulator);      ◁─┐
  }
  // ...                      Instantiates a class
}                           instead of an interface
```

b Otherwise, add the method that is causing the error to the interface.

Listing 5.119 Before

```
class ArraySum {
  // ...
  process(arr: number[]) {
    for (let i = 0; i < arr.length; i++)
      this.processor.processElement(arr[i]);
    return this.processor.getAccumulator();
  }
}
interface SumProcessor {
}
```

Listing 5.120 After (3/3)

```
class ArraySum {
  // ...
  process(arr: number[]) {
    for (let i = 0; i < arr.length; i++)
      this.processor.processElement(arr[i]);   │
    return this.processor.getAccumulator();    │
  }                          Adding the methods
}                              to the interface
interface SumProcessor {
  processElement(e: number): void;   │
  getAccumulator(): number;          │
}
```

Now that everything works, we should rename the interface to something more fitting, like `ElementProcessor`, and rename the class back to `SumProcessor`. We can also make the `MinimumProcessor` from earlier implement the interface and then replace the `accumulator` parameter in `ArraySum` with the processor and rename that to `BatchProcessor`. Thereby the two batch processors are identical, and we can delete one of them. Doing all of this results in the following code.

Listing 5.121 After

```
class BatchProcessor {
  constructor(private processor: ElementProcessor) { }
  process(arr: number[]) {
    for (let i = 0; i < arr.length; i++)
      this.processor.processElement(arr[i]);
    return this.processor.getAccumulator();
  }
}
interface ElementProcessor {
  processElement(e: number): void;
  getAccumulator(): number;
}
class MinimumProcessor implements ElementProcessor {
  constructor(private accumulator: number) { }
```

```
    getAccumulator() { return this.accumulator; }
    processElement(e: number) {
      if (this.accumulator > e)
        this.accumulator = e;
    }
  }
  class SumProcessor implements ElementProcessor {
    constructor(private accumulator: number) { }
    getAccumulator() { return this.accumulator; }
    processElement(e: number) {
      this.accumulator += e;
    }
  }
}
```

FURTHER READING

To my knowledge, this is the first description of this technique as a refactoring pattern.

5.5 *Unifying similar functions*

Another place we have similar code is in the two functions removeLock1 and removeLock2.

Listing 5.122 removeLock1

```
function removeLock1() {
  for (let y = 0; y < map.length; y++) {
    for (let x = 0; x < map[y].length; x++) {
      if (map[y][x].isLock1()) {
        map[y][x] = new Air();
      }
    }
  }
}
```

Listing 5.123 removeLock2

```
function removeLock2() {
  for (let y = 0; y < map.length; y++) {
    for (let x = 0; x < map[y].length; x++) {
      if (map[y][x].isLock2()) {
        map[y][x] = new Air();
      }
    }
  }
}
```

The only difference

As it turns out, we can use INTRODUCE STRATEGY PATTERN to unify these as well. They are not identical, so we handle them by pretending we have the first one and need to introduce the second: that is, we want to add variance.

1 Start by performing EXTRACT METHOD on the code we want to isolate.

Listing 5.124 Before

```
function removeLock1() {
  for (let y = 0; y < map.length; y++)
    for (let x = 0; x < map[y].length; x++)
      if (map[y][x].isLock1())
        map[y][x] = new Air();
}
```

Listing 5.125 After (1/3)

```
function removeLock1() {
  for (let y = 0; y < map.length; y++)
    for (let x = 0; x < map[y].length; x++)
      if (check(map[y][x]))
        map[y][x] = new Air();
}
function check(tile: Tile) {
  return tile.isLock1();
}
```

New method and call

2 Make a new class.

Listing 5.126   A new class

```
class RemoveStrategy {
}
```

3 In this case, we have no constructor where we can instantiate this new class. Instead, we instantiate it directly in the function.

Listing 5.127   Before

```
function removeLock1() {

  for (let y = 0; y < map.length; y++)
    for (let x = 0; x < map[y].length; x++)
      if (check(map[y][x]))
        map[y][x] = new Air();
}
```

Listing 5.128   After (2/3)

```
function removeLock1() {
  let shouldRemove = new RemoveStrategy();   ◁──┐
  for (let y = 0; y < map.length; y++)
    for (let x = 0; x < map[y].length; x++)
      if (check(map[y][x]))
        map[y][x] = new Air();        Initializing
}                                     the new class
```

4 Move the method.

Listing 5.129   Before

```
function removeLock1() {
  let shouldRemove = new RemoveStrategy();
  for (let y = 0; y < map.length; y++)
    for (let x = 0; x < map[y].length; x++)
      if (check(map[y][x]))
        map[y][x] = new Air();
}

function check(tile: Tile) {
  return tile.isLock1();
}
```

Listing 5.130   After (3/3)

```
function removeLock1() {
  let shouldRemove = new RemoveStrategy();
  for (let y = 0; y < map.length; y++)
    for (let x = 0; x < map[y].length; x++)
      if (shouldRemove.check(map[y][x]))   ◁──┐
        map[y][x] = new Air();
}
class RemoveStrategy {
  check(tile: Tile) {                       ◁──┤
    return tile.isLock1();
  }                                   Moved
}                                     method
```

5 There are no dependencies on any fields and no errors in the new class.

Having introduced a strategy, we can use EXTRACT INTERFACE FROM IMPLEMENTATION in preparation to introduce the variance:

1 Create a new interface with the same name as the class we are extracting from.

Listing 5.131   Before

```
interface RemoveStrategy {
}
```

2 Rename the class from which we want to extract the interface, and make it implement the new interface.

Listing 5.132   Before

```
class RemoveStrategy {
  // ...
}
```

Listing 5.133   After (1/3)

```
class RemoveLock1 implements
RemoveStrategy
{
  // ...
}
```

3 Compile, and go through the errors:

    a If it is a **new**, change it to the new class name.

Listing 5.134   Before

```
function removeLock1() {
  let shouldRemove = new RemoveStrategy();
  for (let y = 0; y < map.length; y++)
    for (let x = 0; x < map[y].length; x++)
      if (shouldRemove.check(map[y][x]))
        map[y][x] = new Air();
}
```

Listing 5.135   After (2/3)

```
function removeLock1() {
  let shouldRemove = new RemoveLock1();
  for (let y = 0; y < map.length; y++)
    for (let x = 0; x < map[y].length; x++)
      if (shouldRemove.check(map[y][x]))
        map[y][x] = new Air();
}
```

**Instantiating a class
instead of an interface**

    b Otherwise, add the method that is causing the error to the interface.

Listing 5.136   Before

```
interface RemoveStrategy {
}
```

Listing 5.137   After (3/3)

```
interface RemoveStrategy {
  check(tile: Tile): boolean;
}
```

At this point, it is trivial to make RemoveLock2 from a copy of RemoveLock1. We then only need to move shouldRemove out as a parameter. I'll spare you the details, but we do the following:

1 Extracting from removeLock1 everything but the first line, we get remove.
2 The local variable shouldRemove is used only once, so we inline it.
3 INLINE METHOD on removeLock1.

These refactorings result in us having only one remove.

Listing 5.138 Before

```
function removeLock1() {


  for (let y = 0; y < map.length; y++)
    for (let x = 0; x < map[y].length; x++)
      if (map[y][x].isLock1())
        map[y][x] = new Air();
}
class Key1 implements Tile {
  // ...
  moveHorizontal(dx: number) {
    removeLock1();
    moveToTile(playerx + dx, playery);
  }
}
```

Listing 5.139 After

```
function remove(
    shouldRemove: RemoveStrategy)
{
  for (let y = 0; y < map.length; y++)
    for (let x = 0; x < map[y].length; x++)
      if (shouldRemove.check(map[y][x]))
        map[y][x] = new Air();
}
class Key1 implements Tile {
  // ...
  moveHorizontal(dx: number) {
    remove(new RemoveLock1());
    moveToTile(playerx + dx, playery);
  }
}
interface RemoveStrategy {
  check(tile: Tile): boolean;
}
class RemoveLock1 implements RemoveStrategy
{
  check(tile: Tile) {
    return tile.isLock1();
  }
}
```

Just like earlier, this makes remove more general, but this time without limiting us. It also enables change by addition: if we want to remove another type of tile, we can simply make another class that implements RemoveStrategy without modifying anything.

In some applications, we like to avoid calling **new** inside a loop, because doing so can slow down our application. If that is the case here, then we can easily store the RemoveLock strategy in an instance variable and initialize it in the constructor. However, we are not finished with Key1.

5.6   *Unifying similar code*

We also have some duplication in Key1 and Key2, and Lock1 and Lock2. In each case, the twin classes are almost identical.

Listing 5.140 Key1 and Lock1

```
class Key1 implements Tile {
  // ...
  draw(g: CanvasRenderingContext2D,
    x: number, y: number)
  {
    g.fillStyle = "#ffcc00";
    g.fillRect(x * TILE_SIZE, y * TILE_SIZE,
      TILE_SIZE, TILE_SIZE);
  }
```

Listing 5.141 Key2 and Lock2

```
class Key2 implements Tile {
  // ...
  draw(g: CanvasRenderingContext2D,
    x: number, y: number)
  {
    g.fillStyle = "#00ccff";
    g.fillRect(x * TILE_SIZE, y * TILE_SIZE,
      TILE_SIZE, TILE_SIZE);
  }
```

```
moveHorizontal(dx: number) {                 moveHorizontal(dx: number) {
  remove(new RemoveLock1());                   remove(new RemoveLock2());
  moveToTile(playerx + dx, playery);           moveToTile(playerx + dx, playery);
}                                            }
}                                          }
class Lock1 implements Tile {              class Lock2 implements Tile {
  // ...                                     // ...
  isLock1() { return true; }                isLock1() { return false; }
  isLock2() { return false; }               isLock2() { return true; }
  draw(g: CanvasRenderingContext2D,         draw(g: CanvasRenderingContext2D,
    x: number, y: number)                     x: number, y: number)
  {                                         {
    g.fillStyle = "#ffcc00";                  g.fillStyle = "#00ccff";
    g.fillRect(x * TILE_SIZE, y * TILE_SIZE,  g.fillRect(x * TILE_SIZE, y * TILE_SIZE,
      TILE_SIZE, TILE_SIZE);                    TILE_SIZE, TILE_SIZE);
  }                                         }
}                                          }
```

We first use UNIFY SIMILAR CLASSES on both locks and both keys.

Listing 5.142   Before

```
class Key1 implements Tile {




  // ...
  draw(g: CanvasRenderingContext2D,
    x: number, y: number)
  {
    g.fillStyle = "#ffcc00";
    g.fillRect(x * TILE_SIZE, y * TILE_SIZE,
      TILE_SIZE, TILE_SIZE);
  }
  moveHorizontal(dx: number) {
    remove(new RemoveLock1());
    moveToTile(playerx + dx, playery);
  }
}
class Lock1 implements Tile {




  // ...



class Key1 implements Tile {
```

Listing 5.143   After

```
class Key implements Tile {
  constructor(
    private color: string,
    private removeStrategy: RemoveStrategy)
  { }
  // ...
  draw(g: CanvasRenderingContext2D,
    x: number, y: number)
  {
    g.fillStyle = this.color;
    g.fillRect(x * TILE_SIZE, y * TILE_SIZE,
      TILE_SIZE, TILE_SIZE);
  }
  moveHorizontal(dx: number) {
    remove(this.removeStrategy);
    moveToTile(playerx + dx, playery);
  }
}
class Lock implements Tile {
  constructor(
    private color: string,
    private lock1: boolean,
    private lock2: boolean) { }
  // ...
  isLock1() { return this.lock1; }
  isLock2() { return this.lock2; }
class Key implements Tile {
  constructor(
    private color: string,
    private removeStrategy: RemoveStrategy)
  { }
```

```
  // ...                                       // ...
  draw(g: CanvasRenderingContext2D,            draw(g: CanvasRenderingContext2D,
    x: number, y: number)                        x: number, y: number)
  {                                            {
    g.fillStyle = "#ffcc00";                     g.fillStyle = this.color;
    g.fillRect(x * TILE_SIZE, y * TILE_SIZE,     g.fillRect(x * TILE_SIZE, y * TILE_SIZE,
      TILE_SIZE, TILE_SIZE);                        TILE_SIZE, TILE_SIZE);
  }                                            }
  moveHorizontal(dx: number) {                 moveHorizontal(dx: number) {
    remove(new RemoveLock1());                   remove(this.removeStrategy);
    moveToTile(playerx + dx, playery);           moveToTile(playerx + dx, playery);
  }                                            }
}                                            }
class Lock1 implements Tile {                class Lock implements Tile {
                                               constructor(
                                                 private color: string,
                                                 private lock1: boolean,
                                                 private lock2: boolean) { }
  // ...                                        // ...
                                               isLock1() { return this.lock1; }
                                               isLock2() { return this.lock2; }
  draw(g: CanvasRenderingContext2D,            draw(g: CanvasRenderingContext2D,
    x: number, y: number)                        x: number, y: number)
  {                                            {
    g.fillStyle = "#ffcc00";                     g.fillStyle = this.color;
    g.fillRect(x * TILE_SIZE, y * TILE_SIZE,     g.fillRect(x * TILE_SIZE, y * TILE_SIZE,
      TILE_SIZE, TILE_SIZE);                        TILE_SIZE, TILE_SIZE);
  }                                            }
}                                            }
function transformTile(tile: RawTile) {      function transformTile(tile: RawTile) {
  switch (tile) {                              switch (tile) {
    // ...                                       // ...
    case RawTile.KEY1:                          case RawTile.KEY1:
      return new Key1();                          return new Key("#ffcc00",
                                                    new RemoveLock1());
    case RawTile.LOCK1:                          case RawTile.LOCK1:
      return new Lock1();                         return new Lock("#ffcc00",
                                                    true, false);
  }                                            }
}                                            }
```

This code works, but we can take advantage of some structure that we already know.
We introduced the methods isLock1 and isLock2: they came from two values in an
enum, so we know that only one of these methods can return **true** for any given class.
We therefore need only one parameter to represent both methods. The same is true
for the Lock methods.

Listing 5.144 Before

```
class Lock implements Tile {
  constructor(
    private color: string,
    private lock1: boolean,
    private lock2: boolean) { }
  // ...
  isLock1() { return this.lock1; }
  isLock2() { return this.lock2; }
}
```

Listing 5.145 After

```
class Lock implements Tile {
  constructor(
    private color: string,
    private lock1: boolean
    ) { }
  // ...
  isLock1() { return this.lock1; }
  isLock2() { return !this.lock1; }
}
```

It also seems as though there is a connection between the parameters color, lock1, and removeStrategy of our constructors in Key and Lock. When we want to unify things across two classes, we use our favorite new trick: INTRODUCE STRATEGY PATTERN.

Listing 5.146 Before

```
class Key implements Tile {
  constructor(
    private color: string,
    private removeStrategy: RemoveStrategy)
  { }
  // ...
  draw(g: CanvasRenderingContext2D,
    x: number, y: number)
  {
    g.fillStyle = this.color;
    g.fillRect(x * TILE_SIZE, y * TILE_SIZE,
      TILE_SIZE, TILE_SIZE);
  }
  moveHorizontal(dx: number) {
    remove(this.removeStrategy);
    moveToTile(playerx + dx, playery);
  }
  moveVertical(dy: number) {
    remove(this.removeStrategy);
    moveToTile(playerx, playery + dy);
  }
}
class Lock implements Tile {
  constructor(
    private color: string,
    private lock1: boolean) { }
  // ...
  isLock1() { return this.lock1; }
  isLock2() { return !this.lock1; }
  draw(g: CanvasRenderingContext2D,
    x: number, y: number)
  {
    g.fillStyle = this.color;
    g.fillRect(x * TILE_SIZE, y * TILE_SIZE,
```

Listing 5.147 After

```
class Key implements Tile {
  constructor(

    private keyConf: KeyConfiguration)
  { }
  // ...
  draw(g: CanvasRenderingContext2D,
    x: number, y: number)
  {
    g.fillStyle = this.keyConf.getColor();
    g.fillRect(x * TILE_SIZE, y * TILE_SIZE,
      TILE_SIZE, TILE_SIZE);
  }
  moveHorizontal(dx: number) {
    remove(this.keyConf.getRemoveStrategy());
    moveToTile(playerx + dx, playery);
  }
  moveVertical(dy: number) {
    remove(this.keyConf.getRemoveStrategy());
    moveToTile(playerx, playery + dy);
  }
}
class Lock implements Tile {
  constructor(

    private keyConf: KeyConfiguration) { }
  // ...
  isLock1() { return this.keyConf.is1(); }
  isLock2() { return !this.keyConf.is1(); }
  draw(g: CanvasRenderingContext2D,
    x: number, y: number)
  {
    g.fillStyle = this.keyConf.getColor();
    g.fillRect(x * TILE_SIZE, y * TILE_SIZE,
```

```
      TILE_SIZE, TILE_SIZE);                        TILE_SIZE, TILE_SIZE);
  }                                              }
}                                              }
function transformTile(tile: RawTile) {        class KeyConfiguration {
  switch (tile) {                                constructor(
    // ...                                         private color: string,
    case RawTile.KEY1:                             private _1: boolean,
      return new Key("#ffcc00",                    private removeStrategy: RemoveStrategy)
        new RemoveLock1());                      { }
    case RawTile.LOCK1:                           getColor() { return this.color; }
      return new Lock("#ffcc00", true);           is1() { return this._1; }
  }                                              getRemoveStrategy() {
}                                                  return this.removeStrategy;
                                                 }
                                               }
                                               const YELLOW_KEY =
                                                 new KeyConfiguration("#ffcc00", true,
                                                   new RemoveLock1());
                                               function transformTile(tile: RawTile) {
                                                 switch (tile) {
                                                   // ...
                                                   case RawTile.KEY1:
                                                     return new Key(YELLOW_KEY);
                                                   case RawTile.LOCK1:
                                                     return new Lock(YELLOW_KEY);
                                                 }
                                               }
```

Imagine that at this point, we want to introduce a third and fourth key + lock pair. We do this by changing the `boolean` in `keyConfiguration` to a `number` and changing the `isLock` methods to a single `fits(id: number)`. We can now introduce as many key + locks as we want. Of course, after this, we rewrite the `number` to an enum and then use REPLACE TYPE CODE WITH CLASSES—and you know the rest.

Again, note that this transformation made explicit something we have not spent time investigating: the colors and the lock IDs are connected. We might have expected this due to the intuitive nature of the example. However, even if we were working on a complex financial system, we would slowly discover connections like these embedded in the code's existing structure. Some connections discovered this way are coincidental, so we have to be careful and ask ourselves whether this grouping makes sense. Such a grouping could also expose some nasty bugs in the code stemming from things being linked that are not supposed to be linked.

The `KeyConfiguration` class we introduced is currently pretty bare and boring. In the next chapter, we remedy this, and we further expose and exploit links by encapsulating data.

Summary

- When we have similar code that should converge, we should unify it. We can unify classes with UNIFY SIMILAR CLASSES (P5.1.1), ifs with COMBINE ifs (P5.2.1), and methods with INTRODUCE STRATEGY PATTERN (P5.4.2).

- The rule USE PURE CONDITIONS (R5.3.2) states that conditions should not have side effects because if they do not, we can use conditional arithmetic. We saw how to use a Cache to separate side effects from conditions.

- UML class diagrams are commonly used to illustrate specific architectural changes to a codebase.

- Interfaces with a single implementing class are a form of unnecessary generality. The rule NO INTERFACE WITH ONLY ONE IMPLEMENTATION (R5.4.3) states that we should not have these. Instead, we should introduce the interface later with the refactoring pattern EXTRACT INTERFACE FROM IMPLEMENTATION (P5.4.4).

Defend the data

In chapter 2, we discussed the advantage of localizing invariants. We have already done that when introducing classes because they pull together functionality concerning the same data and thereby also pull invariants closer and localize them. In this chapter, we focus on encapsulation—limiting access to data and functionality—such that invariants can only be broken locally and therefore are much easier to prevent.

6.1 *Encapsulating without getters*

At this point, the code follows our rules and is already much more readable and extendable. However, we can do even better by introducing another rule: DO NOT USE GETTERS OR SETTERS.

6.1.1 *Rule: DO NOT USE GETTERS OR SETTERS*

STATEMENT

Do not use setters or getters for non-Boolean fields.

EXPLANATION

When we say *setters or getters*, we mean methods that directly assign or return a non-Boolean field, respectively. For C# programmers, we also include properties in this definition. Notice that this has nothing to do with a method's name—it may or may not be called getX.

Getters and setters are often taught alongside encapsulation as a standard method for getting around private fields. However, if we have getters for object fields, we immediately break encapsulation, and we are making our invariant global. After we return an object, the receiver can further distribute it, which we have no control over. Anyone who gets the object can call its public methods, possibly modifying it in a way we did not expect.

Setters present a similar issue. In theory, setters introduce another layer of indirection where we can change our internal data structure and modify our setter so it still has the same signature. Following our definition, such methods are no longer setters and thus are not a problem. However, what happens in practice is that we modify the getter to return the new data structure. Then the receiver has to be modified to accommodate this new data structure. This is exactly the form of tight coupling we want to avoid.

This is only a problem with mutable objects; however, the rule only specifies Booleans as an exception due to another effect of private fields that also applies to immutable fields: the architecture they suggest. One of the biggest advantages of making fields private is that doing so encourages a push-based architecture. In a push-based architecture, we push computations as close to the data as possible, whereas in a pull-based architecture, we fetch data and then do computations at a central point.

A pull-based architecture leads to a lot of "dumb" data classes without any interesting methods, and some big "manager" classes doing all the work and mixing data from a lot of places. This approach imposes a tight coupling between the data and the managers and, implicitly, between the data classes as well.

In a push-based architecture, instead of "getting" data, we pass data as arguments. As a result, all of our classes have functionality, and the code is distributed according to its utility.

In this example, we want to generate a link to a blog post. Both sides do the same thing, but one is written with a pull-based architecture and the other with a push-based architecture. The call structure of the pull-based code is illustrated in listing 6.1 and of the push-based code in listing 6.2.

Listing 6.1 Pull-based architecture

```
class Website {
  constructor (private url: string) { }
  getUrl() { return this.url; }
}
class User {
  constructor (private username: string) { }
  getUsername() { return this.username; }
}
class BlogPost {
  constructor (private author: User,
    private id: string) { }
  getId() { return this.id; }
  getAuthor() { return this.author; }
}
function generatePostLink(website: Website,
  post: BlogPost)
{
  let url = website.getUrl();
  let user = post.getAuthor();
  let name = user.getUsername();
  let postId = post.getId();
  return url + name + postId;
}
```

Listing 6.2 Push-based architecture

```
class Website {
  constructor (private url: string) { }
  generateLink(name: string, id: string) {
    return this.url + name + id;
  }
}
class User {
  constructor (private username: string) { }
  generateLink(website: Website, id: string)
  {
    return website.generateLink(
      this.username,
      id);
  }
}
class BlogPost {
  constructor (private author: User,
    private id: string) { }
  generateLink(website: Website) {
    return this.author.generateLink(
      website,
      this.id);
  }
}
function generatePostLink(website: Website,
  post: BlogPost)
{
  return post.generateLink(website);
}
```

In the push-based example, we would most likely inline `generatePostLink`, as it is just a single line with no added information.

SMELL

This rule is derived from something called the *Law of Demeter*, which is often summarized as "Don't talk to strangers." A *stranger* in this context is an object that we do not have direct access to but can obtain a reference to. In object-oriented languages, this happens most commonly through getters—and therefore, we have this rule.

INTENT

The issue with interacting with objects to which we can obtain a reference is that we are now tightly coupled to the way we get the object. We know something about the internal structure of the owner of the object. The owner of the field cannot change the data structure without still supporting a way to get the old data structure; otherwise, it breaks our code.

In a push-based architecture, we expose methods like services. The users of those methods should not care about the internal structure of how we deliver them.

REFERENCES

The Law of Demeter is described extensively online. For a thorough exercise that uses it, I recommend the Fantasy Battle refactoring kata by Samuel Ytterbrink, available at https://github.com/Neppord/FantasyBattle-Refactoring-Kata.

6.1.2   Applying the rule

In our code, we have only three getters, and two of them are in KeyConfiguration: getColor and getRemoveStrategy. Luckily they are not too difficult to deal with. We start with getRemoveStrategy:

1 Make getRemoveStrategy private to get errors everywhere we use it.

Listing 6.3   Before

```
class KeyConfiguration {
  // ...
  getRemoveStrategy() {
    return this.removeStrategy;
  }
}
```

Listing 6.4   After (1/3)

```
class KeyConfiguration {
  // ...
  private getRemoveStrategy() {    ⟵
    return this.removeStrategy;
  }
}
```
                                          **Method made
                                          private**

2 To fix the errors, use PUSH CODE INTO CLASSES (P4.1.5) on the failing lines.

Listing 6.5   Before

```
class Key implements Tile {
  // ...
  moveHorizontal(dx: number) {

remove(this.keyConf.getRemoveStrategy());
    moveToTile(playerx + dx, playery);
  }
  moveVertical(dy: number) {

remove(this.keyConf.getRemoveStrategy());
    moveToTile(playerx, playery + dy);
  }
}
class KeyConfiguration {
  // ...
}
```
                                    **New
                                    method**

Listing 6.6   After (2/3)

```
class Key implements Tile {
  // ...
  moveHorizontal(dx: number) {
    this.keyConf.removeLock();      ⟵
    moveToTile(playerx + dx, playery);
  }
  moveVertical(dy: number) {
    this.keyConf.removeLock();      ⟵
    moveToTile(playerx, playery + dy);
  }
}
class KeyConfiguration {
  // ...
  removeLock() {
    remove(this.removeStrategy);
  }
}
```
                                    **Previously
                                    failing lines**

3 getRemoveStrategy is inlined as part of PUSH CODE INTO CLASSES. It is therefore unused, and we can delete it to avoid other people trying to use it.

Listing 6.7 Before

```
class KeyConfiguration {
  // ...
  private getRemoveStrategy() {
    return this.removeStrategy;
  }
}
```

Listing 6.8 After (3/3)

```
class KeyConfiguration {
  // ...

}
```

◁—— **getRemoveStrategy is deleted.**

After repeating this process for getColor, we have the following.

Listing 6.9 Before

```
class KeyConfiguration {
  // ...
  getColor() {
    return this.color;
  }
  getRemoveStrategy() {
    return this.removeStrategy;
  }
}
class Key implements Tile {
  // ...
  draw(g: CanvasRenderingContext2D,
    x: number, y: number)
  {
    g.fillStyle = this.keyConf.getColor();
    g.fillRect(x * TILE_SIZE, y * TILE_SIZE,
      TILE_SIZE, TILE_SIZE);
  }
  moveHorizontal(dx: number) {
   remove(this.keyConf.getRemoveStrategy());
   moveToTile(playerx + dx, playery);
  }
  moveVertical(dy: number) {
   remove(this.keyConf.getRemoveStrategy());
   moveToTile(playerx, playery + dy);
  }
}
class Lock implements Tile {
  // ...
  draw(g: CanvasRenderingContext2D,
    x: number, y: number)
  {
    g.fillStyle = this.keyConf.getColor();
    g.fillRect(x * TILE_SIZE, y * TILE_SIZE,
      TILE_SIZE, TILE_SIZE);
  }
}
```

Method that replaces getRemoveStrategy

Listing 6.10 After

```
class KeyConfiguration {
  // ...
  setColor(g: CanvasRenderingContext2D) {
    g.fillStyle = this.color;
  }
  removeLock() {
    remove(this.removeStrategy);
  }
}
class Key implements Tile {
  // ...
  draw(g: CanvasRenderingContext2D,
    x: number, y: number)
  {
    this.keyConf.setColor(g);
    g.fillRect(x * TILE_SIZE, y * TILE_SIZE,
      TILE_SIZE, TILE_SIZE);
  }
  moveHorizontal(dx: number) {
    this.keyConf.removeLock();
    moveToTile(playerx + dx, playery);
  }
  moveVertical(dy: number) {
    this.keyConf.removeLock();
    moveToTile(playerx, playery + dy);
  }
}
class Lock implements Tile {
  // ...
  draw(g: CanvasRenderingContext2D,
    x: number, y: number)
  {
    this.keyConf.setColor(g);
    g.fillRect(x * TILE_SIZE, y * TILE_SIZE,
      TILE_SIZE, TILE_SIZE);
  }
}
```

Method that replaces getColor

Notice that `setColor` is not a setter in the sense described earlier. Also notice that we are in violation of the rule EITHER CALL OR PASS (R3.1.1) since we are both passing g and calling `g.fillRect`. We can solve this by either pushing the `fillRect` into the `KeyConfiguration` along with the color or extracting the `fillRect` into a method. If we did this, we would likely encapsulate g at some later point and push that method into a custom graphics object instead of `CanvasRenderingContext2D`. I'll leave this as an exercise for the eager reader.

Even though eliminating a getter is another simple process, having two names that suggest we should get rid of getters helps accentuate the importance of doing so. We call this refactoring pattern ELIMINATE GETTER OR SETTER.

6.1.3   *Refactoring pattern: ELIMINATE GETTER OR SETTER*

DESCRIPTION

This refactoring lets us eliminate getters and setters by moving the functionality closer to the data. Conveniently, because getters and setters are so similar, the same process can eliminate either; but for ease of reading, we assume getters for the remainder of the description.

We have localized invariants many times by pushing code closer to the data. That is also the solution here. Usually, when we do so, we introduce a lot of similar functions instead of the getter. These are introduced based on how many contexts the getter is used in. Having many methods means we can name them based on the specific call context instead of the data context.

We saw an example of this issue in chapter 4. In the `TrafficLight` example, the car has a public method called `drive` that `TrafficLight` ends up calling. The `drive` method is named for the effect it has on the car, but we could instead name it based on the context it is called in: `notifyGreenLight`. The effect on the car is the same.

Listing 6.11   Before

```
class Green implements TrafficLight {
  // ...
  updateCar() { car.drive(); }
}
```

Listing 6.12   After

```
class Green implements TrafficLight {
  // ...
  updateCar() { car.notifyGreenLight(); }  ◁─
}
```
After renaming the method based on the context

PROCESS

1   Make the getter or setter private to get errors everywhere it is used.
2   Fix the errors with PUSH CODE INTO CLASSES.
3   The getter or setter is inlined as part of PUSH CODE INTO CLASSES. It is therefore unused, so delete it to avoid other people trying to use it.

EXAMPLE

Continuing the previous example, we can pick any getter to eliminate.

Listing 6.13   Initial

```
class Website {
  constructor (private url: string) { }
  getUrl() { return this.url; }
}
class User {
  constructor (private username: string) { }
  getUsername() { return this.username; }
}
class BlogPost {
  constructor (private author: User, private id: string) { }
  getId() { return this.id; }
  getAuthor() { return this.author; }
}
function generatePostLink(website: Website, post: BlogPost) {
  let url = website.getUrl();
  let user = post.getAuthor();
  let name = user.getUsername();
  let postId = post.getId();
  return url + name + postId;
}
```

Here we demonstrate eliminating getAuthor. We follow the process:

1 Make the getter private to get errors everywhere it is used.

Listing 6.14   Before

```
class BlogPost {
  // ...
  getAuthor() {
    return this.author;
  }
}
```

Listing 6.15   After (1/3)

```
class BlogPost {
  // ...
  private getAuthor() {        ⟵── Added
    return this.author;              private
  }
}
```

2 Fix the errors with PUSH CODE INTO CLASSES.

Listing 6.16   Before

```
function generatePostLink(website:
Website,
  post: BlogPost)
{
  let url = website.getUrl();
  let user = post.getAuthor();
  let name = user.getUsername();
  let postId = post.getId();
  return url + name + postId;
}
```

Listing 6.17   After (2/3)

```
function generatePostLink(website: Website,
  post: BlogPost)
{
  let url = website.getUrl();

  let name = post.getAuthorName();
  let postId = post.getId();
  return url + name + postId;
}
```

```
class BlogPost {                        class BlogPost {                │  New
  // ...                                  // ...                        │  method
}                                         getAuthorName() {         ◁───┘
                                            return this.author.getUsername();
                                          }
                                        }
```

3 The getter is inlined as part of PUSH CODE INTO CLASSES. It is therefore unused, so we delete it to avoid other people trying to use it.

| Listing 6.18   Before | Listing 6.19   After (3/3) |

```
class BlogPost {                        class BlogPost {
  // ...                                  // ...
  private getAuthor() {                 }                      ◁───┐ getAuthor is
    return this.author;                                              deleted.
  }
}
```

Following the same process for the other getters results in the push-based version described in section 6.1.

6.1.4   *Eliminating the final getter*

The final getter is `FallStrategy.getFalling`. We follow the same process to get rid of it:

1 Make the getter private to get errors everywhere it is used.

| Listing 6.20   Before | Listing 6.21   After (1/3) |

```
class FallStrategy {                    class FallStrategy {
  // ...                                  // ...
  getFalling() {                          private getFalling() {   ◁───┐ Added
    return this.falling;                    return this.falling;        private
  }                                       }
}                                       }
```

2 Fix the errors with PUSH CODE INTO CLASSES.

Listing 6.22   Before

```
class Stone implements Tile {
  // ...
  moveHorizontal(dx: number) {
    this.fallStrategy.getFalling()
      .moveHorizontal(this, dx);
  }
}
class Box implements Tile {
  // ...
  moveHorizontal(dx: number) {
    this.fallStrategy.getFalling()
      .moveHorizontal(this, dx);
  }
}
class FallStrategy {
  // ...
}
```

New method

Listing 6.23   After (2/3)

```
class Stone implements Tile {
  // ...
  moveHorizontal(dx: number) {
    this.fallStrategy
      .moveHorizontal(this, dx);
  }
}
class Box implements Tile {
  // ...
  moveHorizontal(dx: number) {
    this.fallStrategy
      .moveHorizontal(this, dx);
  }
}
class FallStrategy {
  // ...
  moveHorizontal(tile: Tile, dx: number) {
    this.falling
      .moveHorizontal(tile, dx);
  }
}
```

3 The getter is inlined as part of PUSH CODE INTO CLASSES. It is therefore unused, so we delete it to avoid other people trying to use it.

Listing 6.24   Before

```
class FallStrategy {
  // ...
  private getFalling() {
    return this.falling;
  }
}
```

Listing 6.25   After (3/3)

```
class FallStrategy {
  // ...

}
```

getFalling is deleted.

This results in FallStrategy looking as follows.

Listing 6.26   Before

```
class Stone implements Tile {
  // ...
  moveHorizontal(dx: number) {
    this.fallStrategy.getFalling()
      .moveHorizontal(this, dx);
  }
}
class Box implements Tile {
  // ...
  moveHorizontal(dx: number) {
    this.fallStrategy.getFalling()
```

Listing 6.27   After

```
class Stone implements Tile {
  // ...
  moveHorizontal(dx: number) {
    this.fallStrategy
      .moveHorizontal(this, dx);
  }
}
class Box implements Tile {
  // ...
  moveHorizontal(dx: number) {
    this.fallStrategy
```

New pushed code

```
    .moveHorizontal(this, dx);
  }
}
class FallStrategy {
  constructor(private falling: FallingState)
  { }
  getFalling() { return this.falling; }
  update(tile: Tile, x: number, y: number) {
    this.falling = map[y + 1][x].isAir()
      ? new Falling()
      : new Resting();
    this.drop(tile, x, y);
  }
  private drop(tile: Tile,
    x: number, y: number)
  {
    if (this.falling.isFalling()) {
      map[y + 1][x] = tile;
      map[y][x] = new Air();
    }
  }
}
```

getFalling is deleted.

```
    .moveHorizontal(this, dx);
  }
}
class FallStrategy {
  constructor(private falling: FallingState)
  { }

  update(tile: Tile, x: number, y: number) {
    this.falling = map[y + 1][x].isAir()
      ? new Falling()
      : new Resting();
    this.drop(tile, x, y);
  }
  private drop(tile: Tile,
    x: number, y: number)
  {
    if (this.falling.isFalling()) {
      map[y + 1][x] = tile;
      map[y][x] = new Air();
    }
  }
  moveHorizontal(tile: Tile, dx: number) {
    this.falling.moveHorizontal(tile, dx);
  }
}
```

New pushed code

Looking at `FallStrategy`, we realize that we can make a few other improvements. First, the ternary operator ? : violates NEVER USE **if** WITH **else** (R4.1.1). Second, the **if** in drop seems more concerned with `falling`. If we start with the ternary, we can get rid of it by pushing the line into `Tile`.

Listing 6.28 Before

```
interface Tile {
  // ...




}
class Air implements Tile {
  // ...






}
class Stone implements Tile {
  // ...




}
```

Listing 6.29 After

```
interface Tile {
  // ...
  getBlockOnTopState(): FallingState;
}
class Air implements Tile {
  // ...
  getBlockOnTopState() {
    return new Falling();
  }
}
class Stone implements Tile {
  // ...
  getBlockOnTopState() {
    return new Resting();
  }
}
```

Pushed code

```
class FallStrategy {
  // ...
  update(tile: Tile, x: number, y: number) {
    this.falling = map[y + 1][x].isAir()
      ? new Falling()
      : new Resting();
    this.drop(tile, x, y);
  }
}
```

```
class FallStrategy {
  // ...
  update(tile: Tile, x: number, y: number) {
    this.falling =
      map[y + 1][x].getBlockOnTopState();    ◁─┐
                                                │
    this.drop(tile, x, y);              Pushed │
  }                                       code  │
}
```

In `FallStrategy.drop`, we can get rid of the `if` entirely by pushing the method into
`FallingState` and inlining `FallStrategy.drop`.

Listing 6.30   Before

```
interface FallingState {
  // ...




}
class Falling {
  // ...




}
class Resting {
  // ...


}
class FallStrategy {
  // ...
  update(tile: Tile, x: number, y: number) {
    this.falling =
      map[y + 1][x].getBlockOnTopState();
    this.drop(tile, x, y);
  }
  private drop(tile: Tile,
    x: number, y: number)
  {
    if (this.falling.isFalling()) {
      map[y + 1][x] = tile;
      map[y][x] = new Air();
    }
  }
}
```

Listing 6.31   After

```
interface FallingState {
  // ...
  drop(
    tile: Tile, x: number, y: number): void;    ◁─┐
}                                                  │
class Falling {                                    │
  // ...                                           │
  drop(tile: Tile, x: number, y: number) {    ◁──┤
    map[y + 1][x] = tile;                          │
    map[y][x] = new Air();                         │
  }                                                │
}                                        Pushed    │
class Resting {                            code    │
  // ...                                           │
  drop(tile: Tile, x: number, y: number) { }  ◁──┤
}                                                  │
class FallStrategy {                               │
  // ...                                           │
  update(tile: Tile, x: number, y: number) {      │
    this.falling =                                 │
      map[y + 1][x].getBlockOnTopState();          │
    this.falling.drop(tile, x, y)         ◁────────┘
  }
}                 ◁─┐  drop is
                   │  deleted.
```

6.2 *Encapsulating simple data*

Once again, we are in a position where our code abides by all of our rules. So, we again introduce a new rule.

6.2.1 *Rule:* NEVER HAVE COMMON AFFIXES

STATEMENT

Our code should not have methods or variables with common prefixes or suffixes.

EXPLANATION

We often postfix or prefix methods and variables with something that hints at their context, such as `username` for the name of the user or `startTimer` for a timer's start action. We do this to communicate the context. Although doing so makes the code more readable, when multiple elements have the same affix, it indicates coherence of these elements. There is a better way to communicate such structure: classes.

The advantage of using classes to group such methods and variables is that we have complete control over the external interface. We can hide helper methods so they do not pollute our global scope. This is especially valuable since our five-line rule introduces a lot of methods.

It can also be the case that not every method can be safely called from everywhere. If we extract the middle part of a complicated computation, it may require some setup before it works. In our game, this is the case for `updateMap` and `drawMap`, both of which require that `transformMap` has been called.

Most important, by hiding the data, we ensure that its invariants are maintained in the class. Doing so makes them local invariants, which are easier to maintain.

Consider the bank example from chapter 4, where we could deposit money without withdrawing it if we called `deposit` directly. Since we never want to call `deposit` directly, a better way to implement this functionality is to put both methods in a class and make `deposit` private.

Listing 6.32 Bad

```
function accountDeposit(
  to: string, amount: number)
{
  let accountId = database.find(to);
  database.updateOne(
    accountId,
    { $inc: { balance: amount } });
}

function accountTransfer(amount: number,
  from: string, to: string)
{
  accountDeposit(from, -amount);
  accountDeposit(to, amount);
}
```

Listing 6.33 Good

```
class Account {
  private deposit(
    to: string, amount: number)
  {
    let accountId = database.find(to);
    database.updateOne(
      accountId,
      { $inc: { balance: amount } });
  }

  transfer(amount: number,
    from: string, to: string)
  {
    this.deposit(from, -amount);
    this.deposit(to, amount);
  }
}
```

SMELL

The smell that this rule is derived from is called the *single responsibility principle*. It is the same as the "Methods should do one thing" smell that we discussed earlier, but for classes. Classes should have a single responsibility.

INTENT

Designing classes with a single responsibility requires discipline and overview. This rule helps to identify sub-responsibilities. The structure hinted at by a common affix suggests that those methods and variables share the responsibility of the common affix; therefore, those methods should be in a separate class dedicated to this common responsibility.

This rule also helps us identify responsibilities even when they emerge over time as our application evolves. Classes often grow over time.

REFERENCES

The single responsibility principle is covered extensively on the internet. It is a standard design principle for classes. Unfortunately, this means it is often presented as something to design up front. But here, we take a different approach and focus on a symptom that can be seen in the code.

6.2.2 Applying the rule

We have a clear group with the same affix, the method and variables:

- `playerx`
- `playery`
- `drawPlayer`

This suggests that we should put these in a class called `Player`. We already have a `Player` class, but it has a completely different purpose. There are two easy solutions. One is to enclose all tile types in a namespace and make them public. Although this is our preferred solution, it leads to a lot of TypeScript-specific tinkering. Since this is not a book about TypeScript, we choose the other easy solution and simply rename the existing `Player`.

Listing 6.34 Before

```
class Player implements Tile { ... }
```

Listing 6.35 After

```
class PlayerTile implements Tile { ... }
```
Append Tile to the name.

We can now make a new `Player` class for the group mentioned earlier:

1 Create a `Player` class.

Listing 6.36 New class

```
class Player { }
```

2 Move the variables `playerx` and `playery` into `Player`, replacing **let** with **private**. Remove `player` from their names. Also make getters and setters for the variables, which will be dealt with later.

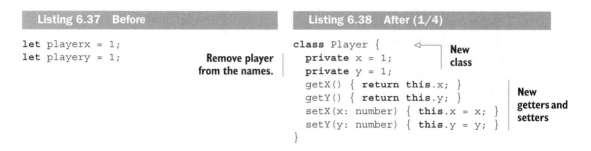

Listing 6.37 Before

```
let playerx = 1;
let playery = 1;
```

Remove player from the names.

Listing 6.38 After (1/4)

```
class Player {
  private x = 1;
  private y = 1;
  getX() { return this.x; }
  getY() { return this.y; }
  setX(x: number) { this.x = x; }
  setY(y: number) { this.y = y; }
}
```

New class

New getters and setters

3 Because `playerx` and `playery` are no longer in the global scope, the compiler helps us find all the references by giving errors. We fix these errors in the following five steps:

    a Pick a good variable name for an instance of the `Player` class: that is, `player`.

    b Pretending that we have a `player` variable, use its getters or setters.

Listing 6.39 Before

```
function moveToTile(
  newx: number, newy: number)
{
  map[playery][playerx] =
    new Air();
  map[newy][newx] = new PlayerTile();
  playerx = newx;
  playery = newy;
}
/// ...
```

Access and assignment are changed everywhere.

Listing 6.40 After (2/4)

```
function moveToTile(
  newx: number, newy: number)
{
  map[player.getY()][player.getX()] =
    new Air();
  map[newy][newx] = new PlayerTile();
  player.setX(newx);
  player.setY(newy);
}
/// ...
```

Access changed to getters

Assignment changed to setters

    c If we have errors in two or more different methods, we add `player: Player` as the first parameter and add `player` as the argument, causing new errors.

Listing 6.41 Before

```
interface Tile {
  // ...
  moveHorizontal(
    dx: number): void;
  moveVertical(
    dy: number): void;
}
```

player is added as a parameter to many methods, even those in the interfaces.

Listing 6.42 After (3/4)

```
interface Tile {
  // ...
  moveHorizontal(
    player: Player, dx: number): void;
  moveVertical(
    player: Player, dy: number): void;
}
```

d Repeat until only one method errors.

e Because we encapsulated variables, put **let** player = **new** Player(); at the point where the variables used to be.

Listing 6.43 After (4/4)

```
let player = new Player();
```

This transformation made changes throughout the codebase. The following are some of the important effects.

Listing 6.44 Before

```
interface Tile {
  // ...
  moveHorizontal(
    dx: number): void;
  moveVertical(
    dy: number): void;
}
/// ...
function moveToTile(
  newx: number, newy: number)
{
  map[playery][playerx] =
    new Air();
  map[newy][newx] = new PlayerTile();
  playerx = newx;
  playery = newy;
}
/// ...

let playerx = 1;
let playery = 1;
```

> **Added player as a parameter to lots of methods**

> **New class with getters and setters**

Listing 6.45 After

```
interface Tile {
  // ...
  moveHorizontal(
    player: Player, dx: number): void;
  moveVertical(
    player: Player, dy: number): void;
}
/// ...
function moveToTile(
  newx: number, newy: number)
{
  map[player.getY()][player.getX()] =
    new Air();
  map[newy][newx] = new PlayerTile();
  player.setX(newx);
  player.setY(newy);
}
/// ...
class Player {
  private x = 1;
  private y = 1;
  getX() { return this.x; }
  getY() { return this.y; }
  setX(x: number) { this.x = x; }
  setY(y: number) { this.y = y; }
}
let player = new Player();
```

> **Access changed to getters**

> **Assignments switched to setters**

> **New declaration in place of the encapsulated variables**

Having introduced a class, we can now push any method with a Player affix into this class without any issues. In this case, we only need to push drawPlayer into the class.

Listing 6.46   Before

```
function drawPlayer(player: Player,
  g: CanvasRenderingContext2D)
{
  g.fillStyle = "#ff0000";
  g.fillRect(
    player.getX() * TILE_SIZE,
    player.getY() * TILE_SIZE,
    TILE_SIZE,
    TILE_SIZE);
}
class Player {
  // ...
}
```

Listing 6.47   After

```
function drawPlayer(player: Player,
  g: CanvasRenderingContext2D)
{
  player.draw(g);
}
class Player {
  // ...
  draw(g: CanvasRenderingContext2D) {
    g.fillStyle = "#ff0000";
    g.fillRect(
      this.x * TILE_SIZE,
      this.y * TILE_SIZE,
      TILE_SIZE,
      TILE_SIZE);
  }
}
```

> **Notice that we have inlined the getters.**

As usual, we perform INLINE METHOD (P4.1.7) on drawPlayer. The new class violates our new rule, DO NOT USE GETTERS OR SETTERS. So we use its related refactoring, ELIMINATE GETTER OR SETTER. We start with getX.

1 Make the getter private to get errors everywhere it is used.

Listing 6.48   Before

```
class Player {
  // ...
  getX() { return this.x; }
}
```

Listing 6.49   After (1/3)

```
class Player {
  // ...
  private getX() { return this.x; }
}
```

> **Make the getter private.**

2 Fix the errors with PUSH CODE INTO CLASSES.

Listing 6.50   Before

```
class Right implements Input {
  handle(player: Player) {
    map[player.getY()][player.getX() + 1]
      .moveHorizontal(player, 1);
  }
}
class Resting {
  // ...
  moveHorizontal(
    player: Player, tile: Tile, dx: number)
  {
    if (map[player.getY()]
          [player.getX()+dx + dx].isAir()
      && !map[player.getY() + 1]
          [player.getX()+dx].isAir())
    {
```

Listing 6.51   After (2/3)

```
class Right implements Input {
  handle(player: Player) {
    player.moveHorizontal(1);
  }
}
class Resting {
  // ...
  moveHorizontal(
    player: Player, tile: Tile, dx: number)
  {
    player.pushHorizontal(tile, dx);
  }
}
/// ...
  player.move(0, dy);
/// ...
```

> **Methods pushed into Player**

```
        map[player.getY()]                     function moveToTile(player: Player,
          [player.getX()+dx + dx] = tile;        newx: number, newy: number)
        moveToTile(player,                      {
          player.getX()+dx,                       player.moveToTile(newx, newy);
          player.getY());                       }
      }                                         /// ...
    }                                           class Player {
  }                                               // ...
/// ...                                           moveHorizontal(dx: number) {
      moveToTile(player,                            map[this.y][this.x + dx]
        player.getX(), player.getY() + dy);             .moveHorizontal(this, dx);
/// ...                                            }
function moveToTile(player: Player,               move(dx: number, dy: number) {
  newx: number, newy: number)                       this.moveToTile(this.x+dx, this.y+dy);
{                                                 }
  map[player.getY()][player.getX()] =             pushHorizontal(tile: Tile, dx: number) {
    new Air();                                      if (map[this.y]
  map[newy][newx] = new PlayerTile();                   [this.x+dx + dx].isAir()
  player.setX(newx);                                  && !map[this.y + 1]
  player.setY(newy);                                      [this.x+dx].isAir())
}                                                     {
/// ...                                                map[this.y][this.x+dx + dx] = tile;
class Player {                                         this.moveToTile(this.x+dx, this.y);
  // ...                                              }
}                                                   }
                                                    moveToTile(newx: number, newy: number) {
                                                      map[this.y][this.x] = new Air();
                                                      map[newy][newx] = new PlayerTile();
                                                      this.x = newx;
                                                      this.y = newy;
                                                    }
                                                  }
```

3 The getter is inlined as part of PUSH CODE INTO CLASSES. It is therefore unused, so delete it to avoid other people trying to use it.

Listing 6.52 Before	Listing 6.53 After (3/3)

```
class Player {              class Player {
  // ...                       // ...            Delete
  getX() { return this.x; }  }                   getX.
}
```

Luckily, getX and getY were so closely connected that getY simply disappeared with getX, along with (amazingly) the two setters. We now have the following.

Listing 6.54 Before	Listing 6.55 After

```
class Player {
  // ...
  getX() { return this.x; }
  getY() { return this.y; }
  setX(x: number) { this.x = x; }
  setY(y: number) { this.y = y; }
}
```

New methods pushed into Player

```
class Player {                    Getters and
  // ...                          setters deleted
  moveHorizontal(dx: number) {
    map[this.y][this.x + dx]
      .moveHorizontal(this, dx);
  }
  move(dx: number, dy: number) {
    moveToTile(this.x + dx, this.y + dy);
  }
  pushHorizontal(tile: Tile, dx: number) {
    if (map[this.y][this.x + dx + dx].isAir()
      && !map[this.y + 1][this.x + dx].isAir())
    {
      map[this.y][this.x + dx + dx] = tile;
      moveToTile(this.x + dx, this.y);
    }
  }
  moveToTile(newx: number, newy: number) {
    map[this.y][this.x] = new Air();
    map[newy][newx] = new PlayerTile();
    this.x = newx;
    this.y = newy;
  }
}
```

Since moveToTile was pushed entirely into Player, we INLINE METHOD on the original moveToTile, thereby removing it from the global scope. The new method Player .moveToTile is now only called from inside the Player class, so we can make it **private**. Doing so makes the growing interface for Player slightly cleaner.

The process of moving variables and methods into a class is called ENCAPSULATE DATA.

6.2.3   *Refactoring pattern: ENCAPSULATE DATA*

DESCRIPTION

As mentioned earlier, we encapsulate variables and methods to limit where they can be accessed from and to make structure explicit. Encapsulating methods helps simplify their names and makes cohesion clearer. This leads to nicer classes—and it often also leads to more and smaller classes, which is beneficial as well. In my experience, people are much too reserved about making classes.

The most significant benefit, however, comes from encapsulating variables. As discussed in chapter 2, we often assume certain properties about our data. These properties become harder to maintain if the data can be accessed from more places. Limiting the scope means only methods inside the class can modify data, and therefore only those methods can affect properties. If we need to verify an invariant, we need only check the code inside the class.

Note that in some situations, we have only methods with a common affix, without variables. It can still make sense to use this refactoring in that situation, but we then need to push the methods into the class before we perform the inner steps.

PROCESS

1 Create a class.

2 Move the variables into the new class, replacing `let` with `private`. Simplify the variables' names; also make getters and setters for the variables.

3 Because the variables are no longer in the global scope, the compiler helps us find all the references by giving errors. Fix these errors in the following five steps:

   a Pick a good variable name for an instance of the new class.

   b Replace access with getters or setters on the pretend variable.

   c If we have errors in two or more different methods, add a parameter with the variable name from earlier as the first parameter, and put the same variable as the first argument at call sites.

   d Repeat until only one method errors.

   e If we encapsulated variables, instantiate the new class at the point where the variables were declared. Otherwise, put the instantiation in the method that errors.

EXAMPLE

This is a constructed example; it simply increments a variable 20 times, printing the variable's value at every step. Even these few lines are enough to show a potential pitfall of refactorings similar to this one.

Listing 6.56 Initial

```
let counter = 0;
function incrementCounter() {
  counter++;
}
function main() {
  for (let i = 0; i < 20; i++) {
    incrementCounter();
    console.log(counter);
  }
}
```

We follow the process:

1 Create a class.

Listing 6.57 New class

```
class Counter { }
```

2 Move the variables into the new class, replacing `let` with **private**. Simplify the variables' names; also make getters and setters for the variables.

Listing 6.58 Before	Listing 6.59 After (1/4)

```
let counter = 0;
class Counter {




}
```

Encapsulated variable

```
class Counter {                      New getter
  private counter = 0;
  getCounter() { return this.counter; }
  setCounter(c: number) {
    this.counter = c;                New
  }                                  setter
}
```

3 Because counter is no longer in the global scope, the compiler helps us find all the references by giving errors. Fix these errors in the following five steps:

  a Pick a good variable name for an instance of the new class: counter.

  b Replace access with getters or setters on the pretend variable.

Listing 6.60 Before	Listing 6.61 After (2/4)

```
function incrementCounter() {
  counter++;


}
function main() {
  for (let i = 0; i < 20; i++) {
    incrementCounter();
    console.log(counter);
  }
}
```

```
function incrementCounter() {      Assigning
  counter.setCounter(              replaced with
    counter.getCounter() + 1);     setter
}
function main() {
  for (let i = 0; i < 20; i++) {
    incrementCounter();
    console.log(counter.getCounter());
  }
}                                  Accessing replaced
                                   with getter
```

c If we have errors in two or more different methods, add a parameter with the variable name from earlier as the first parameter, and put the same variable as the first argument at call sites.

Listing 6.62 Before	Listing 6.63 After (3/4)

```
function incrementCounter()
{
  counter.setCounter(
    counter.getCounter() + 1);
}
function main() {
  for (let i = 0; i < 20; i++) {
    incrementCounter();
    console.log(counter.getCounter());
  }
}
```

```
function incrementCounter(counter: Counter)
{                                  Parameter
  counter.setCounter(              added
    counter.getCounter() + 1);
}
function main() {
  for (let i = 0; i < 20; i++) {
    incrementCounter(counter);
    console.log(counter.getCounter());
  }
}                                  Artificial variable
                                   passed as an argument
```

d Repeat until only one method errors. In this case, we have only one error at this point.

e Now we can inadvertently make a mistake by initializing the class inside the loop. It is not always easy to know whether the code is somehow run inside a loop. Notice how the following code would not work properly, although it would compile.

Listing 6.64 Incorrect

```
function main() {
  for (let i = 0; i < 20; i++) {
    let counter = new Counter();        ←— Incorrect
    incrementCounter(counter);              instantiation
    console.log(counter.getCounter());      location
  }
}
```

To ensure that we do not make this mistake, we determine whether we encapsulated variables. In this case, we did, so we instantiate the new class at the point where the variable was.

Listing 6.65 Before

```
class Counter { ... }
```

Listing 6.66 After (4/4)

```
class Counter { ... }
let counter = new Counter();    ←—   Instantiating a
                                      variable at the
                                      place where the
                                      old variable was
```

After this, we can easily push in `incrementCounter` with the same suffix. The resulting code in this example also breaks one of our rules: can you spot which one and how to fix it? Hint: Look at how we use `counter` in listing 6.63.

FURTHER READING

This refactoring is very closely related to one called "Encapsulate field" in Martin Fowler's *Refactoring* that makes a public field private and introduces a getter and setter for it. The difference is that our version also replaces the public access to the field with parameters. This, in turn, allows this pattern to also encapsulate methods without a field.

Converting to parameters has the added benefit that we can more easily move the instantiation around if we see fit. Because of the parameters, we are forced to instantiate the class before we use it, thereby avoiding a possible null reference error that might have occurred when it was globally accessed.

6.3 *Encapsulating complex data*

In our game codebase, we have another clear group in the methods and variables:

- `map`
- `transformMap`

- updateMap
- drawMap

These are asking to be in a map class, so we use ENCAPSULATE DATA.

1 Create a `Map` class.

Listing 6.67   New class

```
class Map { }
```

2 Move the variable `map` into `Map`, and replace **let** with **private**. In this case, we cannot simplify the name. We also make a getter and setter for `map`.

Listing 6.68   Before

```
let map: Tile[][];
```

Add a getter and
setter for map.

Listing 6.69   After (1/4)

```
class Map {
  private map: Tile[][];      ◁──  Move in the variable,
  getMap() { return this.map; }      changing let to private.
  setMap(map: Tile[][]) { this.map = map; }
}
```

3 Because `map` is no longer in the global scope, the compiler helps us find all the references by giving errors. We fix these errors in the following five steps:

a Pick a good variable name for an instance of the `Map` class: `map`.

b Replace access with getters or setters on the pretend variable.

Listing 6.70   Before

```
function remove(
  shouldRemove: RemoveStrategy)
{
  for (let y = 0;
      y < map.length;
      y++)
    for (let x = 0;
        x < map[y].length;
        x++)
      if (shouldRemove.check(
        map[y][x]))
        map[y][x] = new Air();
}
```

Access map
through
getMap.

Listing 6.71   After (2/4)

```
function remove(
  shouldRemove: RemoveStrategy)
{
  for (let y = 0;
      y < map.getMap().length;
      y++)
    for (let x = 0;
        x < map.getMap()[y].length;
        x++)
      if (shouldRemove.check(
        map.getMap()[y][x]))
        map.getMap()[y][x] = new Air();
}
```

c If we have errors in two or more different methods, add a parameter with the variable name from earlier as the first parameter, and put the same variable as the first argument at call sites.

Listing 6.72   Before

```
interface Tile {
  // ...
  moveHorizontal(
    player: Player, dx: number): void;
  moveVertical(
    player: Player, dy: number): void;
  update(
    x: number, y: number): void;
}
/// ...
```

Listing 6.73   After (3/4)

```
interface Tile {
  // ...
  moveHorizontal(map: Map,                ◁
    player: Player, dx: number): void;        map
  moveVertical(map: Map,                  ◁   added
    player: Player, dy: number): void;        as an
  update(map: Map,                        ◁   argument.
    x: number, y: number): void;
}
/// ...   ◁
```

map is added in lots of places.

d   Repeat until only one method errors.

e   We encapsulated a variable, so we put **let** map = **new** Map(); at the point where map used to be.

Listing 6.74   After (4/4)

```
let map = new Map();
```

The result is the following transformation.

Listing 6.75   Before

```
interface Tile {
  // ...
  moveHorizontal(player: Player, dx: number): void;
  moveVertical(player: Player, dy: number): void;
  update(x: number, y: number): void;
}
/// ...
function remove(shouldRemove: RemoveStrategy)
{
  for (let y = 0; y < map.length; y++)
    for (let x = 0; x < map[y].length; x++)
      if(shouldRemove.check(map[y][x]))
        map[y][x] = new Air();
}
/// ...
let map: Tile[][];
```

Listing 6.76   After

```
interface Tile {
  // ...
  moveHorizontal(map: Map, player: Player, dx: number): void;
  moveVertical(map: Map, player: Player, dy: number): void;
  update(map: Map, x: number, y: number): void;
}
/// ...
```

map added as an argument

```
function remove(map: Map, shouldRemove: RemoveStrategy)
{
  for (let y = 0; y < map.getMap().length; y++)
    for (let x = 0; x < map.getMap()[y].length; x++)
      if (shouldRemove.check(map.getMap()[y][x]))
        map.getMap()[y][x] = new Air();
}
/// ...
class Map {
  private map: Tile[][];
  getMap() { return this.map; }
  setMap(map: Tile[][]) { this.map = map; }
}
```

> **Accesses map through getMap**

> **New class with a getter and setter for map**

Handling the methods mentioned earlier is now easy: PUSH CODE INTO CLASSES simplifies their names in the process, and we use INLINE METHOD, as we have done so many times before.

Listing 6.77   Before

```
function transformMap(map: Map) {
  map.setMap(new Array(rawMap.length));
  for (let y = 0; y < rawMap.length; y++) {
    map.getMap()[y] = new Array(rawMap[y].length);
    for (let x = 0; x < rawMap[y].length; x++)
      map.getMap()[y][x] = transformTile(rawMap[y][x]);
  }
}
function updateMap(map: Map) {
  for (let y = map.getMap().length - 1; y >= 0; y--)
    for (let x = 0; x < map.getMap()[y].length; x++)
      map.getMap()[y][x].update(map, x, y);
}
function drawMap(map: Map, g: CanvasRenderingContext2D) {
  for (let y = 0; y < map.getMap().length; y++)
    for (let x = 0; x < map.getMap()[y].length; x++)
      map.getMap()[y][x].draw(g, x, y);
}
```

Listing 6.78   After

```
class Map {
  // ...
  transform() {
    this.map = new Array(rawMap.length);
    for (let y = 0; y < rawMap.length; y++) {
      this.map[y] = new Array(rawMap[y].length);
      for (let x = 0; x < rawMap[y].length; x++)
        this.map[y][x] = transformTile(rawMap[y][x]);
    }
  }
  update() {
    for (let y = this.map.length - 1; y >= 0; y--)
      for (let x = 0; x < this.map[y].length; x++)
```

```
          this.map[y][x].update(this, x, y);
    }
    draw(g: CanvasRenderingContext2D) {
      for (let y = 0; y < this.map.length; y++)
        for (let x = 0; x < this.map[y].length; x++)
          this.map[y][x].draw(g, x, y);
    }
  }
```

As we did with `Player`, we have a getter and a setter, so we again ELIMINATE GETTER OR SETTER. Luckily the setter is unused, so it is trivial to delete. The getter requires some pushing; therefore, I have split the before and after code up into multiple bites.

Listing 6.79 Before

```
class Falling {
  // ...
  drop(map: Map, tile: Tile,
    x: number, y: number)
  {
    map.getMap()[y + 1][x] = tile;
    map.getMap()[y][x] = new Air();
  }
}
class Map {
  // ...



}
```

Listing 6.80 After

```
class Falling {
  // ...
  drop(map: Map, tile: Tile,
    x: number, y: number)
  {
    map.drop(tile, x, y);           ◁──┐  Code is
  }                                     │  pushed
}                                       │  into Map.
class Map {
  // ...
  drop(tile: Tile, x: number, y: number) {
    this.map[y + 1][x] = tile;
    this.map[y][x] = new Air();
  }
}
```

Listing 6.81 Before

```
class FallStrategy {
  // ...
  update(map: Map, tile: Tile,
    x: number, y: number)
  {
    this.falling =
      map.getMap()[y + 1][x].isAir()
      ? new Falling()
      : new Resting();
    this.falling.drop(map, tile, x, y);
  }
}
class Map {
  // ...



}
```

Listing 6.82 After

```
class FallStrategy {
  // ...
  update(map: Map, tile: Tile,           Code is
    x: number, y: number)                pushed
  {                                      into Map.
    this.falling =
      map.getBlockOnTopState(x, y + 1);  ◁──┘
    this.falling.drop(map, tile, x, y);
  }
}
class Map {
  // ...
  getBlockOnTopState(x: number, y: number) {
    return this.map[y][x]
      .getBlockOnTopState();
  }
}
```

Listing 6.83   Before

```
class Player {
  // ...
  moveHorizontal(map: Map, dx: number) {
    map.getMap()[this.y][this.x + dx]
      .moveHorizontal(map, this, dx);
  }
  moveVertical(map: Map, dy: number) {
    map.getMap()[this.y + dy][this.x]
      .moveVertical(map, this, dy);
  }
  pushHorizontal(map: Map, tile: Tile,
    dx: number)
  {
    if (map.getMap()
      [this.y][this.x + dx + dx].isAir()
      && !map.getMap()
      [this.y + 1][this.x + dx].isAir())
    {
      map.getMap()[this.y][this.x + dx + dx]
        = tile;
      this.moveToTile(
        map, this.x + dx, this.y);
    }
  }
  private moveToTile(map: Map,
    newx: number, newy: number)
  {
    map.getMap()[this.y][this.x] =
      new Air();
    map.getMap()[newy][newx] =
      new PlayerTile();
    this.x = newx;
    this.y = newy;
  }
}
class Map {
  // ...
}
```

Listing 6.84   After

```
class Player {
  // ...
  moveHorizontal(map: Map, dx: number) {
    map.moveHorizontal(this,
      this.x, this.y, dx);
  }
  moveVertical(map: Map, dy: number) {
    map.moveVertical(this,
      this.x, this.y, dy);
  }
  pushHorizontal(map: Map, tile: Tile,
    dx: number)
  {
    if (map.isAir(this.x + dx + dx, this.y)
      && !map.isAir(this.x + dx, this.y + 1))
    {
      map.setTile(this.x + dx + dx, this.y,
        tile);
      this.moveToTile(
        map, this.x + dx, this.y);
    }
  }
  private moveToTile(map: Map,
    newx: number, newy: number)
  {
    map.movePlayer(this.x, this.y,
      newx, newy);



    this.x = newx;
    this.y = newy;
  }
}
class Map {
  // ...
  isAir(x: number, y: number) {
    return this.map[y][x].isAir();
  }
  setTile(x: number, y: number, tile: Tile)
  {
    this.map[y][x] = tile;
  }
  movePlayer(x: number, y: number,
    newx: number, newy: number)
  {
    this.map[y][x] = new Air();
    this.map[newy][newx] = new PlayerTile();
  }
  moveHorizontal(player: Player,
    x: number, y: number, dx: number)
  {
    this.map[y][x + dx]
```

Code is pushed into Map.

```
      .moveHorizontal(this, player, dx);
  }
  moveVertical(player: Player,
    x: number, y: number, dy: number)
  {
    this.map[y + dy][x].moveVertical(
      this, player, dy);
  }
}
```

Listing 6.85 Before

```
function remove(map: Map,
  shouldRemove: RemoveStrategy)
{
  for (let y = 0;
       y < map.getMap().length;
       y++)
    for (let x = 0;
         x < map.getMap()[y].length;
         x++)
      if (shouldRemove.check(
          map.getMap()[y][x]))
        map.getMap()[y][x] = new Air();
}
class Map {
  // ...
  getMap() {
    return this.map;
  }
}
```

Listing 6.86 After

```
class Map {
  // ...
```
← **getMap is removed.**
```
  remove(shouldRemove: RemoveStrategy) {
    for (let y = 0;
         y < this.map.length;
         y++)
      for (let x = 0;
           x < this.map[y].length;
           x++)
        if (shouldRemove.check(
          this.map[y][x]))
          this.map[y][x] = new Air();
  }
}
```
Code is pushed into Map.

The original remove is now a single line, so we use INLINE METHOD.

Usually, we are not fans of introducing a strong method like setTile into our public interface. It very nearly gives complete control to the private field map. However, we should not be afraid to add code; we soldier on.

We notice that all the lines but one in Player.pushHorizontal use map, so we decide to push the code into map.

Listing 6.87 Before

```
class Player {
  // ...
  pushHorizontal(map: Map, tile: Tile,
    dx: number)
  {
    if (map.isAir(this.x + dx + dx, this.y)
    && !map.isAir(this.x + dx, this.y + 1))
    {
      map.setTile(this.x + dx + dx, this.y,
        tile);
      this.moveToTile(
```

Listing 6.88 After

```
class Player {
  // ...
  pushHorizontal(map: Map, tile: Tile,
    dx: number)
  {
    map.pushHorizontal(
      this, tile, this.x, this.y, dx);
  }
  moveToTile(map: Map,
    newx: number, newy: number)
  {
```
Code pushed into Map
Method is made public

```
            map, this.x + dx, this.y);                map.movePlayer(this.x, this.y,
    }                                                     newx, newy);
  }                                                    this.x = newx;
  private moveToTile(map: Map,                         this.y = newy;
    newx: number, newy: number)                      }
  {                                                 }
    map.movePlayer(this.x, this.y,               class Map {
       newx, newy);                                 // ...
    this.x = newx;                                 pushHorizontal(player: Player, tile: Tile,
    this.y = newy;                                   x: number, y: number, dx: number)
  }                                                  {
}                                                      if (this.map[y][x + dx + dx].isAir()
                                                       && !this.map[y + 1][x + dx].isAir())
                                                       {
                                                         this.map[y][x + dx + dx] = tile;
                                                         player.moveToTile(this, x + dx, y);
                                                       }
                                                     }
                                                   }
```

This `setTile` is only used inside `Map`. We can make it private or—even better—remove it since we love deleting code.

6.4   *Eliminating a sequence invariant*

We notice that the map is initialized with a call to `map.transform`. But in an object-oriented setting, we have a different mechanism for initialization: the constructor. In this case, we are lucky because we can replace `transform` with **constructor** and remove the call to `transform`.

Listing 6.89 Before	Listing 6.90 After

```
class Map {                   class Map {
  // ...                        // ...
  transform() {                 constructor() {        ◁──┐ transform
    // ...                        // ...                  │ changed to
  }                             }                         │ constructor
}                             }
/// ...                       /// ...
window.onload = () => {       window.onload = () => {
  map.transform();
  gameLoop(map);                gameLoop(map);         ◁──┐ Call to transform
}                             }                            │ removed
```

Doing this has the significant effect of removing the invariant that we have to call `map.transform` before the other methods. When something needs to be called before something else, we call it a *sequence invariant*. It is impossible not to call the constructor first, so the invariant is eliminated. This technique can always be used to make sure things happen in a specific sequence. We call this refactoring ENFORCE SEQUENCE.

6.4.1 Refactoring pattern: ENFORCE SEQUENCE

DESCRIPTION

I think the coolest type of refactoring is when we can "teach" the compiler something about how we want our program to run, so it can help make sure that happens. This is one of those situations.

Object-oriented languages have a built-in property that constructors are always called before methods on objects. We can take advantage of this property to make sure things happen in a specific order. It is even fairly straightforward to do, although it means introducing one class per step that we want to enforce. But after performing this transformation, the sequence is no longer an invariant because it is enforced! We don't need to remember to call one method before the other because it is impossible not to do so. Amazing!

By using the constructor to ensure that some code is run, the instance of the class becomes proof that the code was run. We cannot get an instance without running the constructor successfully.

This example shows how to use this technique to make sure a string is capitalized before it is printed.

Listing 6.91   Before

```
function print(str: string) {
  // string should be capitalized
  console.log(str);
}
```

Listing 6.92   After

```
class CapitalizedString {
  private value: string;
  constructor(str: string) {
    this.value = capitalize(str);
  }
  print() {                          The invariant
                                     disappeared.

    console.log(this.value);
  }
}
```

The ENFORCE SEQUENCE transformation has two variants: internal and external. The previous example demonstrates the internal version: the target function is moved inside the new class. Here is a side-by-side comparison of the two variants, which mostly offer the same advantages.

Listing 6.93   Internal

```
class CapitalizedString {
  private value: string;
  constructor(str: string) {
    this.value = capitalize(str);
  }
  print() {
    console.log(this.value);
  }
}
```

Private vs. public

Method vs. function with a specific parameter type

Listing 6.94   External

```
class CapitalizedString {
  public readonly value: string;
  constructor(str: string) {
    this.value = capitalize(str);
  }
}
function print(str: CapitalizedString) {
  console.log(str.value);
}
```

This refactoring pattern focuses on the internal version because it leads to stronger encapsulation by not having a getter or a public field.

PROCESS

1 Use ENCAPSULATE DATA on the method that should run last.

2 Make the constructor call the first method.

3 If arguments of the two methods are connected, make these arguments into fields, and remove them from the method.

EXAMPLE

Let's look at an example similar to the earlier one about a bank. We want to make sure money is always first subtracted from the sender before it's added to the receiver. The sequence is thus a `deposit` with a negative amount followed by a `deposit` with a positive amount.

Listing 6.95   Initial

```
function deposit(
  to: string, amount: number)
{
  let accountId = database.find(to);
  database.updateOne(
    accountId,
    { $inc: { balance: amount } });
}
```

1 Use ENCAPSULATE DATA on the method that should run last.

Listing 6.96   Before

```
function deposit(
  to: string, amount: number)
{
  let accountId = database.find(to);
  database.updateOne(
    accountId,
    { $inc: { balance: amount } });
}
```

Listing 6.97   After (1/2)

```
class Transfer {          ◁——┐  New class
  deposit(
    to: string, amount: number)
  {
    let accountId = database.find(to);
    database.updateOne(
      accountId,
      { $inc: { balance: amount } });
  }
}
```

2 Make the constructor call the first method.

Listing 6.98 Before	Listing 6.99 After (2/2)

```
class Transfer {




  deposit(to: string, amount: number) {
    let accountId = database.find(to);
    database.updateOne(
      accountId,
      { $inc: { balance: amount } });
  }
}
```

```
class Transfer {
  constructor(
    from: string, amount: number)
  {
    this.deposit(from, -amount);
  }
  deposit(to: string, amount: number) {
    let accountId = database.find(to);
    database.updateOne(
      accountId,
      { $inc: { balance: amount } });
  }
}
```

New constructor calling the first method

We have now guaranteed that deposit is called with a negative amount from the sender, but we can go further. We can connect the two amounts by making this argument a field and removing amount from the method. Because we need the amount to be negated in one case, we introduce a helper method. The result looks like the following.

Listing 6.100 After

```
class Transfer {
  constructor(from: string, private amount: number) {
    this.depositHelper(from, -this.amount);
  }
  private depositHelper(to: string, amount: number) {
    let accountId = database.find(to);
    database.updateOne(accountId, { $inc: { balance: amount } });
  }
  deposit(to: string) {
    this.depositHelper(to, this.amount);
  }
}
```

We have made sure that we cannot create money, but money can disappear if we forget to call deposit with a receiver. Therefore, we might want to wrap this class in another class to ensure that a positive transfer also occurs.

FURTHER READING

I am not familiar with any formal description of a pattern like this. There are undoubtedly people familiar with this way of using objects as proof that something has happened, but I have not come across such a discussion.

6.5 *Eliminating enums another way*

One last method that feels distinct is transformTile, because of the Tile suffix. We already have a class (or, more specifically, an enum) with the same suffix: RawTile. The name transformTile suggests that this method should be moved to the RawTile enum. However, this is not possible in many languages, including TypeScript: enums cannot have methods.

6.5.1   *Enumeration through private constructors*

If our language does not support methods on enums, there is a technique we can use to get around that by using a private constructor. Every object must be created by invoking a constructor. If we make the constructor **private**, objects can only be created inside our class. Specifically, we can control how many instances exist. If we put these instances in public constants, we can use them as enums.

Listing 6.101   Enum

```
enum TShirtSize {
  SMALL,
  MEDIUM,
  LARGE,

}
function sizeToString(s: TShirtSize) {
  if (s === TShirtSize.SMALL)
    return "S";
  else if (s === TShirtSize.MEDIUM)
    return "M";
  else if (s === TShirtSize.LARGE)
    return "L";
}
```

Listing 6.102   Private constructor

```
class TShirtSize {
  static readonly SMALL = new TShirtSize();
  static readonly MEDIUM = new TShirtSize();
  static readonly LARGE = new TShirtSize();
  private constructor() { }
}
function sizeToString(s: TShirtSize) {
  if (s === TShirtSize.SMALL)
    return "S";
  else if (s === TShirtSize.MEDIUM)
    return "M";
  else if (s === TShirtSize.LARGE)
    return "L";
}
```

The only exception is that we cannot use **switch** with this construction, but we have a rule preventing us from doing so anyway. Note that some weird behavior happens if we serialize and deserialize our data, but that is out of the scope of this book.

Now TShirtSize is a class (which is awesome), and we can push code into it. Unfortunately, we cannot simplify away the **if**s in this setup, because unlike last time, we do not have a class for each value: we have only one class. To gain the full benefit, we need to remedy this situation: we need to REPLACE TYPE CODE WITH CLASSES (P4.1.3).

Listing 6.103   Classes replacing the type code values

```
interface SizeValue { }
class SmallValue implements SizeValue { }
class MediumValue implements SizeValue { }
class LargeValue implements SizeValue { }
```

Again, we could simplify these names with namespaces or packages. We can skip the is methods this time because we never create new instances on the fly, so === is enough. We then use these new classes as an argument for each value in the private-constructor class. We also store the argument as a field.

<table>
<tr><td>

Listing 6.104 Before

```
class TShirtSize {
  static readonly SMALL = new TShirtSize();
  static readonly MEDIUM = new TShirtSize();
  static readonly LARGE = new TShirtSize();
  private constructor() { }
}
```

Parameter
and field for
the values

</td><td>

Listing 6.105 After

```
class TShirtSize {
  static readonly SMALL =
    new TShirtSize(new SmallValue());   ◁┐
  static readonly MEDIUM =
    new TShirtSize(new MediumValue());  ◁┤
  static readonly LARGE =
    new TShirtSize(new LargeValue());   ◁┤
  private constructor(
    private value: SizeValue)
  { }
}
```

**Passing new classes
as arguments**

</td></tr>
</table>

Now, whenever we push something into TShirtSize, we can push it further into all the classes and resolve === TShirtSize., thereby getting rid of the **ifs**. This could have been a pattern, but I have chosen not to make it one for two reasons. First, this process does not apply equally to all programming languages—in particular, Java. Second, we already have a pattern for eliminating enums, which should take preference.

In the game, one enum remains: RawTile. We have already performed REPLACE TYPE CODE WITH CLASSES on it, but we could not eliminate this enum since we use the indices in places. However, we can use the previous transformation to eliminate it anyway.

We introduce a new RawTile2 class with a private constructor with a field for each value of the enum. We also create a new RawTileValue interface and classes for each of the enum's values, which we pass as arguments for the fields in RawTile2.

Listing 6.106 New class

```
interface RawTileValue { }
class AirValue implements RawTileValue { }
// ...
class RawTile2 {
  static readonly AIR = new RawTile2(new AirValue());
  // ...
  private constructor(private value: RawTileValue) { }
}
```

We are one step closer to eliminating the enum. Now we need to switch to using the classes instead of the enums.

6.5.2 Remapping numbers to classes

In some languages, enums cannot have methods because they are handled like named integers. In our game, we store our rawMap as integers and can then interpret the integers as enums. To replace the enums, we need a way to convert the numbers to our new RawTile2 instances. The easiest way to do this is to make an array with all the values in the same order as in the enum.

Listing 6.107   Before

```
enum RawTile {
  AIR,
  FLUX,
  UNBREAKABLE,
  PLAYER,
  STONE, FALLING_STONE,
  BOX, FALLING_BOX,
  KEY1, LOCK1,
  KEY2, LOCK2
}
```

Listing 6.108   After

```
const RAW_TILES = [
  RawTile2.AIR,
  RawTile2.FLUX,
  RawTile2.UNBREAKABLE,
  RawTile2.PLAYER,
  RawTile2.STONE, RawTile2.FALLING_STONE,
  RawTile2.BOX, RawTile2.FALLING_BOX,
  RawTile2.KEY1, RawTile2.LOCK1,
  RawTile2.KEY2, RawTile2.LOCK2
];
```

With this, we can easily map numbers to the correct instance. With `RawTile` gone, we change the remaining references of `RawTile` to `RawTile2`—or, if that is impossible, to `number`.

Listing 6.109   Before

```
let rawMap: RawTile[][] = [
  // ...
];
class Map {
  private map: Tile[][];
  constructor() {
    this.map = new Array(rawMap.length);
    for (let y = 0;
         y < rawMap.length;
         y++)
    {
      this.map[y] =
        new Array(rawMap[y].length);
      for (let x = 0;
           x < rawMap[y].length;
           x++)
        this.map[y][x] =
          transformTile(
            rawMap[y][x]);
    }
  }
  // ...
}
function transformTile(tile: RawTile) {
  // ...
}
```

Listing 6.110   After

```
let rawMap: number[][] = [        ◁─┐  Impossible
  // ...                             │  to put
];                                   │  RawTile2
class Map {
  private map: Tile[][];
  constructor() {
    this.map = new Array(rawMap.length);
    for (let y = 0;
         y < rawMap.length;
         y++)
    {
      this.map[y] =
        new Array(rawMap[y].length);
      for (let x = 0;
           x < rawMap[y].length;
           x++)
        this.map[y][x] =
          transformTile(
            RAW_TILES[rawMap[y][x]]);  ◁─┐
    }
  }
  // ...
}                                      Maps the number
/// ...                                  to the class
function transformTile(tile: RawTile2) {  ◁─┐
  // ...
}
                                      Parameter
                                 changed to a class
```

Now we get an error in `transformTile`. The **switch** that remains from earlier is an issue because, as mentioned, the private constructor method does not work with **switch**. All this work was to eliminate the enum and with it this **switch**. We therefore PUSH CODE INTO CLASSES through `RawTile2` and into all the classes.

Listing 6.111 Before	Listing 6.112 After

```
interface RawTileValue { }
class AirValue implements RawTileValue { }
class StoneValue implements RawTileValue { }
class Key1Value implements RawTileValue { }
/// ...
class RawTile2 {
  // ...
}
/// ...
function assertExhausted(x: never): never {
  throw new Error(
    "Unexpected object: " + x);
}
function transformTile(tile: RawTile2) {
  switch (tile) {
    case RawTile.AIR:
      return new Air();
    case RawTile.STONE:
      return new Stone(new Resting());
    case RawTile.KEY1:
      return new Key(YELLOW_KEY);
    // ...
    default: assertExhausted(tile);
  }
}
```

The magical assertExhausted is no longer needed.

```
interface RawTileValue {
  transform(): Tile;
}
class AirValue implements RawTileValue {
  transform() {
    return new Air();
  }
}
class StoneValue implements RawTileValue {
  transform() {
    return new Stone(new Resting());
  }
}
class Key1Value implements RawTileValue {
  transform() {
    return new Key(YELLOW_KEY);
  }
}
/// ...
class RawTile2 {
  // ...
  transform() {
    return this.value.transform();
  }
}

function transformTile(tile: RawTile2) {
  return tile.transform();
}
```

The code is pushed right through into the values.

At last, the switch has disappeared. transformTile is a single line, so we INLINE METHOD. Finally, we rename RawTile2 to its permanent name: RawTile.

Summary

- To help enforce encapsulation, avoid exposing data. The rule DO NOT USE GET-TERS OR SETTERS (R6.1.1) states that we should not expose private fields indirectly through getters and setters either. We can use the refactoring pattern ELIMINATE GETTER OR SETTER (P6.1.3) to get rid of getters and setters.
- The rule NEVER HAVE COMMON AFFIXES (R6.2.1) states that if we have methods and variables with a common prefix or suffix, they should be in a class together. We can use the refactoring pattern ENCAPSULATE DATA (P6.2.3) to achieve this.
- By using classes, it is possible to make the compiler enforce a sequence invariant, thereby eliminating it with the refactoring ENFORCE SEQUENCE (P6.4.1).
- Another method for dealing with enums is to use a class with a private constructor. Doing so can further eliminate enums and switches.

This concludes part 1 of the book. We can continue to encapsulate things, like `inputs` and `handleInputs`; we can even encapsulate `player` and `map` in a `Game` class, but I'll leave that to you.

We can also extract constants, improve variable and method naming, and introduce namespaces, or go all out on type codes and convert some or all booleans to enums and then REPLACE TYPE CODE WITH CLASSES (P4.1.3)—and thus the snowball has started rolling. The point is, this is not the end of the refactoring. Rather, it is a strong start! In part 2 of the book, we discuss some of the general principles that enable us to do great refactoring.

I claim that everything we've done with the example game in part 1 has already resulted in a much better architecture for three primary reasons:

1 It is now much quicker and safer to extend the game with new `Tile` types.
2 It is much easier to reason about the code because related variables and functionality are grouped in classes and methods with helpful names.
3 We now have control over the scope of our data, with much finer granularity. Therefore it is harder to program something that breaks non-local invariants—which, as discussed in chapter 2, is the cause of most bugs.

In a few places, we have investigated the code a bit to give things good names or decide whether elements should stay together. But these investigations were quick: we never had to spend time figuring out weird quirks in the code, like why one of the **for** loops in update goes backward, or why we push the inputs on a stack instead of executing the moves directly (we might not even have noticed the stack). Answering questions like these requires much more time to gain an understanding that we didn't require for our refactoring efforts.

Part 2

Taking what you have learned into the real world

In part 2, we take a deeper look at how to bring the rules and refactoring patterns into the real world by adding context. We dive into practices that enable us to take full advantage of the tools now at our disposal and discuss how they came to be as they are.

We raise the level of abstraction; rather than discussing concrete rules and refactoring, we examined socio-technical subjects affecting refactoring and code quality. At the same time, I provide actionable advice relating to skills, culture, and tools.

Figure 1   Skills, culture, and tools

Collaborate
with the compiler

This chapter covers

- Understanding the strengths and weaknesses of compilers
- Using compiler strengths to eliminate invariants
- Sharing responsibility with the compiler

When we are just learning to program, the compiler can feel like an endless source of nagging and nitpicking. It takes things too literally, it gives no leeway, and it freaks out over even the tiniest slip-ups. But used correctly, the compiler is one of the most important elements of our daily work. Not only does it transform our code from a high-level language to a lower-level one, but it also validates several properties and guarantees that certain errors will not occur when we run our program.

In this chapter, we start getting to know our compiler so we can actively use it and build on its strengths. Similarly, we will learn what it cannot do so we do not build on a weak foundation.

When we are intimately familiar with the compiler, we should make it part of our team by sharing the responsibility for correctness with it, letting it help build the software right. If we fight the compiler or trip it up, we are accepting a higher risk of bugs in the future, usually with minimal benefit.

Once we have accepted sharing the responsibility, we must trust the compiler. We need to make an effort to keep dangerous invariants to a minimum, and we need to listen to the compiler's output—including its warnings.

The final stage of this journey is accepting that the compiler is better at predicting program behavior than we are. It is quite literally a robot; it does not fatigue even when dealing with hundreds of thousands of lines of code. It can validate properties that no human realistically could. It is a powerful tool, so we should use it!

7.1 Getting to know the compiler

There are more compilers in the world than I can count, and new ones are invented all the time. So instead of focusing on a specific compiler, we discuss properties that are common to most compilers, including the mainstream Java, C#, and TypeScript variety.

A compiler is a program. It is good at certain things, like consistency; contrary to common folklore, compiling more than once will not yield different results. Likewise, it is bad at certain things, like judgment; compilers follow the common idiom "When in doubt, ask."

Fundamentally, the compiler's goal is to generate a program in some other language that is equivalent to our source program. But as a service, modern compilers also verify whether specific errors can occur during run time. This chapter focuses on the latter.

Like most things in programming, we get the best understanding from practicing. We need a deep understanding of what our compiler can and cannot do and how it can be fooled. Therefore, I always have an experimental project ready, to check how the compiler deals with something. Can it guarantee that this is initialized? Can it tell me whether x can be null here?

In the following sections, we answer both these questions by detailing some of the most common strengths and weaknesses of modern compilers.

7.1.1 Weakness: The halting problem limits compile-time knowledge

The reason we cannot say exactly what will happen during run time is called the *halting problem*. In a nutshell, it states that without running a program, we cannot know how the program will behave—and even then, we observe only one path through our program.

> **The halting problem**
> In general, programs are fundamentally unpredictable.

For a quick demonstration of why this is true, consider the following program.

Listing 7.1 Program without run-time errors

```
if (new Date().getDay() === 35)
    5.foo();
```

We know that getDay will never return 35. So whatever is inside the **if** will never be run and thus doesn't matter, even though it would fail because there is no method foo defined on the number 5.

Some programs will definitely fail and will be rejected. Some will definitely not fail and will be allowed. The halting problem means compilers have to decide how to deal with the programs in between. Sometimes the compiler allows programs that might not behave as expected, including failing during run time. Other times, the compiler disallows a program if it cannot guarantee the program is safe; this is called a *conservative* analysis.

Conservative analyses prove that there is no possibility of some specific failure in our program. We can only rely on conservative analyses.

Note that the halting problem is not specific to any compiler or language; it is an inherent property of programming languages. In fact, being subject to the halting problem is the very definition of being a programming language. Where languages and compilers differ is when they are conservative and when not.

7.1.2 *Strength: Reachability ensures that methods return*

One of the conservative analyses checks whether a method **return**s in every path. We are not allowed to run off the end of a method without hitting a **return** statement.

In TypeScript, it is legal to run off the end of a method; but if we use the method assertExhausted from chapter 4, we can get the desired behavior. Although the following looks like a run-time error, the never keyword forces the compiler to analyze whether there is any possible way to reach assertExhausted. In this example, the compiler figures out that we have not checked all values of the enum.

Listing 7.2   Compiler error due to reachability

```
enum Color {
  RED, GREEN, BLUE
}
function assertExhausted(x: never): never {
  throw new Error("Unexpected object: " + x);
}
function handle(t: Color) {
  if (t === Color.RED) return "#ff0000";
  if (t === Color.GREEN) return "#00ff00";
  assertExhausted(t);           ◁——  The compiler errors
}                                     because we have not
                                      handled Color.BLUE.
```

We used this particular check to verify that our **switch** covered all cases in section 4.32. This is called an *exhaustiveness check* in typed functional languages, where it is much more common.

In general, this is a challenging analysis to take advantage of—especially when we follow the five-lines rule, since then it is easy to spot how many **return**s we have and where they are.

7.1.3   *Strength: Definite assignment prevents accessing uninitialized variables*

Another property that compilers are good at verifying is whether variables have definitely been assigned values before they are used. Note that this does not mean they contain anything useful; but they have been explicitly assigned *something*.

This check applies to local variables, specifically in cases where we want to initialize locals inside an `if`. In this case, we run the risk of not having initialized the variable in all paths. Consider this code to find an element whose name is John. At the `return` statement, there is no guarantee that we will have initialized the `result` variable; thus the compiler will not allow this program.

Listing 7.3   Uninitialized variable

```
let result;
for (let i = 0; i < arr.length; i++)
  if (arr[i].name === "John")
    result = arr[i];
return result;
```

We may know that in this code, `arr` definitely contains an element whose name is John. In this case, the compiler is overly cautious. The optimal way to deal with this is to teach the compiler what we know: that it will find an element named John.

We can teach the compiler by taking advantage of the other target of the definite assignment analysis: read-only (or final) fields. A read-only field is required to be initialized at the termination of the constructor; that means we need to assign it either in the constructor or at the declaration directly.

We can use this strictness to ensure that specific values exist. In the earlier example, we can wrap our array in a class with a read-only field for the object whose name is John. Thereby we even avoid having to iterate through the list. Making this change does, of course, mean that we have to alter how the list is created. Still, by making this change, we prevent anyone from ever causing the John object to disappear unnoticed, thereby eliminating an invariant.

7.1.4   *Strength: Access control helps encapsulate data*

The compiler is also excellent at access control, which we use when we have encapsulated data. If we make a member private, we can be sure that it does not escape accidentally. We saw plenty of examples of how and why to use this technique in chapter 6, so we will not go into further detail here, except for clearing up a common misconception among junior programmers: `private` applies to the class, *not* the object. This means we can inspect another object's private members if it is of the same class.

If we have methods that are sensitive to invariants, we can protect them by making them private, like this.

Listing 7.4 Compiler error due to access

```
class Class {
  private sensitiveMethod() {
    // ...
  }
}
let c = new Class();
c.sensitiveMethod();
```
Compiler error here

7.1.5 *Strength: Type checking proves properties*

The final strength of compilers that I want to highlight is the strongest of them all: the type checker. The type checker is responsible for checking that variables and members exist, and we used this functionality whenever we renamed something to get errors in part 1 of the book. It was also the type checker that enabled ENFORCE SEQUENCE (P6.4.1).

In this example, we have encoded a list data structure that cannot be empty because it can only be made up of one element or an element followed by a list.

Listing 7.5 Compiler error due to types

```
interface NonEmptyList<T> {
  head: T;
}
class Last<T> implements NonEmptyList<T> {
  constructor(public readonly head: T) { }
}
class Cons<T> implements NonEmptyList<T> {
  constructor(
    public readonly head: T,
    public readonly tail: NonEmptyList<T>) { }
}
function first<T>(xs: NonEmptyList<T>) {
  return xs.head;
}
first([]);
```
Type error

Contrary to common jargon, being strongly typed is not a binary property. Programming languages can be more or less strongly typed; it is a spectrum. The subset of TypeScript that we consider in this book limits its type strength to be equivalent to Java's and C#'s. This level of type strength is sufficient to teach the compiler complex properties like not being able to pop something off an empty stack. However, this requires some mastery of type theory. Several languages have even stronger type systems, the most interesting of which are as follows, in generally increasing order of strength:

- Borrowing types (Rust)
- Polymorphic type inference (OCaml and F#)
- Type classes (Haskell)

- Union and intersection types (TypeScript)
- Dependent types (Coq and Agda)

In languages with a decent type checker, teaching it properties of our program is the highest level of security we can get. It equals using the most sophisticated static analyzers or proving the properties manually, which is much harder and more error prone. Learning how to do this is out of the scope of this book, but considering the strength of this analysis and the benefits to be gained, I hope I have piqued your interest enough for you to seek it out on your own.

7.1.6 *Weakness: Dereferencing null crashes our application*

At the other end of the spectrum is null. null is dangerous because it causes failure if we try to invoke methods on it. Some tools can detect some of these cases, but they can rarely detect all of them, which means we cannot rely on the tools blindly.

If we turn off TypeScript's strict null check, it behaves like other mainstream languages. In many modern languages, code like this is accepted, even though we can call it with average(null) and crash the program.

Listing 7.6 Potential null dereference, yet no compiler error

```
function average(arr: number[]) {
  return sum(arr) / arr.length;
}
```

The risk of run-time errors means we should be extra careful when dealing with nullable variables. I like to say that if you cannot see a null check of a variable, then it probably is null. Better to check it one time too many than too few.

Some IDEs might tell us that a null check is redundant, and I know how much that semitransparency or strike-through hurts the eyes. However, I urge you not to remove these checks unless you are absolutely sure that they are too expensive or will never catch an error.

7.1.7 *Weakness: Arithmetic errors cause overflows or crashes*

Something compilers usually do not check is the dreaded division (or modulo) by zero. A compiler does not even check whether something can overflow. These are called *arithmetic errors*. Dividing an integer by zero causes a program to crash; even worse, overflows silently cause programs to behave strangely.

Repeating the earlier example, even if we know our program does not call average with null, almost no compiler will spot the potential division by zero if we call it with an empty array.

Listing 7.7 Potential division by zero, yet no compiler error

```
function average(arr: number[]) {
  return sum(arr) / arr.length;
}
```

Because the compiler is not much help, we need to be very careful when doing arithmetic. Make sure the divisor cannot be zero and that we are not adding or subtracting numbers that are large enough to cause over- or underflow, or use some variation of BigIntegers.

7.1.8 Weakness: Out-of-bounds errors crash our application

Yet another place where the compiler is in hot water is when we directly access data structures. When we attempt to access an index that is not within the bounds of the data structure, it causes an out-of-bounds error.

Imagine that we have a function to find the index of the first prime in an array. We can use the function to find the first prime as follows.

Listing 7.8 Potential access out of bounds, yet no compiler error

```
function firstPrime(arr: number[]) {
  return arr[indexOfPrime(arr)];
}
```

However, if there is no prime in the array, such a function will return −1, which causes an out-of-bounds error.

There are two solutions to circumvent this limitation. Either traverse the entire data structure, if there is a risk of not finding the element we expect, or use the approach from the earlier discussion of definite assignment to prove that the element definitely exists.

7.1.9 Weakness: Infinite loops stall our application

A completely different way our programs can fail is when nothing happens, and we are left staring at a blank screen as our program loops quietly. Compilers generally do not help with this kind of error.

In this example, we want to detect whether we are inside a string. However, we erroneously forgot to pass the previous quotePosition to the second call to indexOf. If s contains a quote, this is an infinite loop, but the compiler does not see it.

Listing 7.9 Potential infinite loop, yet no compiler error

```
let insideQuote = false;
let quotePosition = s.indexOf("\"");
while(quotePosition >= 0) {
  insideQuote = !insideQuote;
  quotePosition = s.indexOf("\"");
}
```

These issues are being reduced by transitioning away from **while** to **for** and then foreach, and recently to higher-level constructions such as forEach in TypeScript, stream operations in Java, and LINQ in C#.

7.1.10 Weakness: Deadlocks and race conditions cause unintended behavior

A final category of trouble comes from multithreading. A sea of issues can arise from having multiple threads that share mutable data: race conditions, deadlocks, starvation, etc.

TypeScript does not support multiple threads, so I cannot write examples of these errors in TypeScript. However, I can demonstrate them using pseudo-code.

A race condition is the first problem we run into with threads. It occurs when two or more threads compete to read and write a shared variable. What can happen is that the two threads read the same value before updating it.

Listing 7.10 Pseudo-code for a race condition	Listing 7.11 Example output

```
class Counter implements Runnable {
  private static number = 0;
  run() {
    for (let i = 0; i < 10; i++)
      console.log(this.number++);
  }
}
let a = new Thread(new Counter());
let b = new Thread(new Counter());
a.start();
b.start();
```

```
1
2
3
4
5     Both repeating
5     numbers ...
7  ◁
8     ... and skipping
...   numbers
```

To solve this issue, we introduce locks. Let's give each thread a lock and check that the other thread's lock is indeed free before proceeding.

Listing 7.12 Pseudo-code for a deadlock	Listing 7.13 Example output

```
class Counter implements Runnable {
  private static number = 0;
  constructor(
    private mine: Lock, private other: Lock) { }
  run() {
    for (let i = 0; i < 10; i++) {
      mine.lock();
      other.waitFor();
      console.log(this.number++);
      mine.free();
    }
  }
}
let aLock = new Lock();
let bLock = new Lock();
let a = new Thread(new Counter(aLock, bLock));
let b = new Thread(new Counter(bLock, aLock));
a.start();
b.start();
```

```
1
2
3
4  ◁   Nothing
       happens
```

The problem we have just stumbled upon is called a *deadlock*: both threads are locked, waiting for each other to unlock before continuing. A common metaphor for this is two people meeting at a door, and both insisting that the other should go through first.

We can expose a final category of multithreading errors if we make the loops infinite and just print out which thread is running.

Listing 7.14 Pseudo-code for starvation

```
class Printer implements Runnable {
  constructor(private name: string,
    private mine: Lock, private other: Lock) { }
  run() {
    while(true) {
      other.waitFor();
      mine.lock();
      console.log(this.name);
      mine.free();
    }
  }
}
let aLock = new Lock();
let bLock = new Lock();
let a = new Thread(
  new Printer("A", aLock, bLock));
let b = new Thread(
  new Printer("B", bLock, aLock));
a.start();
b.start();
```

Listing 7.15 Example output

```
A
A
A
A
```
◁—┘ **Continues forever**

The problem here is that B is never allowed to run. This situation is quite rare but technically possible. It is called *starvation*. The metaphor for it is a one-lane bridge where one side has to wait, but the stream of cars from the other side never stops.

Entire books have been written about how to manage these issues. The best advice I can give to help alleviate them is to avoid having multiple threads with shared mutable data whenever possible. Whether this happens by avoiding the "multiple" part, the "sharing" part, or the "mutable" part depends on the situation.

7.2 Using the compiler

Now that we are familiar with our compiler, it is time to include it. The compiler should be part of the development team. Knowing how it can help us, we should design our software to take advantage of its strengths and avoid its weaknesses. We certainly should not fight with or cheat the compiler.

People often draw similarities between software development and construction. But as Martin Fowler has noted on his blog, this is one of the most damaging metaphors in our field. Programming is not construction; it is communication, on multiple levels:

- We communicate with the computer when we tell it what to do.
- We communicate with other developers when they read our code.
- We communicate with the compiler whenever we ask it to read our code.

As such, programming has much more in common with literature. We acquire knowledge about the domain, form a model in our heads, and then codify this model as a code. A beautiful quote states,

> *Data structures are algorithms frozen in time.*
>
> —Someone whose name eludes me

Dan North has noted the similarity that programs are the development team's collective knowledge of the domain frozen in time. A program is a complete, unambiguous description of everything the developers believe is true about the domain. In this metaphor, the compiler is the editor who makes sure our text meets a certain quality.

7.2.1 *Making the compiler work*

As we have seen many times now, there are several ways to design with the compiler in mind, thereby taking full advantage of having it on the team. Here is a short list of some of the ways we have used the compiler in this book.

GAIN SAFETY BY USING THE COMPILER AS A TODO LIST

Probably the most common way we have taken advantage of the compiler in this book is as a todo list whenever we have broken something. When we want to make a change, we simply rename the source method and rely on the compiler to tell us everywhere else we need to do something. This way, we are safe in the knowledge that the compiler does not miss any references. This works well, but only when we don't have other errors.

Imagine that we want to find every location where we use an enum to check whether we use `default`. We can find all usages of the enum, including those with a `default`, by appending something like _handled to the name. Now the compiler errors everywhere we use the enum. And once we have handled a location, we can simply append _handled to get rid of the error.

Listing 7.16 Finding enum usages with compiler errors

```
enum Color_handled {
  RED, GREEN, BLUE
}
function toString(c: Color) {        ⟵┐  Compiler
  switch (c) {                          │  errors
    case Color.RED: return "Red";    ⟵┘
    default: return "No color";
  }
}
```

Once we are finished, we can easily remove _handled everywhere.

GAIN SAFETY BY ENFORCING SEQUENCES

The pattern ENFORCE SEQUENCE is dedicated to teaching the compiler about an invariant in our program, thereby making the invariant a property, instead. This means the invariant can no longer accidentally be broken in the future, because the compiler guarantees that the property still holds every time we compile.

In chapter 6, we discussed both internal and external variants of using classes to enforce sequences. These classes both guarantee that a string has, at some prior point, been capitalized.

Listing 7.17 Internal

```
class CapitalizedString {
  private value: string;
  constructor(str: string) {
    this.value = capitalize(str);
  }
  print() {
    console.log(this.value);
  }
}
```

Private vs. public

Method vs. function with a specific parameter type

Listing 7.18 External

```
class CapitalizedString {
  public readonly value: string;
  constructor(str: string) {
    this.value = capitalize(str);
  }
}

function print(str: CapitalizedString) {
  console.log(str.value);
}
```

GAIN SAFETY BY ENFORCING ENCAPSULATION

By using the compiler's access control to enforce strict encapsulation, we localize our invariants. By encapsulating our data, we can be much more confident that it is kept in the shape we expect.

We already saw how to prevent someone from accidentally calling a helper method depositHelper by making it private.

Listing 7.19 Private helper

```
class Transfer {
  constructor(from: string, private amount: number) {
    this.depositHelper(from, -this.amount);
  }
  private depositHelper(to: string, amount: number) {
    let accountId = database.find(to);
    database.updateOne(accountId, { $inc: { balance: amount } });
  }
  deposit(to: string) {
    this.depositHelper(to, this.amount);
  }
}
```

GAIN SAFETY BY LETTING THE COMPILER DETECT UNUSED CODE

We have also used the compiler to check whether code is unused with the refactoring pattern TRY DELETE THEN COMPILE (P4.5.1). Deleting a flurry of methods at once, the compiler can quickly scan through our entire codebase and let us know which methods are used.

We use this approach to get rid of methods in interfaces. The compiler cannot know whether they are going to be used or are genuinely unused. But if we know that an interface is only used internally, we can simply try deleting methods from the interface and see if the compiler accepts the program.

In this code from chapter 4, we can safely delete both m2 methods and even the m3 method.

Listing 7.20   Example with deletable methods

```
interface A {
  m1(): void;
  m2(): void;
}
class B implements A {
  m1() { console.log("m1"); }
  m2() { m3(); }
  m3() { console.log("m3"); }
}
let a = new B();
a.m1();
```

GAIN SAFETY WITH DEFINITE VALUES

Finally, earlier in this chapter, we showed a list data structure that could not be empty. We guarantee this by using read-only fields. These are in the compiler's definite assignment analysis and must have a value at the termination of the constructor. Even in a language that supports multiple constructors, we cannot end up with an object with uninitialized read-only fields.

Listing 7.21   Non-empty list due to read-only fields

```
interface NonEmptyList<T> {
  head: T;
}
class Last<T> implements NonEmptyList<T> {
  constructor(public readonly head: T) { }
}
class Cons<T> implements NonEmptyList<T> {
  constructor(
    public readonly head: T,
    public readonly tail: NonEmptyList<T>) { }
}
```

7.2.2   Don't fight the compiler

On the other hand, it saddens me every time I see someone deliberately fighting their compiler and preventing it from doing its part. There are several ways to do this; in the following, we give a short account of the most common. They happen primarily due to one of three offenses, each with a section dedicated to it: not understanding types, being lazy, and not understanding architecture.

TYPES

As described earlier, the type checker is the strongest part of the compiler. Therefore, tricking it or disabling it is the worst offense. People misuse the type checker three different ways.

CASTS

The first is using casts. A cast is like telling the compiler that you know better than it does. Casts prevent the compiler from helping you and essentially disable it for the particular variable or expression. Types are not intuitive; they are a skill that must be learned. Needing a cast is a symptom that either we don't understand the types or someone else didn't.

We use a cast when a type is not what we need it to be. Using a cast is like giving a painkiller to someone in chronic pain: it helps right now but does nothing to fix the issue.

A common place for casts is when we get untyped JSON from a web service. In this example, the developer was confident that the JSON in the variable was always a number.

Listing 7.22 Cast

```
let num = <number> JSON.parse(variable);
```

There are two possible situations here: either get the input from somewhere we have control over, such as our own web service, or—a more permanent solution—reuse the same types on the sending side as the receiving side. Several libraries are available to assist. If the input comes from a third party, the safest solution is to parse the input with a custom parser. This is how we handled the key inputs in part 1.

Listing 7.23 Parsing input from string to custom classes

```
window.addEventListener("keydown", e => {
  if (e.key === LEFT_KEY || e.key === "a") inputs.push(new Left());
  else if (e.key === UP_KEY || e.key === "w") inputs.push(new Up());
  else if (e.key === RIGHT_KEY || e.key === "d") inputs.push(new Right());
  else if (e.key === DOWN_KEY || e.key === "s") inputs.push(new Down());
});
```

DYNAMIC TYPES

Even worse than essentially disabling the type checker is *actually* disabling the type checker. This happens when we use dynamic types: in TypeScript, by using any (dynamic in C#). While this may seem useful, especially when sending JSON objects back and forth over HTTP, it opens up myriad potential errors, such as referring to fields that don't exist or that have different types than we expect, so that we end up attempting to multiply two strings.

I recently came across an issue where some TypeScript was running in version ES6, but the compiler was configured as ES5, meaning the compiler didn't know about all the methods in ES6. Specifically, it did not know `findIndex` on arrays. To solve this, a developer cast the variable to any so the compiler allowed any call on it.

Listing 7.24   Using `any`

```
(<any> arr).findIndex(x => x === 2);
```

It was unlikely that this method would not be present at run time, so it was not too dangerous. However, updating the config would have been a safer and more permanent solution.

RUN-TIME TYPES

The third way people fool the compiler is by moving knowledge from compile time to run time. This is the exact opposite of all the advice in this book. Here is a fairly common example of how it happens. Imagine that we have a method with 10 parameters. This is confusing, and every time we add or remove one, we need to correct it everywhere the method is called. So, instead of using 10 parameters, we decide to use only 1: a Map from strings to values. Then we can easily add more values to it without having to change any code. This is a horrible idea because we throw away knowledge. The compiler cannot know what keys exist in the Map and therefore cannot check whether we ever access a key that does not exist. We have moved from the strength of type checking to the weakness of out-of-bounds errors. Tired of laundry? Easy solution: burn all your clothes!

In this example, instead of passing three separate arguments, we pass one map. We can then pull out the values with `get`.

Listing 7.25   Run-time types

```
function stringConstructor(
    conf: Map<string, string>,
    parts: string[]) {
  return conf.get("prefix")
      + parts.join(conf.get("joiner"))
      + conf.get("postfix");
}
```

A safer solution is to make an object with those specific fields.

Listing 7.26   Static types

```
class Configuration {
  constructor(
    public readonly prefix: string,
    public readonly joiner: string,
    public readonly postfix: string) { }
}
function stringConstructor(
    conf: Configuration,
    parts: string[]) {
```

```
    return conf.prefix
        + parts.join(conf.joiner)
        + conf.postfix;
}
```

LAZINESS

The second great offense is laziness. I don't feel as though programmers are to blame for being lazy since it is what got most people into programming in the first place. We happily spend hours or weeks tirelessly working to automate something we are too lazy to do. Being lazy makes us better programmers; staying lazy makes us worse programmers.

Another reason for my leniency in this offense is that developers are often under tremendous stress and tight deadlines to deliver. In that state of mind, everyone takes as many shortcuts as they can. The problem is they are short-term fixes.

DEFAULTS

We discussed default values quite a bit in part 1. Wherever we use a default value, eventually someone will add a value that should not have the default and forget to correct it. Instead of using defaults, have the developer take responsibility every time they add or change something. This is done by not supplying a default value, so the compiler will force the developer to decide. This can even help expose holes in the understanding of the problem to be solved when the compiler asks us a question we do not know the answer to.

In this code, the developer wanted to take advantage of the fact that most animals are mammals and made that the default. However, we can easily forget to override this, especially since we get no help from the compiler.

Listing 7.27 Bug due to default arguments

```
class Animal {
  constructor(name: string, isMammal = true) { ... }
}
let nemo = new Animal("Clown fish");        ⟵──┤ nemo is now
                                                │ a mammal.
```

INHERITANCE

Through the rule ONLY INHERIT FROM INTERFACES (R4.3.2) and section 4.41, I have made my opinion of sharing code through inheritance abundantly clear, and my arguments as well. Inheritance is a form of default behavior and covered by the earlier section. Further, inheritance adds coupling between its implementing classes.

In this example, if we add another method to Mammal, we have to remember to manually check whether this method is valid in all descendent classes. It is easy to miss some or forget to check. In this code, we have added a laysEggs method to the Mammal superclass, which works for most descendants—except Platypus.

Listing 7.28   Problem due to inheritance

```
class Mammal {
  laysEggs() { return false; }
}
class Dolphin extends Mammal { }
/// ...
class Platypus extends Mammal {

}                       ⊲─┐  Should have
                          │  overwritten laysEggs
```

UNCHECKED EXCEPTIONS

Exceptions often come in two flavors: those we are forced to handle and those we are not. But if an exception can happen, we should handle it somewhere or at least let the caller know that we have not handled it. This is exactly the behavior of checked exceptions. We should use unchecked exceptions only for things that cannot happen, such as when we know some invariant to be true, but we cannot express the invariant in the language. Having one unchecked exception called `Impossible` seems sufficient. But as with all invariants, we risk that one day it will be broken and we will have an unhandled `Impossible` exception.

In this example, we can see the issue with using an unchecked exception for something that is not impossible. We reasonably check whether the input array is empty because that would cause an arithmetic error. However, because we use an unchecked exception, the caller can still call our method with an empty array, and the program will still crash.

Listing 7.29   Using an unchecked exception

```
class EmptyArray extends RuntimeException { }
function average(arr: number[]) {
  if (arr.length === 0) throw new EmptyArray();
  return sum(arr) / arr.length;
}
/// ...
console.log(average([]));
```

A better solution is to use a checked exception. If a local invariant at the call site guarantees that the exception cannot happen, we can easily use the `Impossible` exception mentioned earlier. This is pseudo-code, as TypeScript, unfortunately, does not have checked exceptions.

Listing 7.30   Using an unchecked exception

```
class Impossible extends RuntimeException { }
class EmptyArray extends CheckedException { }
function average(arr: number[]) throws EmptyArray {
  if (arr.length === 0) throw new EmptyArray();
  return sum(arr) / arr.length;
}
```

```
/// ...
try {
  console.log(average(arr));
} catch (EmptyArray e) {
  throw new Impossible();
}
```

ARCHITECTURE

The third way people prevent the compiler from helping is due to a lack of understanding of the architecture: specifically, the micro-architecture. *Micro-architecture* is architecture that affects this team but not other teams.

We discussed the primary way this comes to fruition in part 1: breaking encapsulation with getters and setters. Doing so creates coupling between the receiver and the field and prevents the compiler from controlling the access.

In this stack implementation, we break encapsulation by exposing the internal array. This means external code can depend on it. Even worse, the external code can change the stack by changing the array.

Listing 7.31 Poor micro-architecture with a getter

```
class Stack<T> {
  private data: T[];
  getArray() { return this.data; }
}
stack.getArray()[0] = newBottomElement;          ⊲⎯⎯ This line changes
                                                       the stack.
```

Another way this can happen is if we pass a private field as an argument, which has the same effect. In this example, the method that gets the array can do anything with it, including changing the stack. Never mind that the function is misleadingly named.

Listing 7.32 Poor micro-architecture with a parameter

```
class Stack<T> {
  private data: T[];
  printLast() { printFirst(this.data); }
}
function printFirst<T>(arr: T[]) {            This line changes
  arr[0] = newBottomElement;           ⊲⎯⎯    the stack.
}
```

Instead, we should pass **this** so we can keep our invariants local.

7.3 *Trusting the compiler*

We now actively use the compiler and build software with it in mind. With our knowledge of its strengths and weaknesses, we rarely get into frustrating arguments with the compiler, and we can begin to trust it.

We can move away from the counterproductive feeling that we know better than the compiler, and pay close attention to what it says. We get back what we put into it; and following the last section, we now put a lot into it.

Let's examine the two final frontiers where people tend to distrust the compiler: invariants and warnings.

7.3.1   *Teach the compiler invariants*

The malice of global invariants has been discussed at length throughout the book, so they should be under control by now. But what about local invariants?

Local invariants are easier to maintain because their scope is limited and explicit. However, they come with the same conflicts with the compiler. We know something about the program that our compiler does not.

Let's look at a larger example where this comes into play. Here, we are creating a data structure to count elements. Thus when we add elements, the data structure keeps track of how many of each type of element we have added. For convenience, we also keep track of the total number of elements added.

Listing 7.33   Counting set

```
class CountingSet {
  private data: StringMap<number> = { };
  private total = 0;
  add(element: string) {
    let c = this.data.get(element);
    if (c === undefined)
      c = 0;
    this.data.put(element, c + 1);
    this.total++;
  }
}
```

Keeping track of the total

We want to add a method to pick a random element out of this data structure. We could do this by picking a random number less than the total and returning the element that would have been at that position if this were an array. Because we are not storing an array, we instead need to iterate through the keys and jump forward by that many places in the index.

Listing 7.34   Picking a random element (error)

```
class CountingSet {
  // ...
  randomElement(): string {
    let index = randomInt(this.total);
    for (let key in this.data.keys()) {
      index -= this.data[key];
      if (index <= 0)
        return key;
    }
  }
}
```

Error due to reachability

This method doesn't compile since we fail the reachability analysis described earlier. The compiler does not know that we will always select an element because it does not know the invariant that `total` is the number of elements in the data structure. This is a local invariant, kept true at the termination of every method in this class.

In this case, we can resolve the error by adding an impossible exception.

Listing 7.35 Picking a random element (fixed)

```
class Impossible { }
class CountingSet {
  // ...
  randomElement(): string {
    let index = randomInt(this.total);
    for (let key in this.data.keys()) {
      index -= this.data[key];
      if (index <= 0)
        return key;
    }
    throw new Impossible();          ⊲⎯  Exception to
  }                                        avoid an error
}
```

However, this only solves the immediate issue of the compiler complaining; we have not added any security that this invariant will not be broken later. Imagine implementing a `remove` function and forgetting to decrease `total`. The compiler dislikes our `randomElement` method because it is dangerous.

Whenever we have invariants in a program, we go through an adapted version of "If you can't beat them, join them":

1 Eliminate them.
2 If you can't, then teach the compiler about them.
3 If you can't, then teach the runtime about them with an automated test.
4 If you can't, then teach the team about them by documenting them extensively.
5 If you can't, then teach the tester about them, and test them manually.
6 If you can't, then start praying because nothing earthbound can help you.

Can't in this context means infeasible rather than impossible. There is a time for each of these solutions. But note that the lower we go on the list, the longer we commit ourselves to maintaining the solution. Documentation requires more deliberate time to maintain than tests do because tests tell you when they grow out of sync with the software; documentation offers no such courtesy. The higher each option is on the list, the cheaper it is in the long term. This should disarm the all-too-common excuse that we have no time to write tests, as not doing it is sure to be more time-expensive in the long term.

Note that if your software has a short lifetime, you can permit yourself to select an option lower on the list: for example, if you are building a prototype that is to be thrown out after testing it manually.

7.3.2   *Pay attention to warnings*

The other area where people tend to distrust the compiler is when it gives warnings. In hospitals, there is a term called *alarm fatigue*: health care workers become desensitized to noises because they are the norm rather than the exception. The same effect happens in software: each time we ignore a warning, a run-time error, or a bug, we pay a little less attention to them in the future. Another perspective on warning fatigue is the broken window theory, which states that if something is in pristine condition, people strive to keep it that way, but as soon as something is bad, we are less reluctant to put something bad next to it.

Even if some warnings are unjustified, the danger is that we might miss a crucial one because the insignificant warnings drown it out. This is one of the most critical dangers to understand. Insignificant errors or warnings can shadow more significant errors.

The fact of the matter is, warnings are there for a reason: to help us make fewer mistakes. Therefore, only one number of warnings is healthy: zero. In some codebases, this seems impossible because warnings have run rampant for too long; in such situations, we set an upper limit on the number of warnings that we allow in the codebase and then decrease this number bit by bit every month. This is a daunting task, especially since we won't reap any significant benefits in the beginning before the number is low. Once we are at zero, we should enable the language configuration for disallowing warnings, to ensure that they never raise their ugly heads again.

7.4   *Trusting the compiler exclusively*

Will this work?

—Every programmer

The final stage of this journey is when we have a pristine codebase and we listen to and trust the compiler and design with it in mind. At this stage, we are so intimately familiar with its strengths and weaknesses that instead of having to trust our judgment, we can be satisfied with the compiler's. Instead of straining ourselves, wondering whether something will work, we can just ask the compiler.

If we have taught our compiler the structure of our domain, have encoded the invariants, and are used to warning-free output that we can trust, successful compiling should give us more confidence than we could have gotten simply from reading the code. Of course, the compiler cannot know whether our code solves the problem we expect it to, but it can tell us whether the program can crash, which is never what we expect.

Getting more confidence from the compiler than from reading the code ourselves does not happen overnight. It requires lots of practice and discipline on the journey. It also requires the proper technologies (that is, programming language). This quote includes the compiler:

If you're the smartest person in the room, you're in the wrong room.

—Origin unknown

Summary

- Know the common strengths and weaknesses of modern compilers. We can adjust our code to avoid the weaknesses and take advantage of the strengths:
  - Use reachability to ensure that `switch` covers all cases.
  - Use definite assignment to ensure that variables have values.
  - Use access control to protect methods with sensitive invariants.
  - Check to make sure variables are not `null` before dereferencing them.
  - Check that numbers are not zero before dividing with them.
  - Check that operations will not over- or underflow or use BigIntegers.
  - Avoid out-of-bounds errors by traversing the entire data structure, or use definite assignment.
  - Avoid infinite loops by using higher-level constructions.
  - Avoid threading issues by not having multiple threads share mutable data.
- Learn to use the compiler instead of fighting it, to reach higher levels of safety:
  - Use compiler errors as a todo list when refactoring.
  - Use the compiler to enforce sequence invariants.
  - Use the compiler to detect unused code.
  - Don't use type casts or dynamic or run-time types.
  - Don't use defaults, inheritance from classes, or unchecked exceptions.
  - Pass `this` instead of private fields to avoid breaking encapsulation.
- Trust the compiler, value its output, and avoid warning fatigue by keeping a pristine codebase.
- Rely on the compiler to predict whether code will work.

Stay away from comments

8

This chapter covers

- Understanding the danger of comments
- Identifying comments that add value
- Dealing with different types of comments

Comments are probably one of the most controversial topics in this book, so let's start by clearing up which comments we are talking about. This chapter considers comments that are inside methods and *not* used by external tools, like Javadoc:

```
interface Color {
  /**
   * Method for converting a color to a hex string.
   * @returns a 6 digit hex number prefixed with hashtag
   */
  toHex(): string;
}
```

Although controversial to some, my opinion aligns almost perfectly with those expressed by many brilliant programmers. Comments are an art form, but unfortunately, not many programmers study how to write good comments. Consequently, they end up writing only poor comments, which devalues the code. Therefore, as a general rule, I recommend avoiding them. Rob Pike presented similar arguments back in 1989 in his series of essays, "Notes on Programming in C":

[Comments are] a delicate matter, requiring taste and judgment. I tend to err on the side of eliminating comments, for several reasons. First, if the code is clear, and uses good type names and variable names, it should explain itself. Second, comments aren't checked by the compiler, so there is no guarantee they're right, especially after the code is modified. A misleading comment can be very confusing. Third, the issue of typography: comments clutter code.

—Rob Pike

Martin Fowler extends this opinion by listing comments as a smell. One of his arguments is that they are often used like deodorant on top of otherwise smelly code. Instead of adding comments, we should clean the code.

Many educators demand that students explain their code through comments so we learn to write comments right from the start. This is like including intermediate calculations in an assignment: good for education but less useful in the real world. Carrying this idea to the real world runs into a problem. The issue of incomprehensible code will probably not be solved by having the same developer add comments, as expressed in this tweet by Kevlin Henney:

A common fallacy is to assume authors of incomprehensible code will somehow be able to express themselves lucidly and clearly in comments.

—Kevlin Henney

Comments are not checked by the compiler, making them easier to write than code since there are no constraints on them. However, precisely because the compiler does not know about them, in systems with a long life span, they have a tendency to grow out of date and become either irrelevant or, worse, downright misleading.

There are many uses for comments, including planning your work, indicating "hacks," documenting code, and removing code. In Robert C. Martin's *Clean Code*, he names around 20 types of comments. That many categories can be overwhelming to keep track of, so here we split comments into five categories, each with a specific suggestion for how to approach it.

In most cases, we should avoid comments in the code we deliver. Intermediate comments are great! Therefore, comments should be dealt with in the refactoring phase of our workflow. Before delivering any comment, always consider if there is a better way to express what it says. I would love to make a rule saying never to use them; but in some cases, a comment can save us from making expensive mistakes, in which case they are usually worth their cost. Some properties are difficult or expensive to enforce through code but can be expressed in a comment in seconds. This take on comments is similar to Kevlin Henney's approach (https://medium.com/@kevlinhenney/comment-only-what-the-code-cannot-say-dfdb7b8595ac):

Comment only what the code cannot say.

—Kevlin Henney

The five categories are ordered from the easiest solution to the hardest. Let's get into it.

8.1   Deleting outdated comments

Here we are generous with our wording because this category also includes downright wrong or misleading comments. We do so with the justification that the comment was probably well intended when written but then grew out of sync with the codebase.

In this example, notice how the comment and the condition disagree about whether it is "or" or "and." This can be dangerous.

Listing 8.2   Outdated comment

```
if (element.hasSelection() || element.isMultiSelect()) {
  // Is has a selection and allows multi selection
  // ...
}
```

The easiest types of comments to deal with are those that have gone out of date. This means the comment is now either irrelevant or incorrect. These comments do not save us any time, but they take time to read, so we should delete them.

A worse effect of such comments is when they mislead us. Not only do we waste time reading them, but if we design our code while relying on something untrue, we may have to do considerable rework. Worst of all, they can cause us to introduce bugs in the code.

8.2   Deleting commented-out code

Sometimes we experiment with removing some code—it is quick and easy to comment it out and see what happens. This is a good way to experiment. But after our experiment, we should delete any commented-out code. Since our code is in version control, it is easy to recover even after we delete it.

In this example, it is easy to see why the comments are there: a first draft of the code was working but suboptimal. A developer thought they could improve it but was not confident about success—understandably, because it is not an easy algorithm—and was not supported by their abilities in version control, either due to inexperience or because branching is expensive. Therefore, instead of deleting the old algorithm, the developer simply commented it out so they could quickly revert if the new algorithm didn't work. To test whether it was working, the developer might have had to merge it with the main branch; and when it tested successfully, it was already there, and there was no time or reason to meddle with something that was working.

Listing 8.3   Commented-out code

```
const PHI = (1 + Math.sqrt(5)) / 2;
const PHI_ = (1 - Math.sqrt(5)) / 2;
const C = 1 / Math.sqrt(5);
```

```
function fib(n: number) {
  // if(n <= 1) return n;
  // else return fib(n-1) + fib(n-2);
  return C * (Math.pow(PHI, n) - Math.pow(PHI_, n));
}
```

This scenario should have played out as follows. The developer creates a branch in Git, deletes the old code, and starts working on the new code. If it turns out the code cannot work, the developer checks out the main branch and deletes the one created for the experiment. If it works, the developer merges with main, and everything is clean. Even with the requirement of merging into main to test, we follow this procedure; then, if the code cannot work, we recover the original code from the version history.

8.3 Deleting trivial comments

Another category is comments that do not add anything. When the code is as easy to read as the comment, we say the comment is *trivial.*

Listing 8.4　Trivial comment

```
/// Log error
Logger.error(errorMessage, e);
```

In this category, we also include comments that we ignore when we scan the code. If no one ever reads a comment, it is just taking up space, and we can get rid of it for free.

8.4 Transforming comments into method names

Some comments document the code rather than the functionality. This is easiest to explain with an example.

Listing 8.5　Comment documenting the code

```
/// Build request url
if (queryString)
  fullUrl += "?" + queryString;
```

In these cases, we can simply extract the block into a method with the same name as the comment. As seen here, after this operation, the comment is trivial, and we deal with it accordingly: we delete it. We saw this solution used twice way back in chapter 3.

Listing 8.6 Before

```
/// Build request url
if (queryString)
  fullUrl += "?" + queryString;
```

Listing 8.7 After

```
/// Build request url          ◁──┐  The comment
fullUrl = buildRequestUrl(          │  is now trivial.
  fullUrl, queryString);
/// ...
function buildRequestUrl(
  fullUrl: string, queryString: string)
{
  if (queryString)
    fullUrl += "?" + queryString;
  return fullUrl;
}
```

People tend not to like such long method names. However, this is only an issue for methods we call frequently. Languages have a property where the words we use most often tend to be the shortest. The same should be true for our codebase. This is also obvious since we need less explanation for something we use all the time.

8.4.1 Using comments for planning

Such comments most often come into being when we use comments to plan our work and break down an elephant. This is a great way to create a road map. I personally always plan out my code with comments like the following.

Listing 8.8 Planning comments

```
/// Fetch data
/// Check something
///   Transform
/// Else
///   Submit
```

Some of these comments are likely to become trivial once the code is implemented, e.g., `Else`. The others will be turned into methods. Whether we decide to turn these into methods up front is a matter of preference; what is important is that once the code is written, we critically evaluate whether they add value.

8.5 Keeping invariant-documenting comments

The final comments are those that document a non-local invariant. As we have discussed multiple times, these are where bugs tend to occur. A way to detect them is to ask, "Will this comment ever prevent someone from introducing a bug?"

When we encounter these comments, we still want to check whether we can make them into code. In some cases, we can eliminate the comments with the compiler, as described in chapter 7. However, this is rare, so our next thought should be whether we can make an automated test to verify this invariant. If both of these turn out to be infeasible, we keep the comment.

In the following example, we see a suspicious statement, `session.logout`, accompanied by a comment explaining the reason for the statement. Authentication—or complex interactions like these—can be dreadfully difficult to test or simulate, and therefore the comment is perfectly justified.

Listing 8.9 Comment documenting an invariant

```
/// Log off used to force re-authentication on next request
session.logout();
```

8.5.1 Invariants in the process

Something that is undone (todo), or (probably) erroneous (fixme), or a workaround of a third-party software (hack) is an invariant: not an invariant in the code, but an invariant of the process. Some people despise these and argue justly that they should be not in the code but rather in our ticket system. I agree that this argument is valid, although I prefer the locality of comments directly in the code. If they are in the code, though, there should be some visual indication of how many there are, and this number better be going down. We should strive to actually fix or do the thing the comment mentions so that we can remove the comment rather than postponing the action further.

The best time to plant a tree was 20 years ago. The second best time is now.

—Chinese proverb

Summary

- Comments can be useful during development, but we should try to remove them before we deliver.
- There are five types of comments:
    - Outdated comments should be deleted, as they can cause bugs.
    - Commented-out code should be deleted, since the code is already in version control.
    - Trivial comments should be deleted, because they do not add readability.
    - Comments that could be a method name should be a method name.
    - Comments that document a non-local invariant should be turned into code or an automatic test; otherwise, we keep the comment.

Love deleting code

9

This chapter covers

- Understanding how code slows development
- Setting limits to prevent accidental waste
- Handling transitions with the strangler fig pattern
- Minimizing waste with the spike and stabilize pattern
- Deleting anything that does not pull its weight

Our systems are useful because of the functionality they provide. The functionality comes from code, so it is easy to think that code is implicitly valuable—but this is not the case. Code is a liability. It is a necessary evil that we have to live with to get the functionality we need.

Another reason we tend to feel that code is valuable is that it is expensive to produce. Writing code requires skilled workers to spend lots of time (and consume lots of caffeine). Attributing value to something because we have spent time or effort on it is called the *sunk-cost fallacy*. Value never comes from investment alone but from the outcome of the investment. This is crucial to understand when working with code since we have to continually put effort into maintaining the code regardless of whether it is valuable.

Every programmer has become bored with a manual task and thought, "I can automate this." In many cases, this is why we became programmers. However, it is easy to get so distracted by the automation code that it steals focus from the original problem, and we end up spending more time automating the problem than it would have taken to solve it manually.

Writing code is fun, and it exercises our creativity and problem-solving skills. But the code itself is an expense for as long as we keep it. To get the best of both worlds, we can do katas and spikes as training throughout our careers and experiment with code that is immediately deleted afterward.

In 1998, Christopher Hsee did a study called "Less Is Better: When Low-Value Options Are Valued More Highly than High-Value Options" (*Journal of Behavioral Decision Making*, vol. 11, pp. 107–121, Dec. 1998, http://mng.bz/l2Do). In the study, he established the value of a 24-piece dinner set. He then added a few broken pieces to the original set, and he found that the overall value decreased! Even though he only added to the set, doing so diminished the value. We need some long-lasting code in our systems; how much we need varies, depending on the underlying complexity of the domain. However, if you take only one thing from this chapter, it should be this: *less is better.*

In this chapter, we look first at how we get into trouble with problematic code through technical ignorance, waste, debt, or drag. Next, we dive into several specific types of code that impose a drag on development, such as version control branches, documentation, and features. We then discuss how to either overcome the drag or get rid of it.

9.1 Deleting code may be the next frontier

Programming has gone through many phases. To predict where we are going, we have to look at where we have been. However, going over all inventions and people who led us to the current state of programming would be overwhelming. Instead, I have constructed a brief chronology of what I believe to be the biggest leaps mainstream programming has taken:

- 1944—Computers were used to perform calculations without any abstractions.
- 1952—Grace Hopper invented the first linker, allowing computers to work with symbols instead of pure calculations.
- 1957—The previous leap led to the invention of the compiler, specifically, Fortran. We could now code using high-level control operators like loops.
- 1972—The next big issue to solve was data abstractions. Enter a new generation of languages: programming languages like C—and later C++ and Java—work with data indirectly, through pointers and references.
- 1994—Another big leap forward came from the Gang of Four (Erich Gamma, Richard Helm, Ralph Johnson, John Vlissides), who created a set of reusable design patterns. Design patterns function as high-level building blocks when we are designing software to be built.

- 1999—Next, Martin Fowler compiled a catalogue of standard refactoring patterns. Unlike design patterns, these do not require up-front design but let us improve the design of existing code.
- 2011—The most recent big leap forward in programming, in my opinion, was the microservices architectures popularized by Sam Newman. A microservices architecture is based on the old principle of loose coupling, but it solves a modern scaling issue. It also allows emerging architecture through indirect communication; we can improve the design of running systems.

We are now proficient at writing code and building systems. The systems we can build are so big and complex that no person can reasonably understand them fully. This makes it challenging to remove things, because to figure out what can be removed, we need to invest time determining what code is being run, how often, and in which versions. We are not yet excellent at deleting code. I believe this could be the next big problem to be solved.

9.2   *Deleting code to get rid of incidental complexity*

It is the nature of systems to grow over time as we add features, do experiments, and handle more corner cases. When we implement something, we need to build a mental model of how the system behaves and then make a change to affect that. A bigger codebase means a more complex model, because of couplings, and a larger library of utilities to keep track of.

This complexity comes in two types: domain complexity and incidental complexity. *Domain complexity* is the result of the underlying domain. That is, the problem we are solving is inherently complicated; for example, a system for calculating taxes will be complicated no matter what we do because the tax law is complicated. *Incidental complexity* is any complexity that is not demanded by the domain but was added incidentally.

Incidental complexity is commonly used as a synonym for *technical debt*. However, I think it is beneficial to use finer-grained terms. In my experience, there are four types of incidental complexity, each with a different origin and a different solution: technical ignorance, technical waste, technical debt, and technical drag. Let's discuss each in turn.

9.2.1   *Technical ignorance from inexperience*

The simplest type of incidental complexity is *technical ignorance*. It comes from unknowingly making bad decisions in the code, resulting in poor architecture. This happens when we lack sufficient skills to solve a problem without adding unnecessary coupling, either because we don't know what we don't know or because we don't have time to learn. Hopefully, this book has helped ease this situation for you. The only sustainable solution to this challenge can be found as the first half of one of the principles in the manifesto for agile software development:

> *Continuous attention to technical excellence and good design enhances agility.*
>
> —Manifesto for Agile Software Development

We must all continuously strive to get better at our craft by reading books and blog posts, watching conferences and tutorials, sharing knowledge through communal programming, and, most importantly, deliberate practicing—nothing is a substitute for practice.

Communal programming

In some situations, we need a boost in our cognitive capacity because we encounter a challenging task to solve, have an urgent bug to fix, or are learning. We can get this cognitive boost by collaborating more closely through communal programming.

As stated beautifully by Llewellyn Falco, the fundamental principle of communal programming is that any idea has to pass through someone else's brain before it makes it into the code ("Llewellyn's strong-style pairing" blog post, June 30, 2014). In practice, this means that the person at the keyboard is not supposed to do anything other than what someone else instructs. Examples of this are *pair programming*—when two people do it—and *ensemble programming* (also sometimes called *mob programming*—with less appealing connotations) when more people instruct or assist.

Communal programming forces us to share knowledge directly. It exposes all sorts of tiny wastes, and it frees up cognitive capacity for the person not instructing, which they can use for learning. It also generally leads to higher quality, as the code is being reviewed live—or synchronously. This means it also eliminates the need for asynchronous code review, making our delivery process more lean.

9.2.2 *Technical waste from time pressure*

The simplest type of incidental complexity is *technical waste*. This comes from making bad decisions in the code, resulting in poor architecture.

Much more commonly, technical waste stems from some form of time pressure. We don't understand the problem or the model well enough and are too busy to figure it out. Or we skip testing or refactoring because we don't have time. Or we circumvent a process to hit a deadline.

These bad decisions are intentional. In all cases, the developer chooses to go against better knowledge, albeit due to external pressure. This is sabotage.

A story from the real world

Once, I was tech lead on a project where we had slowly introduced a set of practices to ensure that we didn't repeat mistakes of the past. We were under a lot of time pressure for the next delivery, so I asked one of my developers whether function X could be done by tomorrow. He replied, "Yes, if I can skip testing." Biting my tongue, I told him that "done" meant following *all* our practices.

The solution is to teach developers that there is absolutely no occasion for skipping best practices. Teach project managers, customers, and other stakeholders that building software right is essential. I do this by asking them something like whether they would want to receive a new car three weeks sooner if it meant the brakes or airbags wouldn't be tested. Some industries have regulations; developers have practices, and we have to stick to them, even when pressured.

9.2.3   *Technical debt from circumstances*

Whereas both technical ignorance and waste can and should be eliminated, technical debt is more nuanced. *Technical debt* is when we temporarily choose a suboptimal solution for some gain. This is also a deliberate decision, but the keyword is *temporary*. If the solution we choose is not temporary, it is not debt; it is waste.

For example, this happens frequently when we implement a hotfix without any regard for proper architecture and push it to fix a critical issue—and then we have to start over to implement a proper fix afterward. I want to underline that incurring technical debt is a strategic decision, and there is nothing inherently wrong with it as long as it has an expiry date.

9.2.4   *Technical drag from growing*

The final type of incidental complexity is the fuzziest. *Technical drag* is anything that makes development slower. It includes all the other categories as well as documentation, tests, and indeed all code.

Automated tests (intentionally) make it harder to change code as we also need to change the tests. This is not necessarily bad, such as in critical systems where we usually prefer being slow and stable over being fast. The opposite is true in situations that benefit from a high level of experimentation, such as during a spike.

Documentation slows us down because we need to update it when we change something. Even the code itself is technical drag because we must consider how changes will affect the rest of the application, and we have to spend time maintaining it.

Technical drag is a side effect of building something. It is not bad in itself, but it *is* bad in situations where we are maintaining sparsely used documentation, features, or code. In such cases, it may be economically beneficial to remove the feature to get rid of the drag.

> **A story from real life**
> Once, as a developer on a project, I was asked to build a specific subsystem. I did so, but when it was done, the customer was not ready to adopt it. The tech lead told me to leave it in there so it would be ready when the customer was. From that day on, in everything we built, we had to consider how new code would react *if* the customer suddenly started using this new subsystem. Of course, they never did.

The all-too-common argument, "It doesn't hurt anything to keep it in there," is false. The solution is to delete as much as possible, but no more. Anything that is not paying for itself should go, even if it is being used a little. Delete every unused or unnecessary feature, piece of code, documentation, wiki page, test, configuration flag, interface, version control branch, etc.

Use it or lose it.

—Proverb

Having established that everything incurs drag—a slowdown in development—we spend the remainder of the chapter going into detail about the most common situations where we can get rid of things without losing value.

9.3 Categorizing code based on intimacy

Before we dive into deleting specific things, we need to take a detour. At the GOTO 2016 conference, Dan North gave a talk called "Software, faster." Here he categorized code based on three levels of intimacy. We are intimately familiar with the code we have recently developed. We are familiar with the libraries and utilities we use often. Everything in between is unknown and therefore expensive to maintain because we need to relearn it.

Relating this idea to technical drag, the code we are familiar with because we use it often can stay. This also underlines the point that using things often is the only way to prevent them from decaying into the unknown. But it also adds a time component. Deleting code we are intimately familiar with is cheaper and safer than deleting code we have to understand first.

Dan North argues anecdotally that after about six weeks, the intimacy of fresh code starts to deteriorate as the code quickly moves into the unknown category. The specific time is not important to me. Being the author of some code naturally gives us an edge in terms of understanding it; but importantly, this advantage diminishes, and at some point, the code's author no longer has any meaningful head start for understanding the code. My experience agrees with Dan North's that this cutoff should be on the scale of weeks rather than months; so when I refer to this later in the chapter, I assume the cutoff is six weeks.

9.4 Deleting code in a legacy system

A common definition of *legacy code* is "code that we are afraid to modify." This situation is often the result of a circus factor. The *circus factor* (also sometimes called the *bus* or *lottery factor*—a more morbid or lucky metaphor, respectively) expresses how many people need to run off and join a circus before so much knowledge is lost that some part of development is halted. If we hear a statement like "Only John knows how to deploy this system," we say the circus factor is one in that system.

We never want to stop development, so we need to minimize risk by keeping the circus factor high. However, even if everyone on a team knows about all the code, sometimes an entire team is let go or taken over from/by consultants. When we lose our circus factor, we inherit unknown code that we are likely reluctant to touch: legacy code.

The code may be working, but the fact that we do not feel comfortable editing it is enough of a negative that we should fix the situation. We need to be comfortable with our code, and we need to take responsibility for it, to be productive. This cannot happen if the code is fragile or unknown. Having some part of the code be dark also means we have no idea when or how it can break. Even worse, who will fix it if it breaks at 3:00 a.m. on a Saturday?

9.4.1   *Using the strangler fig pattern to get insight*

The first step in the solution is to find out how much the legacy code is being used. If it is hardly being used at all, we might be able to remove it without further investigation. If only a small part is being used much, we may only need to fix that part and get rid of the rest. Or if all of it is being heavily used, we need to get comfortable with it and possibly make it stable.

When we're getting insight into legacy code, we need to know how much each part is called. But this is not enough; we also need to know how many of these calls are successful. Some code is called but fails, so the result is never used; this is especially common in legacy code. Finally, we need to know how tightly coupled the legacy code is to the rest of the software. I recommend starting with the latter.

We can use Martin Fowler's *strangler fig* pattern to help with this process. The pattern is named after the strangler fig tree, which seeds on an existing tree and, while growing, envelopes and ultimately strangles its host. In this metaphor, the host is the legacy system. The pattern proceeds as follows.

Listing 9.1   Legacy code

```
class LegacyA {
  static a() { ... }
}
class LegacyB {
  b() { ... }
}

LegacyA.a();
let b = new LegacyB();
b.b();
```

To find out how tightly coupled a piece of code is, we can isolate it, making all accesses go through a virtual gate. We do this by encapsulating the classes in a new package/namespace; we then make a new gate class in the new package. We reduce all public modifiers in the new package to be package-private; and we fix errors by adding a public function in the gate class.

Listing 9.2 Before

```
class LegacyA {
  static a() { ... }
}
class LegacyB {
  b() { ... }
}

LegacyA.a();
let b = new LegacyB();
b.b();
```

Listing 9.3 After

```
namespace Legacy {
  class LegacyA {
    static a() { ... }
  }
  class LegacyB {
    b() { ... }
  }
  export class Gate {
    a() { return LegacyA.a(); }
    bClass() { return new LegacyB(); }
  }
}

let gate = new Legacy.Gate();
gate.a();
let b = gate.bClass();
b.b();
```

At this point, we know exactly how many contact points the legacy code has because they are all functions in the gate class. We also have an easy way to add monitoring by putting it in the gate class: we log every call and whether it was successful. This is just the bare minimum and can be made as sophisticated as desired.

Listing 9.4 Before

```
namespace Legacy {
  // ...
  export class Gate {
    a() { return LegacyA.a(); }
    bClass() { return new LegacyB(); }
  }
}
```

Listing 9.5 After adding monitoring

```
namespace Legacy {
  // ...
  export class Gate {
    a() {
      try {
        let result = LegacyA.a();
        Logger.log("a success");
        return result;
      } catch (e) {
        Logger.log("a fail");
        throw e;
      }
    }
    bClass() {
      try {
        let result = new LegacyB();
        Logger.log("bClass success");
        return result;
      } catch (e) {
        Logger.log("bClass fail");
        throw e;
      }
    }
  }
}
```

We put this code in production and wait. The team has to decide how long to wait, but I don't think it is unreasonable to say that a team won't maintain features that are not used at least once a month. (Certain things have scheduled uses, such as quarterly, biannual, or annual financial reports; but I don't consider them exempt from the following treatment.) After the legacy code has been in production for a while, we know how much each part is used and whether some calls always fail.

9.4.2   *Using the strangler fig pattern to improve the code*

How often something is called is usually a good indicator of how critical it would be if it failed. I like to start with the easy decisions: the most-called parts should almost certainly be migrated, and the least-called parts can almost certainly be deleted, so I handle these extremities first and move toward the middle, where the hard decisions are. We should critically assess the code that is called the least or always fails, to determine whether it is critical or has strategic functionality.

If some legacy code is critical or strategic, we should first make sure the call number reflects this fact. We can increase the number of calls to the functionality by improving the UI or through training or marketing. Once the code's usage reflects its importance, we need to get comfortable with the code. We have two options: either refactor that part of the legacy code, thereby removing coupling and fragility, and move the code into the "recent" category; or rebuild the part and switch to the new version by changing the gate once the rebuilt code is ready.

If some legacy code is not critical and not strategic, delete the method in the gate. Doing so can sometimes make large parts of the legacy code unused, which we can find out with IDE support for methods and TRY DELETE THEN COMPILE (P4.5.1) for interface methods. This also simplifies the calling code, as we remove a coupling, sometimes making that code deletable as well. Figure 9.1 summarizes how to deal with legacy code.

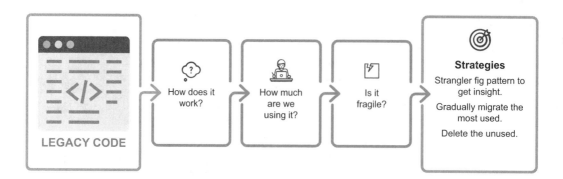

Figure 9.1   How to deal with legacy code

9.5   Deleting code from a frozen project

Sometimes a product stakeholder requests a major feature. We start working on it, but by the time we finish, there is a barrier: getting the necessary access, training the users, etc. Instead of wasting time waiting, we move on and work on the next thing. But now we have a *frozen project.*

Frozen projects aren't limited to code; they can include database tables, integrations, services, and a host of things external to the code. Once the original author forgets about the project, it can be nearly impossible to spot that it even exists—especially if the only thing missing is the user training. There is no trace of that anywhere in the system, so no investigation will discover it.

We may have code on the main branch that is not being used. There is no indication in the code that it is not being used, so we have to consider it whenever we make changes, and we have to maintain it. This adds to the mental overhead; plus, the code risks becoming legacy code. Another problem with a frozen project is that there is no guarantee the functionality will still be relevant when the barrier is removed.

9.5.1   Making the desired outcome the default

Depending on whether the project is exclusively in the code or has effects on databases, services, integration, etc., there are slightly different solutions. We take each in turn.

If the project has no effects outside of the codebase, we can revert the project off the main branch and put it in a separate branch. Then we need to tag it and make a note six weeks in the future to delete the tag. This means if we don't begin using the project within six weeks, it will be removed.

If the project includes changes external to the code, we cannot necessarily put it in a branch. Instead, we should make a ticket in our project management tool, noting all the components to remove, and schedule the ticket for six weeks later. If this happens frequently, it might be beneficial to make scripts that set up and tear down the most frequently used types of components.

In both cases, you will notice that unless deliberate action is taken, the code will disappear. Therefore, in these scenarios, you cannot accidentally add technical drag—it can only be added deliberately.

9.5.2   Minimizing waste with spike and stabilize

Another way to save effort when we have to implement a major change is by using Dan North's *spike and stabilize* pattern (which is where the six-week rule originally came from). In this pattern, we treat the project as a spike, meaning we implement it as separately from the regular application as possible and with no attention to high quality: that is, no automated testing and no refactoring. But, crucially, we include monitoring so we know how much the code is being used.

After six weeks, we return to the code and see if it has been used. If it has, we reimplement it—but the right way, with refactoring and everything. If it has not, we delete it, which is easy because the spike already had minimal integration with the main system. So we save time removing it, but we also save the time we would have spent refactoring or testing the code without knowing whether it would ever be used. Figure 9.2 summarizes how to deal with frozen projects.

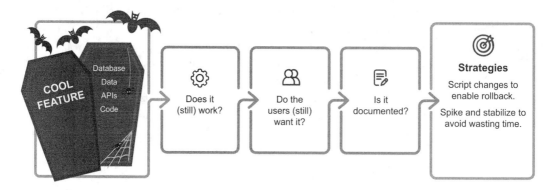

Figure 9.2   How to deal with frozen projects

9.6   *Deleting branches in version control*

Branches behave differently in different version control systems. In centralized version control systems like Subversion, branches duplicate the entire codebase, so they are quite expensive. On the other hand, Git branches require mere bytes, independent of the size of the codebase. In this section, we consider only Git branches because the issue tends to resolve itself if branches are expensive.

When branches are cheap, we tend to be less diligent about removing them; thus, they build up over time. We create branches for many purposes. The main reasons fall into these categories:

- To do a hotfix
- To tag commits we may need to return to later, like releases
- To work on something without interfering with our colleagues' work

The first and third categories should be deleted once we merge into main. In the second category, we should instead use Git's built-in method for tagging. Knowing this, why do branches accumulate? Sometimes it is simply an oversight, like when we forget to tick the Delete Branch option when merging pull requests or forget to remove an experimental branch after we are finished. Sometimes branches host frozen projects, spikes, or prototypes because we think we might need the code someday.

Those situations are relatively easy to deal with. A more difficult type of branch is one that is pending but blocked because it cannot pass the gate to get onto main. This happens if our gate includes a human component like an integration team or asynchronous human code review. Both of these prevent continuous integration and can easily become bottlenecks, slowing development. But if branches only cost a few bytes, what is the harm in leaving them?

Like code, branches in Git are technically almost free but are expensive in terms of mental overhead. We should only have a main branch and possibly a release branch; any other branch should optimally live only days. With long-lived branches, we expose ourselves to expensive, soul-crushing, error-prone merge conflicts. And clutter causes more clutter.

9.6.1 *Minimizing waste by enforcing a branch limit*

To solve this issue, we can adapt an element from the development method Kanban. Kanban uses a concept of work in progress (WIP) limits, which means we have a set ceiling on how many tickets the team can have in progress. Doing so helps expose bottlenecks in development because a bottleneck will eventually hit the WIP limit, preventing people upstream from starting new work. When people upstream can't start new tickets, they are encouraged to investigate the bottleneck and how to resolve the clog. This encourages teamwork and continuous improvement of the process.

The issue of having too many branches exactly mirrors the bottleneck issue, so we can use the same solution: introducing a hard limit on the number of branches. Let's go through a few things to keep in mind when setting a WIP or branch limit. The limit should be equal to at least the number of workstations so everyone can work in parallel; here, a *workstation* is a unit that can work independently, such as one ensemble if we are doing ensemble programming, one pair if we are using pair programming, or one developer otherwise. Setting the limit higher has the effect of building a buffer, which imposes a delay in the system but can be useful if some work tends to be significantly varied in size. We desire as little delay in the system as possible. Most crucially, once a limit is set, it should not be broken or changed for any reason short of changing team size. Figure 9.3 summarizes how to deal with branches in version control.

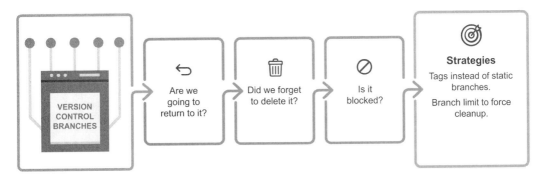

Figure 9.3 How to deal with branches

9.7 *Deleting code documentation*

Code documentation comes in many forms: wiki pages, Javadoc, design documents, tutorials, etc. As we dealt with intra-method comments in the last chapter, we do not consider those here.

Documentation is invaluable when exactly three conditions are met:

- *Relevant*—It needs to answer the right question.
- *Accurate*—The answer needs to be correct.
- *Discoverable*—We need to be able to find the answer.

If any of these properties is missing, the value of the documentation is greatly diminished. Writing good documentation is difficult and requires effort to make sure it stays relevant and accurate. This is because documentation needs to be used at least as often as the subject changes. Otherwise, maintaining it will likely not be cost beneficial. Keeping it up to date can happen through frequent adjustments or by generalizing it up front, abstracting away parts that change frequently.

The danger of keeping outdated documentation depends on which of the three properties it violates. The least significant is if the documentation is not discoverable; in that case, only the research time and writing time are wasted. Worse is keeping irrelevant documentation: writing time is wasted, but we also have to skim past the irrelevant part every time we are looking for answers—and in the end, we still have to do the research. Worst is inaccurate documentation: in the best case, it can cause confusion and doubt; and in the worst case, it can cause errors.

9.7.1 *Algorithm to determine how to codify knowledge*

Documentation can lose its relevance or accuracy, and not everything needs to be documented. It might seem as though documentation saves you from repeating previous research, but that is the case only if the documentation does not drift out of date. When I need to determine whether it makes sense to document something, I go through this process:

1 If the subject changes often, then there is nothing to be gained by documenting it.
2 Else if we will use it rarely, then document it.
3 Else if we can automate it, then automate it.
4 Else learn it by heart.

Notice that a solution can be to increase the usage of documentation, causing the frequent adjustments mentioned earlier. This can be done by making new team members go through it and correct anything inaccurate. Doing so requires some confidence to determine whether the documentation is wrong or the person did something wrong; when in doubt, the person should simply flag the difference.

Figure 9.4 summarizes how to deal with documentation. Another approach to documentation that stays accurate is to use automated test cases as documentation, so let's examine that next.

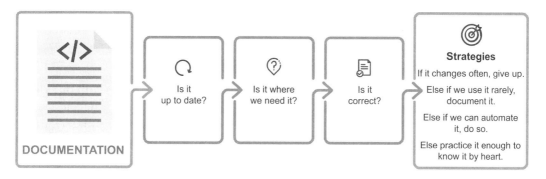

Figure 9.4 How to deal with documentation

9.8 Deleting testing code

Automated tests (simply *tests* in this section) come in many flavors and have many more properties than documentation. Kent Beck describes 12 properties of tests in his "Test Desiderata" (http://mng.bz/BKW2). Different types of tests put different weights on these properties. I will not go through all of them here but will instead focus only on tests that hurt development.

9.8.1 Deleting optimistic tests

Sometimes we write some code like a hash function, and we want to test it, so we come up with a test that says, "Given a = b then hash(a) = hash(b)." This seems like something we want to be true. But we have accidentally stumbled on a tautology: something that is always true.

One necessary property of tests is that they inspire confidence. A green test should make us more confident that code is working. So, tests should test something; a test that cannot fail is worthless.

A nice concept from the test-first community is, "Never trust a test you have not seen fail." This is useful when we discover an error in our code; by making a test before fixing the issue, we can check that it correctly fails, whereas if we make the test afterward, we only ever see it pass.

9.8.2 Deleting pessimistic tests

Similarly, a red test should mean something is broken and we need to fix it. That is why the tolerance for failing tests should be zero. If we have tests that are always red, we risk getting alarm fatigue and missing a critical error, even when the tests catch it.

9.8.3 Fixing or deleting flaky tests

Both optimistic and pessimistic tests are extremes, always passing or always failing. But the same issues apply to tests that are unpredictably red or green, sometimes called *flaky tests*. Like both types discussed earlier, these also do not elicit any action, except perhaps running the tests a few more times. We act if and only if a test is red; any test for which this is not true has no place in our codebase.

9.8.4   *Refactoring the code to get rid of complicated tests*

An entirely different category consists of tests that require delicate setup or exhibit a lot of duplication, so we decide to refactor them or build complicated test setups. These tests are dangerous because we feel like we are doing valuable work: we are simplifying, localizing, doing all the right things. Unfortunately, doing the right things in the wrong place is still wrong. If the test is more complicated than the code, how do we know whether the code or the test is wrong? Even when this is not the case, the need to refactor tests is a sign that the code being tested does not have proper architecture; any refactoring effort should be in the code, not in the test.

9.8.5   *Specializing tests to speed them up*

In some places, we use end-to-end tests to check that certain functionality works. This technique has its place, but these tests can be slow, and having many of them will impact how often we can run them. If some tests cause us to run other tests less often, they are hurting development, and we need to address the situation. There are two ways to do so: separate the slow tests from the fast tests, and keep running the fast tests as often as possible; or observe what causes a slow test to fail and, if the answer is nothing, remove it (it is an optimistic test). There are probably only a few things deeper in the system that tend to go wrong, in which case we can make tests for those places. Those tests will be faster and more specific, so we can correct errors more quickly. Figure 9.5 summarizes how to deal with automated tests.

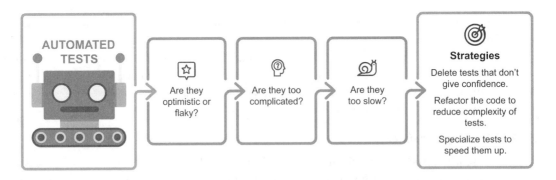

Figure 9.5   How to deal with automated tests

9.9   *Deleting configuration code*

Most programmers know that hardcoding is bad.

The first solution we learn to deal with this is to extract the hardcoded value into a constant. Then, as we mature as developers, we learn this maxim:

> *If you can't make it perfect, at least make it configurable.*
>
> —Maxim

Configurability can increase our software's utility when we can increase our user count without a significant increase in the codebase. When configurability comes in the form of feature flags, it lets us separate *deploy* and *release*, increase deployment frequency, and make *release* a business decision instead of a technical decision.

It does, however, come with a price: each place we add configurability, we also increase the complexity of the code. Even worse, in most cases, we double the testing space because we need to test for each option against all other flags. The testing space grows exponentially. Hopefully, some of the flags are independent and can be tested at the same time. Testing multiple flags in parallel can make testing possible; however, we open ourselves up to potential errors involving complex interactions between those flags.

9.9.1   *Scoping configuration in time*

My solution to dealing with the increase in complexity due to configuration is to consider as much of the configuration temporary as possible. To this end, I categorize configuration based on its expected lifetime. The categories I suggest are experimental, transitional, and permanent.

EXPERIMENTAL CONFIGURATION

We have already talked about an example of experimental configuration: feature flags. These are intended to be removed after the release of the feature; and to ensure that this is an easy task, it should be done within six weeks, as discussed earlier. Another type of experimental configuration comes from testing whether a change is superior. This is sometimes called *beta testing* or *A/B testing*. In the code, these are very similar, but their purposes differ. In this case, the configuration allows some users to experience the change while others do not. This way, we can gauge whether a change will have the desired effect; ultimately, we want to determine whether the code is superior before or after. This technique allows us to adjust to feedback or opt out of a change without affecting all users.

In my experience, testing configuration tends to leak out of the experimental phase and become permanent, splitting the user base into those with the flag on and those with it off, and thus increasing only complexity and not usage. This is bad, so to avoid it, we should be proactive: determine from the beginning whether something is experimental, and, upon completion, create a reminder to remove it immediately after testing is finished (keeping within six weeks).

TRANSITIONAL CONFIGURATION

A transitional configuration is useful while the business or codebase is going through major changes. An example could be moving from a legacy system to a new one. We cannot expect or enforce that making such large-scale changes will happen within six weeks, so we have to deal with a longer-term increase in complexity and a higher cleanup cost. However, longer transitions usually have two properties that we can take advantage of.

First, many types of transition are invisible to the user. Therefore, we can be satisfied with linking *release* and *deploy*. This means we can have the configuration as part of the code instead of something external. Having it in code means we can collect all the configuration tied to the transition in a central spot, separated from the rest, which makes the invariant explicit that these are more closely related than other configuration flags and should be considered a collection.

Second, there is usually a point where the transition is complete and the old part can be removed. Taking advantage of this, we can avoid spending time chipping away at the code and deleting small parts, and simply wait for the whole thing to go at once. To make this approach safe, we should again use the strangler fig pattern to gate *all* access to the legacy component. Not only can this work as an excellent todo list, but when we can delete the gate without getting errors in our code, we know that we can delete the entire legacy component as well. We can discover this either through TRY DELETE THEN COMPILE or by gradually deleting methods in the gate as they become unused; once it is empty, we can delete it.

PERMANENT CONFIGURATION

The final category is permanent configuration. This is special because it should cause an increase in usage or be trivial to maintain. An example of usage-increasing configuration is reusing most of the same software for two different customers by putting their differences behind an in-code configuration flag. Or it could be configuration to enable different tiers of usage, allowing us to cater to different business sizes. Both of these could potentially double our number of users, making the configuration well worth an increase in maintainability.

An example in the trivial-to-maintain subcategory is offering users a light-versus-dark mode flag. It affects only the outermost parts of our code (the styling) and therefore does not affect maintainability, but it can enhance the experience for some users.

We should be very critical of what goes in the permanent category. If it does not cause an increase in usage and is not trivial to maintain, it is probably not worth the cost and should be removed. Figure 9.6 summarizes how to deal with configuration code.

9.10   *Deleting code to get rid of libraries*

A quick way to get a lot of functionality cheaply is by using third-party libraries. Some libraries spare you from writing thousands of lines of code and also provide higher quality or better security than you could have gotten in-house. I have always advised leaving security to people who devote their lives to it, because as laypeople, we are

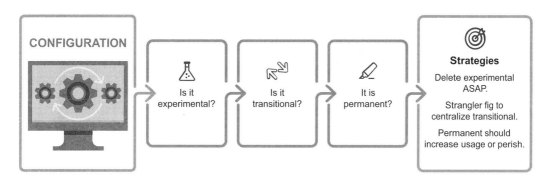

Figure 9.6   How to deal with configuration code

simply not experienced enough to put up a fight against attackers who often also devote their lives to their craft.

Another property of security that supports going with a third-party library is that the quality of our security can easily have a direct impact on the viability of our software. If our software has a major security incident, it may destroy our users' trust and thereby the software.

An additional reason to use a third-party library is to enable doing something that is not feasible otherwise, such as using a frontend framework like Swing (Java), React (TypeScript), or WPF (C#). These all provide a lot of code that required specialized skills to build—graphics programming skills that we may not have on our team.

Unfortunately, using libraries is a double-edged sword because although we don't need to maintain their code, we do have to update them, which sometimes means adapting our code. Doing so can be time consuming and error prone. Using libraries also adds to the team's finite cognitive load because team members must keep at least a working knowledge of them.

We lose some predictability when we use libraries, as we cannot predict when updates are coming or how much time we need to spend adjusting our codebase. Sometimes features we rely on are deprecated or removed, and we have to build something to replace them. Sometimes bugs are introduced, and we need to implement temporary workarounds or hacks to make our software work. Finally, when bugs are fixed in the libraries, we have to undo our workarounds so they don't fester in the code. We are also forced to decide between reading and understanding the library source code or accepting degraded security, because the library is another possible attack vector that we can only vouch for by treating it as we do our own code.

The danger of external libraries is amplified because most modern languages come with a package manager, which makes it easier than ever to add dependencies. And as the previous scenario illustrates, we have to worry not only about our dependencies but also about all the dependencies of our dependencies, and so on.

A famous thought experiment

In a blog post, David Gilbertson presents a thought-provoking fictitious scenario where he releases a small JavaScript library that adds colors to log messages in the console. He reports: "People love pretty colors" and "We live in an age where people install npm packages like they're popping pain killers." With minimal social engineering (some pull requests), he injects his library into other libraries. The library starts getting hundreds of thousands of downloads monthly. However, unbeknownst to the users, the library contains malicious code that steals data from sites using it.

9.10.1 *Limiting our reliance on external libraries*

One method for dealing with the pains just described is to pick libraries from high-quality vendors so we trust their internal quality and security requirements. Such vendors strive to avoid breaking changes. We only need to re-audit for security or adjust our code when there are updates, so if the libraries rarely change, we minimize these costs.

Another way to reduce these pains is to update frequently. In DevOps, there is a saying:

> *If something hurts, do it more.*

> —DevOps proverb

If we do something often, we have more incentive to streamline it and reduce the pains it causes. This argument is behind processes such as continuous integration and delivery. Another advantage of doing something more often is that the amount of work tends to be smaller, spreading the cost and reducing the risk and cost overall.

However, this does not help mitigate the security risk mentioned in the previous section. The final and simplest solution I will suggest is this: make your dependencies visible, and then categorize whether each library is *enhancing* or is *critical*. Use this approach to lower your dependence and ultimately reduce your reliance on libraries.

If an enhancing library breaks, simply remove it, get the application working, and then look for a replacement later. Be cautious about promoting a library from enhancing to critical. If unused libraries are lurking in the codebase, remove them. If they are relatively easy to implement in-house, doing so is often worth it, to remove the uncertainty.

If we have installed the jQuery library, with its hundreds of functions, but we are only using the one to make Ajax calls, it would probably be advantageous to either find a simpler library that fits our needs more precisely or implement an in-house function that does the same thing. In terms of security, we need to audit all the code in the library, even if we don't use it directly. Figure 9.7 summarizes how to deal with third-party libraries.

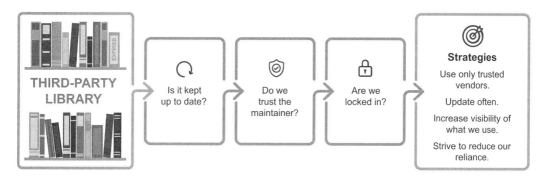

Figure 9.7   How to deal with third-party libraries

9.11   Deleting code from working features

Code is a liability; it costs time to maintain and has a lot of unpredictability, and therefore it comes with risk. Usage is the value that pays for it. It is a common misunderstanding that features are correlated with usage so that adding more features adds more value. Unfortunately, it is not so simple.

As I have tried to illuminate throughout this chapter, many factors are at play when balancing the cost of code with the benefit of functionality: how long we accept an increase in complexity, how we value predictability, how we test new features, how well we onboard people to them, and so on. There are two ways to increase value in any cost/benefit relationship, and given that the benefit of features is so complicated, it is often easier to look for ways to reduce the cost by refactoring or, even better, removing code. This is true even if you remove working features whose cost is higher than the usage increase they cause.

Analogously, anything that is unused, no matter its potential, is only an expense. This is why you should love deleting code: doing so immediately makes the codebase more valuable. Figure 9.8 summarizes how to deal with working features.

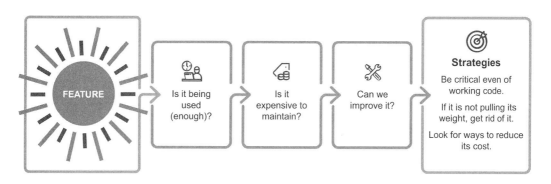

Figure 9.8   How to deal with working features

Summary

- Technical ignorance, technical waste, technical debt, and technical drag are reasons development becomes slower and more difficult. Technical ignorance usually stems from inexperience and is handled only by a continual focus on technical excellence. Technical waste often comes from time pressure, but since it provides no benefit, it is only sabotage. Technical debt arises from circumstances and is perfectly acceptable as long as it is temporary. Technical drag is a side effect of the codebase growing; it is a necessity because our software models a complex world.

- We can use the strangler fig pattern to get insight into and delete code from a legacy system or centralize configuration during a transition period.

- Using the spike and stabilize pattern can reduce some of the waste that comes from a frozen project. Further, by making the default action deleting the project instead of keeping it, we prevent it from becoming a drag.

- By deleting bad automated tests, we increase confidence in them and thereby make the test suite more useful. Bad tests can be optimistic, pessimistic, or flaky. We can also improve the test suite by refactoring the code to get rid of complicated tests and specializing slow tests to make them faster.

- By enforcing a branch limit, we can reduce the cognitive load wasted on keeping track of stale branches in version control.

- By setting and keeping strict time limits on configuration, we keep complexity creep to a minimum.

- By limiting our reliance on external libraries, we save time updating and auditing while increasing predictability.

- For code documentation to be useful, it needs to be relevant, accurate, and discoverable. We can use an algorithm to determine how to codify knowledge.

Never be afraid to add code

This chapter covers

- Recognizing symptoms of fear of adding code
- Overcoming fear of adding code
- Understanding the trade-offs of code duplication
- Committing to backward compatibility
- Lowering risk by using feature toggles

Having discussed the maladies of code in the previous chapter, it is easy to get scared of writing it. After all, the conclusion to chapter 9 was that code adds cost. When talking about code, another source of fear is not writing perfect code. Considering how many ways code can be flawed, perfection is an utterly unrealistic goal. Many considerations play into "perfection": performance, structure, level of abstraction, ease of use, ease of maintenance, novelty, creativity, correctness, security, and so on. Trying to keep all this in our heads while also trying to solve a nontrivial problem is impossible.

I started coding before I got a formal education in computer science. Back then, I was very productive and creative because my only consideration was making the code work. Then I started university and learned about all the ways code can fail or be bad. My productivity plummeted. I would be given a task and begin by contemplating it for hours or days before writing the first line of code. Once I realized how much effect this coding stage fright was having on me, I started combating it—and I have been fighting it ever since, both in myself and in others.

In this chapter, I share the symptoms I use to detect such situations and provide suggestions for overcoming them. Recognizing that adding code is safer than modifying it, we then discuss ways to exploit this fact through, among other things, code duplication or extensibility.

10.1   Accepting uncertainty: Enter the danger

We cannot work effectively if we are scared. Software development is about learning the domain and codifying this knowledge into a programming language. The most effective way to build knowledge is by experimenting, but this takes courage: we need to be explicit about and draw attention to the parts we are most uncertain about. This is why courage is one of five values in the popular framework Scrum. A major study at Google found that the biggest predictor of team productivity was psychological safety: that is, whether team members trusted each other and felt safe taking risks.

To make matters worse, we are often most scared of the areas with the most uncertainty, but this is exactly where we most need to learn. In improvisational theater, there is a concept called *enter the danger*. The concept recognizes that all of us have a natural tendency to avoid uncomfortable situations, but also that the best theater comes from confronting such situations and building on them. Patrick Lencioni talks about "enter the danger" as one of the most important lessons for effective consulting (*At the Table* podcast, April 2017). I think it applies equally to software development.

It doesn't matter how good we are if we produce nothing. I entered the industry right out of university. Filled with youthful arrogance, I thought I was the best—a feeling that instantly evaporated when I had to push my first code into production. The scale of things that could go wrong was overwhelming. As a consultant, I went from place to place, and the first deploy in a new place is always scary. That is why I adopted a strategy that many big companies also use, in line with "enter the danger": I have to deploy something to production on the first day. This immediately takes away the fear and anxiety and teaches me how to deliver value on that team.

Fear is a form of psychological pain. As I mentioned in the last chapter, if something hurts, do it more! If something is scary, do it more—until it isn't scary anymore.

10.2   Using spikes to overcome the fear of building the wrong thing

In my work as a consultant, I often see that the fear of failure is blocking productivity. Fear makes people want to discuss, design, or think about how to build something before they even try. This happens when the fear of building the wrong thing overpowers the fear of building it poorly. Seeing this happening should raise red flags.

The workflow I recommend for programming helps overcome this problem by starting with a spike. In figure 10.1, we start with exploration, which typically takes the form of a spike. Code produced during a spike may not make its way into main, so it does not matter whether it is flawed; thus the fear dissipates.

Figure 10.1 Recommended development workflow

A spike gives us knowledge that we can use to make our first actual version better, along with the confidence to do it. Spikes are powerful, but they can be difficult to introduce since they require discipline. The culture needs to enable and encourage writing code that is going to be thrown out. Stakeholders must realize that the product is *knowledge* rather than code or functionality.

The temptation for stakeholders, and sometimes even developers, is to use the code from a spike. This sends a signal that the product is code, not knowledge, which has the catastrophic side effect that we start trying to make the code better during our spikes. Soon we are facing the same fear as if we were writing code for production—because we are. To preserve the advantage, we have to be strict about not letting spike code into production, and we must promote the idea that the product is knowledge. We can use the spike to test hypotheses, experiments, and user friendliness.

To accommodate this promotion of knowledge, it may help to codify the outcome in a format that is commonly associated with knowledge products, such as a slide show or whitepaper. Having the result of a spike consist of a single slide showing the three most important points and a screenshot or mockup makes it easier to show stakeholders that the time was not wasted. Such slides can then be reused for an easy weekly team knowledge-sharing session, which can serve to reduce the circus factor, strengthen team spirit, and further promote the focus on knowledge.

10.3 Overcoming the fear of waste or risk with a fixed ratio

Another symptom of fearing code is when the surrounding tools and pipeline are significantly more sophisticated than the actual production code. Before writing the first line of business logic, some teams spend vast amounts of time setting up testing environments, innovative branching strategies and repository structures, feature-toggling systems, frontend frameworks, and automated builds and deploys. All of these things have their time and place in software production; however, these tools should be used to reduce risk or waste. Spending too much time on them suggests that the fear of waste or risk is greater than the desire to deliver. When we have no code, we have neither risk nor waste, and thus spending time on these tools is merely procrastination. Setting up these supporting systems can be fun and challenging and can feel important; however, if we push no production code through them, there is nothing to reduce the cost of, and they have no value. The worst scenario is when maintaining or developing these tools takes so much effort that we cannot deliver what matters.

A story from the real world

One time I joined a team that was struggling to deliver. I got the usual introduction to the company and the project. Routinely, I asked what their procedure was for deploying code. Like a match to gasoline, the lead developer lit up and started explaining an amazingly sophisticated build and deployment pipeline. It could do everything but make coffee. Perplexed as to why they were struggling to deliver, I went down my list of possibilities. Now assuming that the problem was an architecture that was too tightly coupled, I asked to see their codebase. "We don't have any code yet. We've been busy building this pipeline."

The solution I recommend to avoid such situations comes from *The DevOps Handbook* by Gene Kim et al. (IT Revolution Press, 2016). The authors recommend setting aside 20% of developers' time for nonfunctional requirements such as maintaining and developing support tools. Setting such a limit works two ways: it ensures that important maintenance tasks do not get drowned out by feature work and, conversely, keeps down the ratio of complexity. Having only 20% of your time to develop something means it can never become more complicated than the production code. I think 80:20 is a reasonable ratio of complexity between production code and supporting tools.

There are multiple ways to implement this solution. You could add 20% to each ticket estimate or a few hours per day. Unfortunately, in my experience, most small time slots are either ignored or wasted due to context switches and other overhead. On the opposite end of the spectrum is reserving every fifth sprint for refactoring and maintenance work. This approach also is not great. The work is too intensive to be fun; and both developers and stakeholders typically crave the feeling of progress, which is difficult to achieve during such sprints. Another reason not to postpone refactoring this way is that during the four preceding sprints, the code will become more and more coupled and tangled, and slower and slower to work with.

The most successful implementation I have seen reserved Fridays for non-ticket work, meaning anything not motivated by a request from the stakeholder. On these Fridays, developers experimented, made major refactorings, or automated development tasks to bring down waste or improve quality. An entire day is sufficient to perform significant tasks and long enough that overhead does not drown the time. It is also often a welcome change of pace from daily ticket work, which can be revitalizing.

10.4   Overcoming the fear of imperfection by embracing gradual improvement

Imposter syndrome is when a person feels unqualified for their job and fears someone will expose them as an imposter. This is prevalent in our industry, even though it is irrational and almost always unjustified. It has a real effect on productivity because to protect ourselves, we try to make our code perfect so there is nothing to expose. Writing perfect code for a nontrivial problem is at best exceptionally difficult, so we end up either procrastinating or taking only trivial tasks.

Developers are sometimes quick to criticize other people's code. It is commonplace to hear developers complaining about some code's usability, performance, stability, architecture, or whatever. Hearing this can make us self-conscious about our code: "Is someone saying those things about my code?" Or "What if that guy saw my code? Is he looking at my code?" It can perhaps even fuel our imposter syndrome.

I have lost my belief in perfect code. Making code more efficient requires skills and profiling; making it easy to use requires testing and experimentation; making it easy to extend requires refactoring and foresight; and making it stable requires testing or typing. All of these take time. However, another property is often just as important: the cost to produce. This means we have to select what to focus on and where to accept imperfection.

Given that there are so many metrics to consider when writing code and that we cannot optimize for all of them at once, which is most important? I have found that one is more useful than the others: optimizing for developer life. That is, try to spend the shortest time possible from getting a task to having something working. That way, we can spend more of our lives on whatever we love to do, such as more coding.

Optimizing for developer life has the added benefits of maximizing practice and minimizing time until we get feedback from tests, testers, stakeholders, and users. Having short feedback loops is known to increase quality because we can use the feedback to guide our improvement efforts. No matter where we start, if we improve more quickly than our competitors, we will eventually overtake them.

This is also the philosophy behind Dan North's spike and stabilize pattern, discussed in chapter 9. In this pattern, we treat a task as a spike and produce code with no regard for metrics. However, we add monitoring to the code, and after six weeks, we see whether the code is being used. If is isn't, we delete it. Otherwise, we rewrite it, guided by the feedback we got from our monitoring. Here we optimize for developer life because we only spend time on code that is being used. We also have feedback to guide our efforts, so we also don't spend time on the wrong metrics.

10.5   How copy and paste effects change velocity

Several times in this book, we have discussed one of the most basic ways to add code: duplicating it. The most notable times were when we duplicated the `draw` code into all the `Tile` classes in section 4.3 and the `update` code into `Stone` and `Box` in section 5.4. In these two instances, we ultimately decided on different follow-up actions. In the draw case, we concluded that the similarity was coincidental and that the code should diverge, so we left it duplicated. In the update case, we concluded that the code was connected and should be linked, so we unified it. Code duplication is a method for encouraging or discouraging divergence in code, but there are two other important properties of code duplication to consider. Let's go through each in turn.

First, when we share code, it is easy to affect all locations where the code is used. This means we can quickly make global changes to behavior. However, it is not straightforward to change behavior in only one of the call sites. On the other hand, if we share behavior by duplicating code, each site is decoupled, which means it is easy to modify only a single site; but, symmetrically, it is difficult to affect this behavior globally since we need to update it at all locations. Sharing code increases global behavior-change velocity, while duplicating code increases local behavior-change velocity.

Second, high global behavior-change velocity means we can affect many different places in the code simultaneously. In chapter 2, we defined *fragility* as the tendency for system changes to cause breakage in seemingly unrelated locations in the code. It is easy to imagine that each call site of a shared function has different local invariants. Whenever we change the shared code, we risk breaking any number of these invariants since they are not local to the shared code. Thus, sharing increases the fragility of the system.

Increasing global behavior-change velocity can be awesome because our code can adapt quickly when needed. Increasing system fragility is the price we pay, alongside the risk of introducing a bad change into the shared code and causing global damage. These two downsides both increase the necessity for testing, proving, or monitoring.

As copied code is completely decoupled, it is easier to experiment with and safer to change because you don't risk breaking anything for anyone else. During a spike, I encourage as much duplication as possible; it is a quick way to test hypotheses. This is true even during the six-week spike period of spike and stabilize. Once the code settles, and before we forget about it, we go back and check whether it makes sense to unify it with the copy source using the refactoring patterns described in chapter 5. That is, we ask these questions: "Should this be coupled with the source? When this changes, should the source change? Is my team owning the unified code?" If the answer to any of these questions is no, then the code should probably stay separate.

10.6 *Modification by addition through extensibility*

Another approach to adding code is through extensibility. If we know some code is receptive to changes, we can make it extensible. This means we push out the variations into separate classes. In this case, adding a new variation may be as simple as adding another class. If our domain is fairly regular, the places that usually vary should become more and more accommodating to further variation over time.

Variation points make our code more complex; it is more difficult to understand how the code flows, so it can be more challenging to modify later. Thus, making everything extensible would be wasteful since doing so would make our code unnecessarily complex. Complexity that is not representative of the underlying domain is called *accidental complexity*. Since code represents the real world, some complexity is inherited from the underlying domain; this is called *essential complexity*.

To limit accidental complexity, we should postpone introducing these variation points until they are needed. Throughout the book, wherever we have had variation, we have followed the same three-step process:

1 Duplicate the code.
2 Work with it and adapt it.
3 If doing so makes sense, unify the code with the source.

This method gives us a lot of freedom when we are working with the code since it is decoupled from any other code. Once we are finished working with it, we can easily unify it to expose the structure.

This workflow is reminiscent of another common refactoring pattern: the Expand-Contract pattern, commonly used to safely introduce breaking changes into databases. Ironically, it is named solely after its two shortest phases. The pattern has three phases, similar to the process just described:

1 In the expand phase, we add new functionality. Doing so is safe since we are only adding, but we now have two copies of the same behavior to maintain.
2 We migrate, slowly moving callers to the new functionality. This is the longest phase.
3 Once all callers have been moved, we execute the contract phase, where we delete the original version of the behavior.

In this book, we have seen two significant ways to make code more extensible: REPLACE TYPE CODE WITH CLASSES (P4.1.3) and INTRODUCE STRATEGY PATTERN (P5.4.2). Both these patterns transform static structure into dynamic structure. REPLACE TYPE CODE WITH CLASSES takes static control flow in the form of **if**s and **switch**es and turns them into method calls on an interface. The control flow through the interface is dynamic as it can be easily extended at any time, meaning we can modify behavior simply by adding another implementing class. INTRODUCE STRATEGY PATTERN unifies two copies of some code, allowing us to add new copies dynamically by adding new strategies.

10.7 Modification by addition enables backward compatibility

Often, we expose functionality externally through public interfaces or APIs. If people rely on our code, we have a responsibility to protect them from unintentional side effects when we update it. To address this responsibility, the standard solution is versioning. When we version our code, we offer callers the option to keep using a familiar version without fear that we might change it.

Microsoft's commitment to backward compatibility

Microsoft famously has a tremendous commitment to backward compatibility, which has likely contributed to the company's success. In the video series *One Dev Question with Raymond Chen*, Chen describes how code from Windows 95 is still running in Windows 10. It can be a fun and awe-inspiring pilgrimage to discover 20+-year-old code still running. In the YouTube video, "Why You Can't Name a File CON in Windows," Tom Scott demonstrates my favorite example—finding the file-selection prompt from Windows 3.1 on Windows 10 systems today:

1 Press Start, type ODBC, and click ODBC Data Source Administrator (32-bit).
2 Click the Add button.
3 Select Driver Do Microsoft Access (*.mdb), and then click Finish.
4 Click the Select button.

I like to remind people that the safest thing to do in code is not to change anything. While this is partially a joke, there is also a profound observation hidden in it. If we are truly committed to offering our callers the greatest possible safety, our code should stay backward compatible throughout its lifetime. This means whenever we make changes, we introduce a new method in our public interface, a new endpoint in our API, or a new event in an event-based system. The original method's functionality stays intact.

Developing this way is surprisingly simple; we simply follow the same process as described previously. We start by duplicating the existing endpoint we wish to change. Then implement any changes, safe in the knowledge that it cannot affect anyone. Next, unify with the code for the original endpoint. This does add some accidental complexity, with "accidental" stemming from version 1.0 not being perfect. To get rid of this complexity, we should make an effort to move people toward the new version by deprecating the old one, adapting tutorial material to use the new version, and loudly announcing the change. Similar to the way we dealt with legacy code in the previous chapter, we should optimally augment the original version with monitoring. Once this monitoring shows no usage of the original version, we can safely remove it.

There is still the question of how to specify which version to use. As I believe in choosing the simplest solution, I recommend putting the versioning directly in the entry point names. Notice that we version only the outermost layer: the interface between our users and us. We do not need to version methods we have control over since we can test them and verify that nothing has broken. We cannot do this with our users' code, and therefore we version it. I also recommend using a consistent naming scheme so we can easily tell which version is the newest. An example of how *not* to name functions can be found in PHP when looking up how to sanitize input for SQL.

Listing 10.1   Three versions of escaping a string in PHP

```
mysql_escape_string
mysql_real_escape_string
mysqli_real_escape_string
```

10.8　*Modification by addition through feature toggles*

Merging our code with our colleagues' is called *integrating* it. We know that integrating our code often and in small batches reduces errors and spares us the time and, more importantly, the dread of merge conflicts. We would prefer to do this multiple times per day or continuously through practices like ensemble programming. But this raises questions like, what if the code is not ready? Or what if the users are not ready for the new functionality?

This line of thought is common when we think of deploying code as also releasing it. It is possible to have code in the codebase without having it run. We can even have it deployed without anyone knowing. The easiest way to have code be ignored is by putting it in an **if (false)**. We can include whatever we want without fear, and as long as it compiles, we can also safely integrate it into the main branch or even deploy it. Notice, though, that there is a minimum requirement: it must compile.

This is the idea behind *feature toggling*. There are amazingly complex systems to handle this, but as a starting point, I always recommend going with the simplest version while learning. A new concept like this requires practice, and using ready-made tools can be both overwhelming and distracting. To get started with feature toggling, here is the progression I recommend:

1　Make a class called `FeatureToggle`, if it doesn't exist.

Listing 10.2　New class

```
class FeatureToggle {
}
```

2　Add a static method for the task you are about to solve, returning **false**. This is called a *feature flag*. In our example, it is `featureA`.

Listing 10.3　Before

```
class FeatureToggle {
}
```

Listing 10.4　After (1/4)

```
class FeatureToggle {
    static featureA() { return false; }    ⟵
}
                                New feature flag
```

3　Find the place where a change should be implemented. Put an empty **if** (FeatureToggle.featureA()) { }, and enclose the existing code in the **else**.

Listing 10.5　Before

```
class Context {
  foo() {
    code();    ⟵  Original code,
  }               unchanged
}
```

Listing 10.6　After (2/4)

```
class Context {
  foo() {
    if (FeatureToggle.featureA()) {    ⟵
    } else {                              New if (false)
      code();    ⟵
    }
  }            Original code,
}              unchanged
```

4   Duplicate the code from the **else** into the **if**.

Listing 10.7 Before	Listing 10.8 After (3/4)

```
class Context {
  foo() {
    if (FeatureToggle.featureA()) {
    } else {
      code();
    }
  }
}
```

```
class Context {
  foo() {
    if (FeatureToggle.featureA()) {
      code();        ◁─┐
    } else {            ├── Same code
      code();        ◁─┘
    }
  }
}
```

5   Make the desired changes to the code inside the **if**. When we are ready to test our new code, we modify the FeatureToggle.featureA to return the value of an environment variable: **false** if the variable does not exist.

Listing 10.9 Before	Listing 10.10 After (4/4)

```
class FeatureToggle {
  static featureA() {
    return false;
  }
}
```

```
class FeatureToggle {
  static featureA() {
    return Env.isSet("featureA");   ◁─┐
  }                                     │
}                    The feature flag uses
                     the environment.
```

Now we can set the variable on our local machine to test it, but it still won't show up for anyone else. We can safely deploy the code. When the customer is ready, we can easily set the environment variable in the production environment to have the code run. Working this way lets us integrate and deploy as often as we like. However, there are a few caveats to take into consideration.

One caveat is that if we forget this process or do it incorrectly, we risk putting something in production unintentionally. As a developer who takes a lot of pride in my work, there are not many things I fear more than not having control over what goes into production. This is one reason I recommend using this primitive version of feature toggling; a simpler process lowers the risk of making mistakes. In the beginning, we can simply add feature toggling on top of our regular workflow and add to our deployment procedure that we set all the environment variables immediately. Doing so should have the same effect as our regular deploys. This way, we can practice and get better without users perceiving any changes, other than the option to roll back features that are correctly feature-toggled without redeploying—which is another value proposition of feature toggling.

Another caveat is that we now have two copies of the same code running. Even worse, we have an **if**. As we have discussed, **if**s add actual complexity, and if we start having dependent features, we must put an **if** in both branches. This approach quickly explodes and becomes unmanageable. But these **if**s are special. They are technical debt because they are temporary. Whenever we close the task that spawned a feature toggle, we should create a scheduled task to remove the toggle. Here again, I recommend scheduling this task at most six weeks in the future. At this time, if the feature is turned on in production, we remove the `else` part; otherwise, we remove the `if` part. This may mean the code never saw the light of day, but in that case, we treat it as a frozen project and delete it from the main branch. Feature flags mustn't be allowed to fester, as they will contaminate the codebase and may cause catastrophic failures.

Toggle trouble at Knight

The blog post "Knightmare: A DevOps Cautionary Tale" by Doug Seven (http://mng .bz/dm0w) reports that in 2012, the high-speed trading company Knight released a new version of its software. A few things conspired to make this probably the worst day in the company's history. Because deploying was a manual process done by a single engineer, the software was not rolled out to all servers, so two versions were running simultaneously. There was no kill switch built into the system, nor were there processes for handling the situation if something went wrong. The only safety feature that activated was a warning email, which was ignored.

All of these were risky decisions, but they didn't cause trouble on their own. The avalanche started because the two running versions were incompatible. The new code repurposed a configuration flag that had been unused for seven years. Unfortunately, the code tied to the flag was still in the codebase running on some of the servers. This caused the program to start trading uncontrollably. Knight lost over $400 million in the 45 minutes it took to stop the program.

Once these two cons are addressed, we feel confident that the toggles are done correctly on everything, and we are routinely removing them. Then—and not a minute sooner—we can begin to further exploit this awesome technology. The first step is probably to move the toggles to a database and create a small UI for them so the business can toggle things on or off. We can also build in a slow rollout: only 10% of users see the new feature at first, to make sure it works, and then the number of users gradually increases. We can take this idea further and couple our toggles to some metric like "did the user buy something": if more users are buying something, we roll it out faster. This is called *A/B testing*, and it can be enormously profitable.

A/B testing Obama's campaign website

For the 2008 US Presidential election, Barack Obama's campaign website needed a photo and a Sign Up button. It was impossible to know which photo or button text would work best, so his team set up an experiment. Using A/B testing, they showed one combination to some visitors and other combinations to other users. They observed that a picture of Obama with his family had the best effect, together with a button saying Learn More. Collectively, this combination did 40% better than before A/B testing, which is estimated to have increased donations by $60 million (http://mng.bz/rmxy).

Notice that this also addresses the last chapter's discussion because then the algorithm automatically phases out code that is less profitable or faulty. We humans only have to perform the actual deletion after looking at whether the flag is on or off, which is trivial.

10.9 Modification by addition through branch by abstraction

At this point, you may be wondering, "Isn't feature toggling breaking the rule NEVER USE `if` WITH `else` (R4.1.1)?" Indeed it is, and there are two ways to address this. The simplest is to say the `if`s are temporary. They are easy to delete, which is our intention, and we are not supposed to extend them, which is the major issue with `if`s. I use this justification if the feature flag is only used in one location.

Some features require changes in multiple locations in the code. This means if we use multiple `if`s, the invariants connected to this change will be spread out across them. In these cases, before I deliver the code, I use REPLACE TYPE CODE WITH CLASSES on the Boolean inside the feature flag. Instead of returning a **true** or **false**, I return a NewA or OldA. This is commonly called *branch by abstraction*: the classes are the abstraction, and having two is the branching. Having them as classes allows us to eliminate the `if`s by pushing them into the classes as we have done repeatedly throughout part 1 of this book.

In this example, we see two versions of the same program: one is using regular feature toggles, and the other is using branch by abstraction.

Listing 10.11   Feature toggles

```
class FeatureToggle {
  static featureA() {
    return Env.isSet("featureA");



  }
}
class ContextA {
  foo() {
    if (FeatureToggle.featureA()) {
      aCodeV2();
    } else {
      aCodeV1();
    }
  }
}
class ContextB {
  bar() {
    if (FeatureToggle.featureA()) {
      bCodeV2();
    } else {
      bCodeV1();
    }
  }
}
```

Listing 10.12   Branch by abstraction

```
class FeatureToggle {
  static featureA() {
    return Env.isSet("featureA")
           ? new Version2()
           : new Version1();
  }
}
class ContextA {
  foo() {
    FeatureToggle.featureA().aCode();
  }
}
class ContextB {
  bar() {
    FeatureToggle.featureA().bCode();
  }
}
interface FeatureA {
  aCode(): void;
  bCode(): void;
}
class Version1 implements FeatureA {
  aCode() { aCodeV1(); }
  bCode() { bCodeV1(); }
}
```

```
class Version2 implements FeatureA {
  aCode() { aCodeV2(); }
  bCode() { bCodeV2(); }
}
```

This approach localizes the invariants of the feature change in those classes. Then, once it is time to remove the feature toggle, we do the following.

1　Delete one of the classes.

Listing 10.13　Before	Listing 10.14　After (1/4)

```
class Version1 implements FeatureA {
  aCode() { aCodeV1(); }
  bCode() { bCodeV1(); }
}
class Version2 implements FeatureA {
  aCode() { aCodeV2(); }
  bCode() { bCodeV2(); }
}
```

    ◁─┐ **Version1**
    　　│ **deleted**

```
class Version2 implements FeatureA {
  aCode() { aCodeV2(); }
  bCode() { bCodeV2(); }
}
```

2　Then, following NO INTERFACE WITH ONLY ONE IMPLEMENTATION (R5.4.3), also delete the interface.

Listing 10.15　Before	Listing 10.16　After (2/4)

```
interface FeatureA {
  aCode(): void;
  bCode(): void;
}
```

    ◁─┐ **FeatureA**
    　　│ **deleted**

3　Finally, inline the methods in the remaining class and the feature flag.

Listing 10.17　Before	Listing 10.18　After (3/4)

```
class ContextA {
  foo() {
    FeatureToggle.featureA().aCode();
  }
}
class ContextB {
  bar() {
    FeatureToggle.featureA().bCode();
  }
}
class Version2 implements FeatureA {
  aCode() { aCodeV2(); }
  bCode() { bCodeV2(); }
}
```

```
class ContextA {
  foo() {
    aCodeV2();      ◁─┐
  }
}                     │ Methods
class ContextB {      │ inlined
  bar() {             │
    bCodeV2();      ◁─┘
  }
}
class Version2 implements FeatureA {
  aCode() { aCodeV2(); }
  bCode() { bCodeV2(); }
}
```

4 Then also delete that class.

Listing 10.19 Before

```
class Version2 implements FeatureA {
  aCode() { aCodeV2(); }
  bCode() { bCodeV2(); }
}
```

Listing 10.20 After (4/4)

← **Version2 deleted**

We are left with this code, containing no trace of the feature toggle.

Listing 10.21 After

```
class FeatureToggle {
}
class ContextA {
  foo() {
    aCodeV2();
  }
}
class ContextB {
  bar() {
    bCodeV2();
  }
}
```

Summary

- Incorporating spikes into our workflow can help us overcome a fear of building the wrong thing.
- Accepting some waste is necessary so we can spend the majority of our time delivering value to our stakeholders.
- Having developer life as our target maximizes practice and productivity.
- Duplicating code encourages experimentation, whereas sharing increases fragility.
- Having a larger body of code exposes more of the underlying structure and gives us a clearer direction for our refactoring.
- Refactoring aims to reduce accidental complexity. Essential complexity is necessary to meaningfully model the underlying domain.
- Modifying by adding supports backward compatibility, which reduces risk.
- Feature toggles support integrating code, which reduces risk.
- Branching by abstraction helps manage complex feature toggles.

Follow the structure
in the code

Software is a model of an aspect of the real world. The real world changes as we learn and grow, and we need to adapt our software to encompass these changes. In this way, as long as the software is being used, it is never finished. This also means connections in the real world must be represented in our code: the code is a codified structure from the real world.

In this chapter, we first discuss where different types of code structure come from. Then we examine three different ways behavior can be embedded in code and how to move behavior between these approaches. Having established the types of structure we are dealing with, we discuss refactoring: when it is helpful and when it may be disadvantageous. Finally, we look at different types of unexploited structures and how to use them with the refactoring patterns we have learned.

11.1 *Categorizing structure based on scope and origin*

In software development, we deal with several types of structure (that is, recognizable patterns). Such a structure could be two similar methods or something people do every day. There is structure in the domain, structure in the program's behavior, structure in our communication, and structure in the code.

I like to split the structure space into four distinct categories: one dimension is whether the structure affects one team or person (intra-team) or multiple teams or people (inter-team); the other dimension is whether the structure is in the code or the people (see table 11.1).

Table 11.1 Structure-space categories

	Inter-team	Intra-team
In code	External API	Data and functions, most refactoring
In people	Organizational chart, processes	Behavior, domain experts

Macro-architecture is about inter-team structure: what our product is and how other code interacts with it. This guides how our external API should look and what data each team owns. It defines our software platforms.

Micro-architecture is about intra-team structure: what the team can do to deliver value, which services we use, how to organize our data, and how our code looks. The refactoring patterns in this book belong in this category.

We also work within processes and a hierarchy defined by the organization: our teams and how they communicate. Here, *processes* refers to Scrum, Kanban, project models, and so on; and *hierarchy* means an organizational chart or similar that defines who should talk to whom.

Finally, there is the structure defined by domain experts. Domain experts are familiar with the patterns in a domain because such patterns repeat their behavior. These experts define how the software should function, which means the system mirrors the experts' behavior.

The mind-blowing thing is that structure tends to be mirrored along the horizontal dimension. Organizational structure tends to constrain how our external API looks; this is called *Conway's law*. Similarly, the structure in domain experts' behavior tends to bleed into the code. This is both fascinating and useful because if we spot inefficiencies in the code, we can often find their real-world source in the way the experts work, in our processes, or somewhere else. Understanding this can be a powerful tool for improvement.

I mention this because user behavior also constrains the code structure. Some changes to the structure of the code require changes in user behavior. We can think of users as another part of the code. If we cannot interact with our users, they are external; therefore, as seen from the point of view of refactoring, they constrain us. If we can retrain the users, they are within the scope of our refactoring. Keep in mind that although changing people's behavior sounds simpler than changing the code, in large organizations or user bases, doing so is often more difficult and usually slow. Therefore, it is often useful to first model user behavior as is, including all its inefficiencies, and then gradually provide more efficient functionality along with training and education, thus refactoring the users' behavior.

11.2 Three ways that code mirrors behavior

Regardless of where behavior comes from, there are three ways we can embed behavior into code:

- In the control flow
- In the structure of the data
- In the data itself

We go through each approach in the following sections. To indicate the differences, I show the famous FizzBuzz program using the different methods. Additionally, I show how to encode infinite loops, as they are an interesting special case. Keep in mind that because refactoring does not change behavior, we either manage duplication or move the structure from one approach to another.

An introduction to FizzBuzz

FizzBuzz is a children's game that teaches multiplication tables. You select two numbers, and then the players take turns saying numbers sequentially. If the next number in the sequence is divisible by your first number, the child says "Fizz"; if it is divisible by your second number, they say "Buzz"; and if it is divisible by both your numbers, they say "FizzBuzz." The game keeps going until someone makes a mistake.

Implementing the game in code usually takes this form: write a program that takes as input a number, N, and outputs all numbers from 0 to N. But if a number is divisible by 3, output "Fizz"; if it is divisible by 5, output "Buzz"; and if it is divisible by both, output "FizzBuzz."

11.2.1 Expressing behavior in the control flow

The control flow is expressed in the text of the code through control operators, method calls, or simply the lines of code. As an example, here is the same loop using the three most common types of control flow:

Listing 11.1 Control operator

```
let i = 0;
while (i < 5) {
  foo(i);
  i++;
}
```

Listing 11.2 Method call

```
function loop(i: number) {
  if (i < 5) {
    foo(i);
    loop(i + 1)
  }
}
```

Listing 11.3 Lines

```
foo(0);
foo(1);
foo(2);
foo(3);
foo(4);
```

Whenever we discuss code duplication, we are almost always talking about moving between these three subcategories of behavior and most commonly away from the rightmost type: lines. These three subcategories are subtly different. Method calls and lines can express non-local structure, whereas a loop can only act locally.

Listing 11.4   Method call

```
function insert(data: object) {
  let db = new Database();
  let normalized = normalize(data);
  db.insert(normalized);
}
function a() {
  // ...
  insert(obj1);      ◁──┐
  // ...                 │ Same
}                        │ method
function b() {           │ call
  // ...                 │
  insert(obj2);      ◁──┘
  // ...
}
```

Listing 11.5   Lines

```
function a() {
  // ...
  let db = new Database();
  let normalized = normalize(obj1);   ┐
  db.insert(normalized);              │
  // ...                              │
}                                     │
function b() {                        │ Same
  // ...                              │ lines
  let db = new Database();            │
  let normalized = normalize(obj2);   ┘
  db.insert(normalized);
  // ...
}
```

On the other hand, control operators and method calls can do something that lines cannot—create infinite loops.

Listing 11.6   Control operator

```
for (;;) { }
```

Listing 11.7   Method call

```
function loop() {
  loop();
}
```

Working with behavior in the control flow, it is easy to make big changes because we can change the flow simply by moving statements. Often we prefer stability and small changes, so we usually refactor away from control flow. But in some situations, we need to make large adjustments. In such cases, it can be beneficial to refactor behavior into control flow, then make the changes, and then refactor the behavior back again.

Many of the refactoring patterns in this book work at this level. Some examples are EXTRACT METHOD (P3.2.1) and COMBINE ifs (P5.2.1).

Most people implement FizzBuzz by encoding it in the control flow.

Listing 11.8   FizzBuzz using control flow

```
function fizzBuzz(n: number) {
  for (let i = 0; i < n; i++) {
    if (i % 3 === 0 && i % 5 === 0) {
      console.log("FizzBuzz");
    } else if (i % 5 === 0) {
```

```
      console.log("Buzz");
    } else if (i % 3 === 0) {
      console.log("Fizz");
    } else {
      console.log(i);
    }
  }
}
```

11.2.2 Expressing behavior in the structure of the data

Another way to encode behavior is in the structure of the data. We have mentioned the parable that data structures are algorithms frozen in time. My favorite example is the connection between the binary search function and a binary search tree (BST) data structure.

Without going into too much detail, binary search is an algorithm to find an element in a sorted list. It does so by repeatedly halving the search space—since the list is sorted, if we compare our search key to the middle element, we can discard half the list. A BST is a tree structure made up of nodes; each node has a value and can have up to two child nodes. The invariant (or behavior) embedded in this data structure is that all children on the left are smaller than the value, and all children on the right are greater than the value. When looking for an element in a BST, we compare the element to the value at the root and then recursively descend into the appropriate child tree. The behavior of a binary search is expressed in the structure of a BST; see figure 11.1.

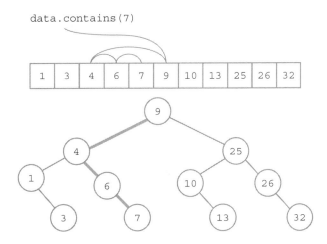

Figure 11.1 Binary search and BST

Let's look at how we can use types instead of **for**, **while**, and recursive functions to define infinite loops. In this example, we use a recursive data structure. Rec has a field f whose type contains Rec; it is thus a recursive data structure. Since the field f is a function, we can define a helper function that takes a Rec object, fetches the function packed inside it, and then calls it with the same Rec object. We can now instantiate a Rec object with the helper function and pass that to the helper function. Notice how no function is calling itself directly in this example: the helper function calls itself through the Rec data structure.

Listing 11.9 Recursive data structure

```
class Rec {
  constructor(public readonly f: (_: Rec) => void) { }
}

function loop() {
  let helper = (r: Rec) => r.f(r);
  helper(new Rec(helper));
}
```

Compared to behavior in the control flow, with this approach it is more difficult to make significant changes unless they align with our existing variation points. However, it is easier and safer to make small changes. This is because we get more type safety and locality. In some cases, we can also gain performance when the data structure allows us to cache and reuse information, as in the example with binary search versus BSTs. The refactoring patterns REPLACE TYPE CODE WITH CLASSES (P4.1.3) and INTRODUCE STRATEGY PATTERN (P5.4.2) both move structure from control flow to data structures.

Encoding FizzBuzz in a data structure is a bit cumbersome because we need to encode the cyclic behavior of %. We can implement natural numbers as a data structure, as well, to get rid of the control operator **for**, but I leave that as an exercise for you. Luckily, the code is easy to read.

Listing 11.10 FizzBuzz using data structures

```
interface FizzAction {
  num(n: number): void;
  buzz(): void;
}
class SayFizz implements FizzAction {       Encoding
  num(n: number) { console.log("Fizz"); }   the fizz
  buzz() { console.log("FizzBuzz"); }        behavior
}
class FizzNumber implements FizzAction {
  num(n: number) { console.log(n); }
  buzz() { console.log("Buzz"); }
}
```

```
interface BuzzAction {
  num(n: number, act: FizzAction): void;
}
class SayBuzz implements BuzzAction {
  num(n: number, act: FizzAction) {
    act.buzz();
  }
}
class BuzzNumber implements BuzzAction {
  num(n: number, act: FizzAction) {
    act.num(n);
  }
}
```

Encoding the buzz behavior

```
interface FizzNum {
  next(): FizzNum;
  action(): FizzAction;
}
class FizzNum1 implements FizzNum {
  next() { return new FizzNum2(); }
  action() { return new FizzNumber(); }
}
class FizzNum2 implements FizzNum {
  next() { return new Fizz(); }
  action() { return new FizzNumber(); }
}
class Fizz implements FizzNum {
  next() { return new FizzNum1(); }
  action() { return new SayFizz(); }
}
```

Encoding % 3

```
interface BuzzNum {
  next(): BuzzNum;
  action(): BuzzAction;
}
class BuzzNum1 implements BuzzNum {
  next() { return new BuzzNum2(); }
  action() { return new BuzzNumber(); }
}
class BuzzNum2 implements BuzzNum {
  next() { return new BuzzNum3(); }
  action() { return new BuzzNumber(); }
}
class BuzzNum3 implements BuzzNum {
  next() { return new BuzzNum4(); }
  action() { return new BuzzNumber(); }
}
class BuzzNum4 implements BuzzNum {
  next() { return new Buzz(); }
  action() { return new BuzzNumber(); }
}
class Buzz implements BuzzNum {
  next() { return new BuzzNum1(); }
  action() { return new SayBuzz(); }
}
```

Encoding % 5

```
function fizzBuzz(n: number) {
  let f = new Fizz();
  let b = new Buzz();
  for (let i = 0; i < n; i++) {
    b.action().num(i, f.action());
    f = f.next();
    b = b.next();
  }
}
```

11.2.3 Expressing behavior in the data

The final approach encodes the behavior in the data. This is the most difficult because we quickly run into the halting-problem blind spot (discussed in section 7.1) of tools and compilers, which means we get no support from them.

In the industry, we most commonly see structure in data through duplicated data. This can lead to consistency challenges, especially if the data is mutable. The performance gain can justify these challenges; however, it can also be a source of errors and waste.

To make an infinite loop in the data, we have to use references in TypeScript, Java, and C# arrays, and objects are handled as references. The idea is to put into memory a function that looks up a reference—which will be itself—and calls it. Notice that the function is again calling itself not directly but indirectly through the heap.

> **Listing 11.11   Recursive data**

```
function loop() {
  let a = [() => { }];
  a[0] = () => a[0]();
  a[0]();
}
```

Unlike the other two methods, here we get no support from our compilers, making this method very difficult to work with safely. One remedy is to use tools to retrieve data and generate data structures from the data. As a consequence, we duplicate the behavior and have to either maintain the tool ourselves or add a third-party dependency.

Because this structure is so difficult to work with, I generally recommend actively transforming it to one of the others. Nonetheless, we have seen an example of refactoring to move the structure from control flow into data in section 6.5.2.

Encoding FizzBuzz in data probably looks a lot simpler than encoding it in a data structure, partly because we went back to having the cyclic behavior in the % operator. This means the cyclic behavior is encoded in the control flow; however, if we want to, we can implement it using pointers or references. I leave that as an exercise for the overachievers among you.

Listing 11.12 FizzBuzz using data structures

```
interface FizzAction {
  num(n: number): void;
  buzz(): void;
}
class SayFizz implements FizzAction {
  num(n: number) { console.log("Fizz"); }
  buzz() { console.log("FizzBuzz"); }
}
class FizzNumber implements FizzAction {
  num(n: number) { console.log(n); }
  buzz() { console.log("Buzz"); }
}

interface BuzzAction {
  num(n: number, act: FizzAction): void;
}
class SayBuzz implements BuzzAction {
  num(n: number, act: FizzAction) {
    act.buzz();
  }
}
class BuzzNumber implements BuzzAction {
  num(n: number, act: FizzAction) {
    act.num(n);
  }
}

const FIZZ = [
  new SayFizz(),
  new FizzNumber(),          Encoding
  new FizzNumber()           the 3
];
const BUZZ = [
  new SayBuzz(),
  new BuzzNumber(),
  new BuzzNumber(),          Encoding
  new BuzzNumber(),          the 5
  new BuzzNumber(),
];

function fizzBuzz(n: number) {
  for (let i = 0; i < n; i++) {
    BUZZ[i % BUZZ.length].num(i, FIZZ[i % FIZZ.length]);
  }
}
```

11.3 Adding code to expose structure

When we refactor, we make some changes easier and other changes more difficult. We refactor to support a particular change vector: the direction we believe the software is taking. The more code we have, the more likely we know this change vector and how the code tends to change because we have more data. As mentioned in chapter 1, if the code should not change, there is no reason to refactor.

Refactoring solidifies the current structure and makes it more receptive to similar changes. It puts variation points in positions where we have seen or expect variation. In stable (sub)systems, this is invaluable, as it accelerates development speed and increases quality. On the other hand, in (sub)systems with a lot of uncertainty, we need experimentation more than solidity.

When we are uncertain about the underlying structure, we should throttle our refactoring efforts and focus first on correctness. Of course, we should never sacrifice team productivity, so we cannot increase fragility. We still need to avoid non-local invariants, as always. When we postpone refactoring, we should encapsulate the un-refactored code so it does not unintentionally affect the rest. But we should not add variation points, because in exchange for their ease of variation, they add complexity—complexity that makes it more difficult to experiment and, more importantly, may hide other structures.

When implementing new features or subsystems, there is bound to be uncertainty. In these situations, it makes sense to use enums and loops rather than classes because they can be changed quickly; and new code is usually under heavy testing, so the risk of introducing mistakes without catching them is low. When the code matures and the structure becomes more stable, so should the code; using refactoring, we should mold the structure to fit. The code's solidity should represent how confident we are in the code's direction.

11.4   *Observing instead of predicting, and using empirical techniques*

In the same vein as the previous section, if we try to predict the change vector, we may hurt the codebase rather than help it. As with most things in our industry, we should not subject our code to conjecture but rather use empirical techniques. Our field is moving toward a more scientific approach with methods for continuous improvement through structured experiments, such as Toyota Kata, Evidence-Based Management, and Popcorn Flow, to name a few.

It is easy to fall into the trap of trying to be smart. When we spot an opportunity to make something extensible or general, solve a more challenging problem, or realize something brilliant, we want to take advantage of this insight. If writing cooler code takes negligible time, it is tempting to take that opportunity. But if we are not sure this generality will be used, we are adding unnecessary code and accidental complexity.

A story from real life

I was once discussing with a developer how to implement chess. I asked how he would implement the pieces. Being well versed in object-oriented programming, he replied, "Using an interface and classes." Leading a horse to water, I asked, "Wouldn't it be easier to hardcode them?" He said, "Sure, but good luck maintaining that," and chuckled as if I'd made a joke—until I replied, "I don't have to; chess hasn't changed in 500 years." His eyes widened.

This story illustrates how even though we have powerful tools, we should not always use them. We should observe how the code tends to change:

- If it doesn't change, do nothing.
- If it changes unpredictably, refactor only to avoid fragility.
- Otherwise, refactor to make accommodations for the types of changes that have happened in the past.

11.5 Gaining safety without understanding the code

You may remember that, in chapter 3, I argued for refactoring without understanding the code. As we have discussed, refactoring moves behavior between control flow, data structures, and data. This is true regardless of the underlying domain or structure because the structure is in the code. We don't need to understand it to work with it, as long as we follow the structure that is already in the code and use sound refactoring patterns without making mistakes.

The last part of that statement is where it can get tricky, because humans make mistakes. Luckily, we don't need to reinvent the wheel, as there are already several steps we can take to protect ourselves. Notice that none of these are failsafe, and generally we use a bit of everything. As with most things in the real world, there is a point at which we have to accept the remaining risk.

11.5.1 Gaining safety through testing

The most common approach to gain safety is to test our code. I believe we should always do this, not only to check correctness but also to walk a mile in our user's shoes. We make software to make someone's world better. How can we do that if we don't know what their world looks like? The issue with testing our code properly is that doing so quickly becomes unmanageable, immensely time consuming, and error prone, since a human is doing it. As with many other monotone tasks in software development, the fix is automation: specifically, the correctness tests also known as *functional tests.* The risk is that our tests may not cover where a mistake happens or not test what we expect them to.

11.5.2 Gaining safety through mastery

Another approach is to reduce the likelihood of mistakes by focusing on the human doing the refactoring. First we need to decompose refactorings into small steps—so small that the risk of failure is negligible. When the steps are small enough, the problem shifts to a risk of overlooking some of the steps. We can reduce this risk by practicing. Wax on, wax off—perform the refactorings in a safe environment so frequently that they become mechanical. In this case, the risk is reduced rather than shifted, so the risk remains the human refactorer.

11.5.3 *Gaining safety through tool assistance*

Speaking of mechanical, we can also reduce human mistakes by removing the human factor. Many modern IDEs come with tool-assisted refactoring built in, so instead of executing the steps to extract a method, we can ask the editor to do it for us. We just have to specify what code to extract. The risk is the tool containing a bug. Luckily, if the tool is widely used, bugs are usually patched quickly, reducing this risk.

11.5.4 *Gaining safety through formal verification*

If we are building software for which failure is exceptionally expensive, such as for an airplane or the next Mars rover, we might go to an extreme and formally verify that the code is bug free. We can even use a proof assistant to mechanically check that our proofs are correct, which is the current state of the art in quality. As this is simply another tool-assisted method, the risk remains the same as in the previous approach: there may be a bug in the proof assistant that aligns with a mistake in our proofs.

11.5.5 *Gaining safety through fault tolerance*

Finally, we can build our code so that even if an error occurs, it self-corrects. One example is feature toggling: as discussed in the last chapter, we can add automatic roll-back on failure. This way, even if we make a mistake while refactoring and our code fails, the feature-toggling system automatically reverts to the old code.

This method can fall through if the feature-toggling system fails to distinguish between a correct response and an error. An example would be having a function return –1 instead of throwing an exception when it fails. The system might expect an integer, and –1 is a perfectly fine integer.

11.6 *Identifying unexploited structures*

There is structure in everything we do. It comes from the domain, from the way we communicate, and from how we think (our biases). Much of this structure bleeds into our codebases. As we have discussed, we can exploit this structure through refactoring to make our code more stable, even with high change velocity.

As we discussed earlier in the chapter, exploiting structure that is coincidental or fleeting often leads to diminished velocity. Always consider whether the foundation is solid, is this structure likely to persist. Generally, the underlying domain tends to be older than the software and therefore more mature and less prone to drastic changes. Therefore, structure that comes from the domain can often be safely exploited.

Our processes and, unfortunately, our teams have significantly shorter lifespans than the software. They are also more unstable, which means if we bake them into the system, we likely have to unwind the process code again, only to bake in a new process, ad infinitum.

Before we can decide whether a structure is worth exploiting, we need to find it. So let's examine the most common places to look for exploitable structures in the code and how to use them.

11.6.1 Exploiting whitespace with extraction and encapsulation

Developers often express perceived structure using blank lines because we have a mental grouping of statements, fields, and so on. When we have to implement something complex, we do so by cutting the proverbial elephant into tiny pieces. Between the pieces, we place a blank line and sometimes a comment, which then serves as a first draft for the grouping's name.

As described in chapter 1, whenever we see groups of statements with whitespace between them, we should consider EXTRACT METHOD. Of course, when developers write new code, they should extract the methods themselves; but this requires effort, and unless it is made trivial through practice, many tend to skip this refactoring. Adding a blank line is cheap and low risk, which means almost everyone does it. Thus this is a reliable insight into the author's mental model of how to solve the task. And luckily, you are now practiced at extracting methods and can easily solidify this structure. In the following example, a function subtracts the minimum value of an array from every element in the array. There are two sections, separated by a blank line.

Listing 11.13 Before

```
function subMin(arr: number[]) {
  let min = Number.POSITIVE_INFINITY;
  for (let x = 0; x < arr.length; x++) {
    min = Math.min(min, arr[x]);
  }

  for (let x = 0; x < arr.length; x++) {
    arr[x] -= min;
  }
}
```

Listing 11.14 After

```
function subMin(arr: number[]) {
  let min = findMin(arr);
  subtractFromEach(min, arr);
}
function findMin(arr: number[]) {
  let min = Number.POSITIVE_INFINITY;
  for (let x = 0; x < arr.length; x++) {
    min = Math.min(min, arr[x]);
  }
  return min;
}
function subtractFromEach(min: number,
  arr: number[])
{
  for (let x = 0; x < arr.length; x++) {
    arr[x] -= min;
  }
}
```

Extracted methods

The second most common place to find unexploited whitespace is when it is used to group fields. In this case, the whitespace suggests what data elements are more related (i.e., change together). We are also practiced at exploiting this structure through the refactoring pattern ENCAPSULATE DATA (P6.2.3). In the following example, we have a particle class with fields for x, y, and color. From the whitespace, we can infer that x and y are more closely connected than color, so we can exploit that.

Listing 11.15   Before

```
class Particle {
  private x: number;
  private y: number;

  private color: number;
  // ...
}
```

Encapsulated
fields

Listing 11.16   After

```
class Vector2D {
  private x: number;
  private y: number;
  // ...
}
class Particle {
  private position: Vector2D;
  private color: number;
  // ...
}
```

Encapsulating
class

11.6.2 Exploiting duplication with unification

We have talked extensively about duplication. We see it in statements, methods, classes, and so on because, like blank lines, it requires little effort and is low risk. Also like blank lines, we already know how to deal with each type of duplication. We follow the structure underlying part 1 of this book: statements into methods, and methods into classes.

We can have duplicated statements either close to each other or spread throughout multiple methods in different classes. In either case, we start by using our fundamental refactoring pattern EXTRACT METHOD. In this example, we have two formatters. The overall flow is different, so we decide to tackle the result += statement that appears in both. We first extract it.

Listing 11.17   Before

```
class XMLFormatter {
 format(vals: string[]) {
   let result = "";
   for (let i = 0; i < vals.length; i++) {
     result +=
`<Value>${vals[i]}</Value>`;
   }
   return result;}
}
class JSONFormatter {
 format(vals: string[]) {
   let result = "";
   for (let i = 0; i < vals.length; i++) {
     if (i > 0) result += ",";
     result += `{ value: "${vals[i]}" }`;
   }
   return result;
 }
}
```

Listing 11.18   After

```
class XMLFormatter {
 format(vals: string[]) {
   let result = "";
   for (let i = 0; i < vals.length; i++) {
     result += this.formatSingle(vals[i]);
   }
   return result;
 }
 formatSingle(val: string) {
   return `<Value>${val}</Value>`;
 }
}
class JSONFormatter {
 format(vals: string[]) {
   let result = "";
   for (let i = 0; i < vals.length; i++) {
     if (i > 0) result += ",";
     result += this.formatSingle(vals[i]);
   }
   return result;
 }
 formatSingle(val: string) {
   return `{ value: "${val}" }`;
 }
}
```

Extracted
method

If the extracted methods are spread across classes, we can centralize them using ENCAPSULATE DATA on the methods this time.

Listing 11.19 Before

```
class XMLFormatter {
  formatSingle(val: string) {
    return `<Value>${val}</Value>`;

  }
  // ...
}
class JSONFormatter {
  formatSingle(val: string) {
    return `{ value: "${val}" }`;

  }
  // ...
}
```

Listing 11.20 After

```
class XMLFormatter {
  formatSingle(val: string) {
    return new XMLFormatSingle()
      .format(val);
  }
  // ...
}
class JSONFormatter {
  formatSingle(val: string) {
    return new JSONFormatSingle()
      .format(val);
  }
  // ...
}
class XMLFormatSingle {
  format(val: string) {
    return `<Value>${val}</Value>`;
  }
}
class JSONFormatSingle {
  format(val: string) {
    return `{ value: "${val}" }`;
  }
}
```

Encapsulated method

If the methods are identical, these classes are also identical, so we can simply delete all but one. If these encapsulating classes are merely similar, and whenever we have duplicated classes, we can use UNIFY SIMILAR CLASSES (P5.1.1).

Listing 11.21 Before

```
class XMLFormatSingle {
  format(val: string) {
    return `<Value>${val}</Value>`;

  }
}
class JSONFormatSingle {
  format(val: string) {
    return `{ value: "${val}" }`;

  }
}
```

Listing 11.22 After

```
class XMLFormatter {
  formatSingle(val: string) {
    return new FormatSingle("<Value>","</Value>")
      .format(val);
  }
  // ...
}
class JSONFormatter {
  formatSingle(val: string) {
    return new FormatSingle("{ value: '","' }")
      .format(val);
  }
  // ...
}
class FormatSingle {
  constructor(
    private before: string,
    private after: string) { }
```

Unified class

```
                                     format(val: string) {
                                       return `${before}${val}${after}`;
                                     }
                                   }
```

If the statements are similar only in flow and not in statements, we can make them identical using INTRODUCE STRATEGY PATTERN. That's why this refactoring pattern is so powerful: it can expose structure even where that structure is hidden.

Listing 11.23 Before	Listing 11.24 After

```
class XMLFormatter {
 format(vals: string[]) {
  let result = "";
  for (let i = 0; i < vals.length; i++) {
    result +=
      new FormatSingle("<Value>","</Value>")
      .format(vals[i]);
  }
  return result;
 }
}
class JSONFormatter {
  format(vals: string[]) {
    let result = "";
    for (let i = 0; i < vals.length; i++) {
      if (i > 0) result += ",";
      result +=
        new FormatSingle("{ value: '","' }")
        .format(vals[i]);
    }
    return result;
  }
}
```

```
class XMLFormatter {
  format(vals: string[]) {
    return new Formatter(
      new
FormatSingle("<Value>","</Value>"),
      new None()).format(vals);
  }
}
class JSONFormatter {
  format(vals: string[]) {
    return new Formatter(
      new FormatSingle("{ value: '","' }"),
      new Comma()).format(vals);
  }
}
class Formatter {
  constructor(
    private single: FormatSingle,
    private sep: Separator) { }
  format(vals: string[]) {
    let result = "";
    for (let i = 0; i < vals.length; i++) {
      result = this.sep.put(i, result);
      result += this.single.format(vals[i]);
    }
    return result;                    Strategy
  }                                    pattern
}
interface Separator {
  put(i: number, str: string): string;
}
class Comma implements Separator {
  put(i: number, result: string) {
    if (i > 0) result += ",";
    return result;
  }
}
class None implements Separator {
  put(i: number, result: string) {
    return result;
  }
}
```

At this point, the two original formatters differ only in constant values, so we can easily unify them.

11.6.3 *Exploiting common affixes with encapsulation*

Another way we see structure in data, methods, and classes is so obvious and reliable that we have a rule for it: NEVER HAVE COMMON AFFIXES (R6.2.1). Similar to a blank line with a comment, we have both a grouping and a suggested name. This approach follows the pattern of requiring little effort and being low risk. And once again, we know how to solidify it because whether we discover the grouping through whitespace, duplication, or naming, the solution remains the same: ENCAPSULATE DATA.

So far, we have only seen how to apply the rule to fields and methods. However, it can also be used to group classes with similar naming. We have not discussed this because the mechanism differs more from language to language; in Java, we can encapsulate classes inside other classes or packages; in C#, we have namespaces; and in TypeScript, we have namespaces or modules. I encourage you to experiment and figure out which mechanism works for your team.

In the following example, we have several protocols for encoding and decoding data that we probably got by introducing a strategy pattern. Their internals are not important.

Listing 11.25 Before

```
interface Protocol { ... }
class StringProtocol implements Protocol { ... }
class JSONProtocol implements Protocol { ... }
class ProtobufProtocol implements Protocol { ... }
/// ...
  let p = new StringProtocol();
/// ...
```

All the classes have the common suffix `Protocol`, which breaks NEVER HAVE COMMON AFFIXES. In this case, we cannot remove `Protocol` directly because `String` would conflict with a built-in class—but not if we encapsulate the three classes and interface in a namespace first.

Listing 11.26 After

```
namespace protocol {
  export interface Protocol { ... }
  export class String implements Protocol { ... }
  export class JSON implements Protocol { ... }
  export class Protobuf implements Protocol { ... }
}
/// ...
  let p = new protocol.String();
/// ...
```

> **In TypeScript ...**
> TypeScript has different keywords to control access at different levels. Inside classes, fields and methods are public by default, and we can use **private** to limit their access. Anything outside a class is private by default, so we can use **export** to widen access to those things (functions, classes, etc.).

11.6.4 *Exploiting the runtime type with dynamic dispatch*

Previously I have only mentioned the final type of structure I want to focus on, which is a very common sign of unexploited structure. I am referring to inspecting the run-time types using typeof, instanceof, reflection, or typecasting.

Object-oriented programming was conceived without any facility to inspect the run-time type because it has a stronger mechanism built in: dynamic dispatch through interfaces. Using interfaces, we can put different types of classes in a variable; then, when we call a method on the variable, we invoke the method in the appropriate class. This is also the way to avoid using run-time type inspection. It is a special case of NEVER USE **if** WITH **else** (R4.1.1).

Now assume we have a variable that can have something of type A or B, and currently, we are inspecting the type directly to determine which case we are in. If we have control over A and B, the solution is simple: we make a new interface, change the variable to have this type, and make both classes implement the interface. We can now use PUSH CODE INTO CLASSES (P4.1.5)—and, like many times before, the **if** disappears.

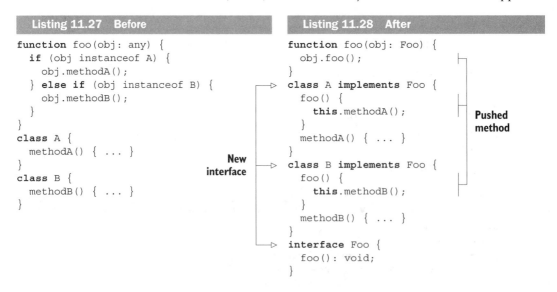

Listing 11.27 Before	Listing 11.28 After

```typescript
function foo(obj: any) {
  if (obj instanceof A) {
    obj.methodA();
  } else if (obj instanceof B) {
    obj.methodB();
  }
}
class A {
  methodA() { ... }
}
class B {
  methodB() { ... }
}
```

```typescript
function foo(obj: Foo) {
  obj.foo();
}
class A implements Foo {
  foo() {
    this.methodA();
  }
  methodA() { ... }
}
class B implements Foo {
  foo() {
    this.methodB();
  }
  methodB() { ... }
}
interface Foo {
  foo(): void;
}
```

New interface

Pushed method

If we don't control the source of A and B, we need to push the type inspection to the edge of our code to ensure that the core of our codebase is pristine. The same advice is described in the rule NEVER USE **if** WITH **else**.

Summary

- Code mirrors behavior from the people involved in its development, the processes, and the underlying domain.
- Control-flow-encoded behavior is conducive to making big changes easily.
- Data-structure-encoded behavior offers advantages such as type safety, locality, performance, and ease of making small changes.
- Data-encoded behavior can be used as a last resort and should be limited, as it is difficult to maintain safely due to a lack of compiler support.
- Refactoring either manages duplication within one of these approaches or moves structures from one approach to another.
- Use code to expose structure so it becomes malleable through refactoring, thus adding more structure.
- Use empirical techniques to guide the refactoring effort and avoid basing it on an ever-shifting foundation.
- Look for unexploited structures that are usually the result of risk aversion. These are most commonly visible through whitespace, duplication, common affixes, or inspection of the runtime type.

Avoid optimizations and generality

This chapter covers
- Minimizing generality to reduce coupling
- Thinking of optimization in terms of invariants
- Managing the fragility from optimizations

Performance optimization and generality are two games programmers play that often hurt more than they help. When we say *optimization* in this chapter, we mean *performance optimization*, which involves increasing the throughput of code or reducing its duration. By *generality*, we mean the code encompasses more functionality, usually through more general parameters. To illustrate what we mean by generality and how it can be harmful, consider the following example.

If someone asks you for a knife, handing them a Swiss Army knife might be a godsend if the recipient is in a survival situation. However, imagine if the recipient is a chef in a professional kitchen; a paring knife might be more welcome. In this parable, as in code, the design accommodating the generality may be more burdensome than the generality is helpful. When it comes to generality, the context is everything.

In this chapter, we begin by exploring how these practices are often harmful. We then take a deep dive into generality and optimization, discussing when to do each and when not to.

In the generality section, 12.2, after discussing how to motivate generality, we focus on how to avoid adding unnecessary generality. Generality can creep in when we add unrequested features to our software. It can also be the result of unifying old code with newer code before it is ready. Both these kinds of generality are challenging to get rid of, so we discuss how to keep them out in the first place. As generality seeps into even the most diligent codebases, we conclude this section by explaining how to seek out and discharge unnecessary generality.

In the optimization section, 12.3, we start again by discussing when we should avoid it and when not. Then we look at preparatory steps to perform before implementing any optimization. First, we ensure that the code is well refactored. Then we make sure our thread scheduling is not wasteful and seek out the bottleneck in the system. Once the bottleneck is found, we use profiling to identify potential candidate methods for optimization. Next, we examine the safest methods to optimize them, such as choosing suitable data structures and algorithms or utilizing caching. Finally, we argue for the importance of isolating any required performance tuning.

12.1 Striving for simplicity

The underlying theme for everything in this chapter, and indeed the entire book, is that we should strive for simplicity. Keeping this as a focus is so essential that it is one of the ideals of software development in Gene Kim's business fable *The Unicorn Project* (IT Revolution Press, 2019). Simplicity is essential because humans have limited cognitive capacity; we can only hold so much information in our heads at one time. Two things quickly fill up our cognitive capacity when working with code: coupled components, because we need to keep both in our head at once; and invariants, which we need to keep track of to understand their functionality. These culprits are often linked to two different common programming exercises. When we make something more general, we increase its possible uses; thus, more things can be coupled to it. When working with generalized code, we have to consider more possible ways it can be called.

In chapter 4, we experienced firsthand the problem with generality. When looking at the following function, it is impossible to determine whether it is called with all possible values for `Tile` or just some of them. Without knowing this, it is impossible to simplify the function.

Listing 12.1 Unnecessarily general function

```
function remove(tile: Tile) {
  for (let y = 0; y < map.length; y++) {
    for (let x = 0; x < map[y].length; x++) {
      if (map[y][x] === tile) {
        map[y][x] = new Air();
      }
    }
  }
}
```

The other culprit activity is optimization, which relies on exploiting invariants; we must keep these in mind whenever we work with this code. It is a fun game and healthy exercise to look for invariants when we work with algorithms or data structures. Let me show you an example: it is easy to see that an invariant of binary search is that the data structure is sorted, but it's easier to miss the invariant that we can efficiently access elements out of order.

We saw an example of how optimizations introduce invariants in chapter 7 when we briefly discussed an implementation of a counting set. This set keeps track of the count of each element. To uniformly select a random element out of this data structure, we generate a random integer smaller than the total number of elements.

Listing 12.2   Unoptimized counting set

```
class CountingSet {
  private data: StringMap<number> = { };

  randomElement(): string {
    let index = randomInt(this.size());
    for (let key in this.data.keys()) {
      index -= this.data[key];
      if (index <= 0)
        return key;
    }
    throw new Impossible();
  }
  add(element: string) {
    let c = this.data.get(element);
    if (c === undefined)
      c = 0;
    this.data.put(element, c + 1);
  }
  size() {
    let total = 0;
    for (let key in this.data.keys()) {
      total += this.data[key];
    }
    return total;
  }
}
```

Listing 12.3   Optimized counting set

```
class CountingSet {
  private data: StringMap<number> = { };
  private total = 0;                          ◁─┐
  randomElement(): string {
    let index = randomInt(this.size());
    for (let key in this.data.keys()) {
      index -= this.data[key];
      if (index <= 0)
        return key;
    }
    throw new Impossible();
  }
  add(element: string) {
    let c = this.data.get(element);
    if (c === undefined)
      c = 0;
    this.data.put(element, c + 1);
    this.total++;                            ◁──┤
  }
  size() {
    return this.total;            ◁───────────┘
  }
}
```

Field to avoid recalculation

Calculating the total number of elements is straightforward, but having to redo this over and over feels wasteful. We can optimize away this waste by introducing a field `total` to keep track of the total number of elements. With this field comes the invariant that we always update it when we add or remove elements. Otherwise, we risk breaking our `randomElement` method. On the other hand, in the unoptimized version, it is impossible to break the existing methods by adding a new method.

Our quest for simplicity doesn't mean we can never optimize or generalize our code, as expert mathematicians can attest: sometimes we *need* a more general lemma to prove our theorem. But it does mean we should always have hard evidence as to *why* we need this generality or optimization. And when we do sacrifice simplicity, we should take precautions to minimize the adverse effects. In the remainder of this chapter, we dive deep into the details.

12.2　When and how to generalize

Before adding generality to our methods or classes, we should understand our motivation for doing so. Luckily, the most straightforward motivation for generality in some cases comes for free if we use the process recommended in this book of first duplicating, then transforming, and finally unifying. The unification step automatically gives us the exact level of generality necessary for the current functionality. Doing this sounds entirely trivial, but a few pitfalls can cause even this method to fail. In the remainder of this chapter, we discuss how to reduce generality and keep it minimized.

12.2.1　Building minimally to avoid generality

The three-step method of duplicate, transform, and unify only guarantees minimal generality if the functionality is minimal. If we build in more features or more general features than necessary, no method can save us. The only way to combat this is through a constant commitment to building minimally.

> *Maximize the amount of work not done.*
>
> —Kent Beck

"Build minimally" is not new advice; it has been said thousands of times in thousands of ways. My favorite iteration is this version from Kent Beck. It is probably the most difficult piece of advice to follow in this chapter, but it is crucial, so it bears repeating.

To build minimally requires first understanding the context—the scope of the behavior we want to implement. Wherever there are holes in our understanding, our brains tend to assume we need to cover everything. We are inclined to think that giving our users or customers a function that solves more things is a gift.

Designing the code to accommodate the generality can be more burdensome than the generality is helpful, as the "Swiss Army knife to a chef" example illustrated. Another reason to build exclusively what is ordered is that requirements tend to change as software evolves, so any effort spent implementing and maintaining unnecessary generality is easily invalidated. Therefore, we should only solve the problem we have, not the problem we can imagine.

A story from real life

I recently worked on a system to calculate and track Ping Pong players' ratings, similar to a chess rating. After finishing the initial design and functionality, I realized that I could use the data to generate the teams that would likely play the most exciting matches. Confident that this was a feature users would use all the time, I implemented it. But as one might have expected, they already had methods to determine matchups, so they did not need the new feature—it was used only a handful of times, and only out of curiosity.

12.2.2 Unifying things of similar stability

In the situation I just described, I could reverse most of the mistakes by exercising my love for deleting code. However, to accommodate the additional functionality, I had to generalize some of the support functions and backend code. This generality is much harder to get rid of, but since it inflates the cognitive price, I had to work it out.

To avoid this problem, we should be careful when unifying things. As a rule of thumb, it is best not to immediately unify something new with something old. Instead, wait until the subjects have reached similar stability. They do not need to have been around for an equal amount of time. Usually, the second instance of something stabilizes much faster, and the third faster still.

12.2.3 Eliminating unnecessary generality

Our final defense against unnecessary generality is to monitor for it regularly and remove it when we spot it. We have seen two refactoring patterns specifically for eliminating unwanted generality: Specialize method and Try delete then compile. When these were introduced, we had found the need for them after lots of refactoring. In practice, Try delete then compile likely does not find all the generality we can remove.

A more fruitful way to look for unnecessary generality is to monitor the runtime arguments passed to functions. It is easy to add some code to log the parameters, as long as our objects are reasonably serializable. We can then inspect the latest N calls of each method and see if some parameter is always called with the same value, in which case we can Specialize method according to this parameter. Even if it is called with a few different values, it may still be worth making a specialized copy of the function for each.

12.3 When and how to optimize

Another common source of high cognitive load is optimization. As with generality, before we do anything, we should motivate its necessity. Unlike generality, there is no simple process that automatically motivates it. Luckily we have another tool at our disposal: to motivate optimization, I always recommend setting up automatic performance tests and only looking for optimizations when the tests fail. The most common types of such tests are as follows:

- "This method should terminate in 14 ms." This type is called a *benchmark test*; it is common in embedded or real-time systems where we have to provide an answer at a specific deadline or interval. Although simple to write, such tests are tightly coupled to the environment; if we have a garbage collector or virus scanner, it might affect the absolute performance and give us a false negative. Therefore, we can only run benchmark tests reliably in production-like environments.
- "This service should be able to handle 1000 requests per second." In *load tests*, we validate our throughput; these are common in web- or cloud-based systems. Compared to benchmark tests, load tests are much more resilient to external factors, but we may still need production-like hardware.
- "Running this test may not be more than 10% slower than the last run." Finally, a *performance approval test* ensures that our performance does not degrade suddenly. These tests are entirely decoupled from external factors, as long as they are consistent between runs. Yet they can still detect if someone adds something too slow to our main loop or accidentally switches one data structure to another, resulting in increased cache misses.

To paraphrase the legal world, code is efficient until proven otherwise. Once our tests have proven that we need to optimize, we must know how to keep the cognitive strain of future maintenance minimal.

12.3.1 *Refactoring before optimizing*

The first step is to make sure the code is adequately refactored. One of the goals of refactoring is to localize invariants, making them clearer. Since optimization relies on invariants, this means it is easier to optimized well-factored code.

In chapter 3, when we introduced the rule EITHER CALL OR PASS (R3.1.1), we saw this refactoring as we extracted `length` into a separate function to avoid breaking the rule.

Listing 12.4   Before

```
function average(arr: number[]) {
  return sum(arr) / arr.length;
}
```

Listing 12.5   After

```
function average(arr: number[]) {
  return sum(arr) / size(arr);
}
```

This refactoring might have seemed like overkill or artificial at the time. However, knowing as we do now that a future step is to encapsulate the methods in a class, we see that these methods define a very nice, minimal public interface for our new data structure. This interface makes it easy to implement the optimizations described later. Adding internal caching is as simple as adding a field in the new class. Alternatively if we want to change the data structure, we can EXTRACT INTERFACE FROM IMPLEMENTATION

(P5.4.4) and then make a new class implementing this interface, which uses the desired data structure.

Listing 12.6   Encapsulated

```
class NumberSequence {
  constructor(private arr: number[]) { }
  sum() {
    let result = 0;
    for(let i = 0; i < this.arr.length; i++)
      result += this.arr[i];
    return result;
  }
  size() { return this.arr.length; }
  average() {
    return this.sum() / this.size();
  }
}
```

Listing 12.7   Cache total

```
class NumberSequence {
  private total = 0;
  constructor(private arr: number[]) {
    for(let i = 0; i < this.arr.length; i++)
      this.total += this.arr[i];
  }
  sum() { return this.total; }
  size() { return this.arr.length; }
  average() {
    return this.sum() / this.size();
  }
}
```

LET THE COMPILER HANDLE IT

Another reason for making the code nice is that compilers continuously work to generate better code. Compiler developers usually decide what to optimize by studying common idioms and usage and focusing on the most common situations. Therefore, in trying to be smart, we accidentally make our code run more slowly merely because the compiler can no longer recognize what we are trying to do. This also echoes the message of chapter 7: work with the compiler, not against it.

In the example from chapter 1, we saw that a good compiler can automatically eliminate the repeated subexpression pow(base, exp / 2) after determining that there are no side effects. Thus both programs should result in the same performance.

Listing 12.8   Unoptimized

```
return pow(base, exp / 2) * pow(base, exp / 2);
```

Listing 12.9   Optimized

```
let result = pow(base, exp / 2);
return result * result;
```

Compiler improvements should mean our code automatically gets faster over time if we write good idiomatic code. This is a good argument for postponing optimization for as long as possible. Working against us is our human desire to seem smart by showing off how we can manage complicated code or demonstrate our creativity through unusual patterns and solutions. I do this myself when I feel intellectually insecure, but never in shared codebases! My favorite way to show off is to replace two common operations with unusual, faster-looking, low-level operations.

Listing 12.10   Idiomatic

```
function isEven(n: number) {
  return n % 2 === 0;
}
```

Listing 12.11   Showing off

```
function isEven(n: number) {
  return (n & 1) === 0;
}
```

Listing 12.12   Idiomatic

```
function half(n: number) {
  return n / 2;
}
```

Listing 12.13   Showing off

```
function half(n: number) {
  return n >> 1;
}
```

The code in listings 12.11 and 12.13 looks much cooler, but the expressions in listings 12.10 and 12.12 are so common that all mainstream compilers automatically optimize them. Therefore the only effect of the "showing off" code is that it is harder to read.

12.3.2 Optimizing according to the theory of constraints

After we have refactored our code, if the tests are still not satisfied, we need to optimize. If we are working in a concurrent system, whether through collaborating threads, processes, or services, we are subject to the *theory of constraints*. In his masterpiece novel *The Goal* (North River Press, 1984), Eliyahu Goldratt illustrates how striving to reduce local inefficiencies rarely affects global efficiency.

To illustrate the theory of constraint, I like to use a metaphor from the real world illustrated in figure 12.1. The system is traffic, where *tasks* are vehicles that need to get from left to right. On the way from left to right, tasks pass through *workstations*, which are like traffic light intersections. Each intersection lets vehicles through at a different rate, which may vary. Between the intersections is a stretch of road where vehicles queue: in the theory of constraint, this stretch is called a *buffer*. If an intersection's right buffer is almost empty while its left buffer is almost full, we call it a *bottleneck*.

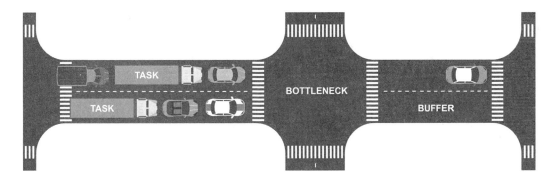

Figure 12.1   Illustration of a system

Whether we look at vehicles, a piece of metal to be shaped, or a piece of data, the theory of constraint works for any system consisting of sequentially linked workstations. As developers, the system is the application, and workstations are the concurrent workers; each worker does some work and passes its result to another worker through a buffer.

In the stream from input to output, there is at any given time precisely one bottleneck worker. Optimizing a worker upstream of the bottleneck only causes a buffer to build up at the bottleneck entrance. Optimizing a worker downstream of the bottleneck does not affect overall performance because the downstream worker cannot get input fast enough. Only optimizations in the bottleneck worker have any effect on system performance.

Optimizing the bottleneck creates a new bottleneck. Maybe a worker downstream cannot keep up with the increased throughput from the previous bottleneck, or maybe an upstream worker cannot produce output fast enough to satisfy the previous bottleneck.

Luckily, in software, we have an exquisite solution for this situation called *resource pooling*. Resource pooling means we put all our available processing resources in a common pool where whoever needs them can use them. Thus the maximum possible capacity is given to the bottleneck. We can implement this approach externally at the service level through load balancers or internally in our application through thread pooling.

Regardless of whether resource pooling is internal or external, the performance effect is the same, so let's briefly examine an internal example. Remember, TypeScript does not have threads, so this is pseudo-code leaning toward Java. In the example, we have a two-stage system where stage B takes twice as long as A; as we know, the order does not matter. To communicate between threads, we use blocking queues, and our workers are threads that never terminate. In the naive implementation, we have one worker per stage; notice the two infinite loops. When we introduce resource pooling, we move the infinite loop out of the stages, thereby making them tasks.

Listing 12.14 Naive threading

```
interface Runnable { run(): void; }
class A implements Runnable {
  // ...
  run() {
    while (true) {
      let result = this.input.dequeue();
      Thread.sleep(1000);
      this.output.enqueue(result);
    }
  }
}
class B implements Runnable {
  // ...
  run() {
    while (true) {
      let result = this.input.dequeue();
      Thread.sleep(2000);
      this.output.enqueue(result);
    }
  }
}
```

Listing 12.15 Resource pooling

```
interface Runnable { run(): void; }
interface Task { execute(): void; }
class A implements Task {
  // ...
  execute() {
    let result = this.input.dequeue();
    Thread.sleep(1000);
    this.output.enqueue(result);       New task
  }                                     abstraction
}
class B implements Task {
  // ...
  execute() {
    let result = this.input.dequeue();
    Thread.sleep(2000);
    this.output.enqueue(result);
  }
}
class Worker implements Runnable {      Runnable
  run() {                               worker
    while (true) {
```

```
let enter = new Queue();              let task = this.tasks.dequeue();
let between = new Queue();            task.run();
let exit = new Queue();          }
let a = new A(enter, between);     }
let b = new B(between, exit);    }
let aThread = new Thread(a);     let enter = new Queue();
let bThread = new Thread(b);     let between = new Queue();
aThread.start();                let exit = new Queue();
bThread.start();                let tasks = new Queue();
                                enter.onEnqueue(element => tasks.enqueue(
                                  new A(enter, between)));
            Task                between.onEnqueue(element =>
         scheduling            tasks.enqueue(
                                  new B(between, exit)));
                                let pool = [
                                  new Thread(new Worker()),
                                  new Thread(new Worker())];      Thread
                                pool.forEach(t => t.start());     pooling
```

As we can see, the code structures are virtually identical. The setup becomes a tiny bit more complicated because we have to create a task every time some work is ready. But the solution with resource pooling has significantly higher throughput. Processing 100 requests with the program in listing 12.14 takes about 201 seconds, whereas listing 12.15 can do it in 150 seconds.

Most important, even with a trivial implementation of resource pooling, we do not have to think about the thread choreography; the system automatically takes care of it. We can even change the threading behavior later without affecting the stages. By merely changing tasks to a priority queue, we can get any order we want. In this case, it is easy to see that optimally we have two B threads for each A, but in practice, we have tens or hundreds of small stages and fluctuating runtime. The price is that we have to maintain the resource pooling code or software; this increases the system's cognitive cost. But, significantly, we have not increased the cognitive cost of the domain code in the stages.

12.3.3 Guiding optimization with metrics

After optimizing the system with resource pooling, we have to optimize inside the bottleneck if we still don't satisfy the performance requirement. We are in a single-threaded situation; we have to make one thread complete its task faster. However, we cannot hope to optimize everything; apart from it being a huge undertaking, we would make our codebase impossible to work with. Instead, we need to focus our efforts on the parts of the code that will have the most significant impact.

To do this, we need to identify hot spots in our code. *Hot spots* are the methods where our thread spends most of its time. Two factors contribute to a method becoming a hot spot: the method taking time to complete, and the method being inside a loop. The only reliable way to discover hot spots is through profiling. *Profiling* means tracking how much accumulated time is spent in a method. Myriad tools exists to assist with profiling. Alternatively, it is easy to manually add timing code starting at the top level and then iteratively drill down into the 20% of the code that is taking 80% of the time.

That the famous 80:20 relationship applies to code also supports my mantra that optimizing should not be part of developers' daily work because optimization comes at the price of a more valuable resource: team productivity. The only exception is developers whose daily work is in a hot spot, like performance specialists or people working with embedded or real-time systems.

There is another reason for using a profiler whenever we think of performance. Many programmers are familiar with basic algorithmics, including asymptotic analysis (usually, big O notation). While being acquainted with such concepts can be very beneficial, it is essential to realize that the asymptotic growth rate is simplified. Therefore, switching to an algorithm or data structure with a better asymptotic growth rate may, in practice, degrade performance due to the same factors that analysis is designed to abstract away, such as cache misses. We can only expose these effects through measurement. Evidence of this is that most library sort functions use the $O(n^2)$ insertion sort for small data in favor of the asymptotically superior quick sort that runs in $O(n \cdot \lg(n))$.

12.3.4 *Choosing good algorithms and data structures*

Having identified the hot spot in the bottleneck component, we can start considering ways to optimize it. The safest way to optimize is to exchange one data structure for another that has an equivalent interface. This optimization is safe because our domain code does not have to change to adapt to the new data structure. In this case, the invariant we introduce is on the usage, meaning the risk is degrading performance if the invariant is broken.

Our performance tests immediately catch the degraded performance, and switching the data structure or algorithm at such a time is easy. Therefore, I generally don't mind baking in such invariants. I do recommend that developers consider behavior when choosing between existing data structures or algorithms. If we implement them ourselves, we should still prefer ease of implementation unless we are in a hot spot.

We can sometimes benefit from locally switching our data structure. This is common practice if we are using data inside a hot spot but we have the data available outside the hot spot. For example, imagine we have some data and need to extract the elements in order in a hot spot. We can do this by repeatedly extracting the minimum element, which is a linear time operation $O(n)$. But if we have the data outside the hot spot, we can put it into a data structure like a minimum heap, from which we can extract it in logarithmic time $O(\lg(n))$. Or even better, if we can sort the data before entering the hot spot, we can extract the minimum element in constant time $O(1)$.

As mentioned, this is commonplace and, indeed, is the motivation for data structures over algorithms. However, we can take this idea further. We may use the data differently at different places in the code: for example, our behavioral invariants are not consistent throughout the code. Here we can locally switch the data structure to suit the specific use. This idea sounds obvious, but in my experience, it is an underused technique.

As an example, imagine that we have implemented a linked list data structure. We want it to have a sort method. We can implement sorting by directly manipulating the linked list. Due to the cache's behavior, it is more efficient to convert the list to an array, sort that, and convert it back into a linked list.

Listing 12.16 Sorting a linked list

```
interface Node<T> { element: T, next: Node<T> }
class LinkedList<T> {
  private root: Node<T> | null;
  // ...
  sort() {
    let arr = this.toArray();
    Array.sort(arr);
    let list = new LinkedList<T>(arr);
    this.root = list.root;
  }
}
```

NOTE Remember that we can access the other object's `list.root` because **private** means class-private, not object-private.

This method is very efficient, and we only had to write code for converting to and from arrays, which we likely needed anyway. Additionally, if we want our linked list data structure to be immutable, we can just change the last line to a **return** instead of an assignment.

12.3.5 *Using caching*

Another optimization that we can often make safely is caching. The idea of caching is simple: instead of doing a calculation multiple times, do it once, store the result, and reuse that instead. Chapter 5 included an example of a caching class that can wrap any function to separate side effects from the return value. An invariant common to all caching is that we call a function with the same arguments multiple times.

Listing 12.17 Cache to separate side effects from the return value

```
class Cacher<T> {
  private data: T;
  constructor(private mutator: () => T) {
    this.data = this.mutator();
  }
  get() {
    return this.data;
  }
  next() {
    this.data = this.mutator();
```

```
  }
}
```

Caching is safest when combined with an idempotence invariant; that is, calling it with the same arguments always gives the same result. In such cases, we can do the caching externally. Here is an example of such a cache. It takes only one argument, for simplicity, but it can be extended to work for multi-argument functions. The only requirement is that the arguments have a `hashCode` method, which is free in many languages.

Listing 12.18   Cache for idempotent functions

```
interface Cacheable { hashCode(): string; }
class Cacher<G extends Cacheable, T> {
  private data: { [key: string]: T } = { };
  constructor(private func: (arg: G) => T) { }
  call(arg: G) {
    let hashCode = arg.hashCode();
    if (this.data[hashCode] === undefined) {
      this.data[hashCode] = this.func(arg);
    }
    return this.data[hashCode];
  }
}
```

Caching is slightly less safe when our function is only temporarily idempotent. Temporary idempotency is common for mutable data: for example, the price of a product likely does not change with every call. This invariant is more fragile because the price may change while cached, resulting in an incorrect cached value. The typical implementation is to add an expiry time to the external cache from above. Notice that this invariant is more fragile because it is more likely that the duration will change than that a fundamental property like idempotency will break.

Listing 12.19   Cache for temporarily idempotent functions

```
interface Cacheable { hashCode(): string; }
class Cacher<G extends Cacheable, T> {
  private data: { [key: string]: { result: T, expiry: number }} = { };
  constructor(private func: (arg: G) => T,
              private duration: number) { }
  call(arg: G) {
    let hashCode = arg.hashCode();
    if (this.data[hashCode] === undefined
      || this.data[hashCode].expiry < Date.now()) {
      this.data[hashCode] = {
        result: this.func(arg),
        expiry: Date.now() + this.duration
      };
    }
    return this.data[hashCode].result;
  }
}
```

Even without idempotency, we can still do caching; however, then it needs to be internal. An example is the `total` field in listing 12.7. As we have discussed, this is the most dangerous because we need to maintain it throughout the class for its entire lifetime.

12.3.6 *Isolating optimized code*

There are rare cases where algorithms, concurrency, and caching are insufficient to satisfy our performance tests. In such cases we turn to performance *tuning*, sometimes called *micro-optimizations*. Here we look for small invariants in the interplay between the runtime and the desired behavior.

An example of tuning is using *magic bit patterns*. These are magic numbers but are usually written in base 16, making them even more challenging to read. Magic bit patterns often satisfy some subtle nuance of the algorithm used: we have to either understand it, at a high cognitive cost, or leave the code alone. To illustrate this point, consider the following C function to calculate the inverse square root from the codebase of the video game Quake III Arena, including original comments. Would you feel comfortable making a change in this function?

> **Listing 12.20 Inverse square root function with a magic bit pattern**

```
float Q_rsqrt( float number )
{
  long i;
  float x2, y;
  const float threehalfs = 1.5F;

  x2 = number * 0.5F;
  y  = number;
  i  = * ( long * ) &y;              // evil floating point bit level hacking
  i  = 0x5f3759df - ( i >> 1 );   // what the fuck?                  ◁─┐ Magic bit
  y  = * ( float * ) &i;                                              │ pattern
  y  = y * ( threehalfs - ( x2 * y * y ) );  // 1st iteration
//y  = y * ( threehalfs - ( x2 * y * y ) );  // 2nd iteration, can be removed
  return y;
}
```

USING METHODS AND CLASSES TO MINIMIZE THE LOCKED AREA

We cannot make any significant changes to a tuned function without understanding it, which is usually tricky (i.e., cognitively expensive). Therefore, the code is essentially locked. Knowing this, we should isolate the tuned code, minimizing how much has to be locked for the tuning to be effective. When the tuning includes data, we have to use a class to isolate it; otherwise, we can extract it to a separate method.

My usual position regarding naming is that we can always improve it later, once we understand the code better. But in the case of tuned code, it is unlikely that anyone will ever have a better understanding than we do when we extract it. So, we should spend some effort to make sure this method or class is well named, well documented, and thoroughly quality controlled. If we do this well, no one will be tempted to look up the source.

USING PACKAGES TO WARN FUTURE DEVELOPERS

We can also benefit from communicating to future developers that this code is tuned and therefore they probably should not drill into it. As we have just isolated it into methods and classes, we need the next level of abstraction: packages or namespaces. As I have said before, different languages have different mechanisms, but the idea in this section works with any of them.

I recommend having a dedicated package for tuned code. This is because when we import and use it, the package becomes invisible. It becomes apparent at the shallowest inspection because it is the first line in the containing file and displayed in most intelligent code completion. The best warning signs only reveal themselves when needed so as not to distract during everyday use.

If you need an inspiration to name such a package, I like to call it `magic`. The famous saying, "Sufficiently advanced technology is indistinguishable from magic," expresses my feelings toward performance tuning. It is also a nice play on the fact that a lot of tuning relies on magic constants, such as the earlier magic bit pattern.

Apart from signaling that this code is difficult to read, putting all the tuned code together also indicates a different quality requirement in this region. Under no circumstances should this package become a trash heap of code no one understands. Instead, it should be an altar for code that a few developers understand exceptionally well, at least at the time of conception. This is useful for users because they know bugs are less likely in this region; but it also affects the author, who must satisfy a higher quality requirement or violate the sanctity of the region. No one wants to be the person to break a streak. We discuss this phenomenon further in the next chapter.

Summary

- Simplicity is about reducing the cognitive load that the code requires.
- Generality increases the risk of coupling.
- By introducing generality through unification combined with building minimally, we avoid introducing unnecessary generality.
- Combining only code of similar stability, we reduce the risk of having to remove generality.
- To discover unnecessary generality or locate candidates for optimization, we use monitoring and profiling.
- All optimization should be motivated by a specification, which in practice is generally some form of performance tests. We should avoid optimizing in our daily work.
- Refactoring localizes invariants. Optimization relies on invariants; so, refactor before optimizing.
- Resource pooling can optimize without increasing the fragility of the domain code.

- Choosing between existing algorithms and data structures is a worthwhile optimization.
- Caching can be a cheap and safe optimization that introduces few invariants.
- When we use performance tuning, we should isolate it to deter people from wasting time trying to understand it.

Make bad code look bad

13

This chapter covers

- Understanding the reasons to separate good and bad code
- Understanding the types of bad code
- Understanding the rules to make code worse safely
- Applying the rules to make bad code worse

At the end of the last chapter, we discussed the advantage of clarifying the quality expectation for code at a glance. In the context of optimization, we did so by putting the code in an isolated namespace or package. In this chapter, we study how to make the quality level clear by making bad code look bad at a glance, a process we will call *anti-refactoring*.

We begin by discussing why anti-refactoring is useful, first from a process perspective and then from a maintenance perspective. Having established the motivation, we look for bad code traits through a brief introduction to some of the most common quality metrics. The last preliminary before beginning to anti-refactor is to establish ground rules that ensure we are not permanently damaging the code's structure but only modifying how it presents itself. Rules in hand, we conclude this chapter with a string of safe, practical methods to make code stand out. This practical section also demonstrates how to use the rules to develop techniques suited to your team.

13.1   *Signaling process issues with bad code*

Sometimes we read or write code that we know is not as good as it should be. However, due to constraints such as the complexity of the code, the problem, or most often simply not having time, we cannot refactor it to the level it should be. In these situations, we sometimes do a little refactoring "just so it is not horrible." We do this because we are proud and don't want to deliver something of poor quality. Regardless, doing so is a mistake. It is better to deliver a horrible mess than to sweep the problems under the proverbial rug in this situation.

Leaving bad code has two advantages: it is easy to find again, and it signals that the constraints are not sustainable. Delivering bad code to signal an issue requires significant psychological safety: we need to trust that we, as the messenger, will not be shot. However, not having such safety is likely a more significant issue than our code's quality. In Project Aristotle, Google and re:Work showed psychological safety to be the most significant productivity factor. As a former tech lead, I followed the mantra "Knowing is always better," meaning messengers were always appreciated. Indeed, I wanted to know if we were not going at a sustainable pace and quality was slipping. As I was busy too, medium-quality code might slip by without me noticing, but code that is obviously bad would not. Consider these two examples with the same functionality; which code needs refactoring the most?

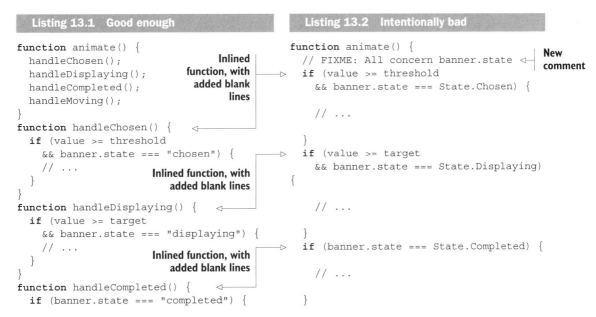

Listing 13.1   Good enough

```
function animate() {
  handleChosen();                          Inlined
  handleDisplaying();              function, with
  handleCompleted();                  added blank
  handleMoving();                           lines
}
function handleChosen() {
  if (value >= threshold
    && banner.state === "chosen") {
    // ...            Inlined function, with
  }                   added blank lines
}
function handleDisplaying() {
  if (value >= target
    && banner.state === "displaying") {
    // ...
  }                   Inlined function, with
}                     added blank lines
function handleCompleted() {
  if (banner.state === "completed") {
```

Listing 13.2   Intentionally bad

```
function animate() {
  // FIXME: All concern banner.state    New
  if (value >= threshold                comment
    && banner.state === State.Chosen) {

    // ...

  }
  if (value >= target
    && banner.state === State.Displaying)
  {

    // ...

  }
  if (banner.state === State.Completed) {

    // ...

  }
```

```
    // ...                                            if (banner.state === State.Moving
  }                  Inlined function, with              && banner.target === banner.current)
}                    added blank lines              {
function handleMoving() {
  if (banner.state === "moving"
    && banner.target === banner.current)              // ...
{
    // ...                                           }                              New
  }                                               }                                enum
}                                                 enum State {
                                                    Chosen, Displaying, Completed, Moving

                                                  }
```

The answer is both. While the methods are small in listing 13.1, they are extracted poorly, hiding the fact that banner.state is repeated. Therefore, it is pretty difficult to see that this method should be pushed into a State class, an exercise journey that I leave to the zealous reader.

13.2   Segregating into pristine and legacy code

The worse code is, the easier it is to spot. Being easy to spot is important since developers are often expending most of their focus trying to solve a problem. If something is not discernible at a glance, we will most likely miss it; whereas if code is obviously bad, we are constantly reminded, making it much more likely that someone will fix it when there is time. I like to say, "If you cannot make it good, make it stand out."

I am not saying that all code should be perfect, but if we think of code as quite good, good enough, or bad, I would rather have bad code than good-enough code. If we don't have the time or skills to raise code past the "quite good" bar, we should instead make it bad. This activity segregates our code into pristine code and legacy code.

Once we can spot at a glance whether code is pristine or legacy, it is easy to estimate a file's ratio between good and bad code—information we can use to guide our refactoring efforts. Specifically, I like to start with the files that are closest to being thoroughly pristine. I do this for two reasons. First, refactoring is often a cascading activity, meaning that to make some code good, we need to make the code around it good, too. When the surrounding code is good already, there is a lower risk of hitting refactoring rabbit holes. The other reason is called the *broken window theory*.

13.2.1   *The broken window theory*

According to the broken window theory, if one window is left broken, soon more will follow. While the broken window theory is disputed, if not disproven entirely, I still think it has merit at the very least as a metaphor. Intuitively, the theory makes sense: while I'm wearing new shoes, I am careful not to mess them up; but as soon as they get dirty, I stop being careful, and the state of my shoes deteriorates quickly. This effect also happens when we are developing code. As soon as we see some bad code, it is much easier to put more bad code next to it. But if we make entire files pristine, they usually stay pristine longer.

13.3 Approaches to defining bad code

Before we discuss how we can make code worse, let's first survey a few different methods for identifying bad code. As we discussed in the introduction, there is no perfect way to determine whether code is good or not by looking at it. Because readability is part of good code, and readability is subjective. However, there are a few different methods that estimate how bad code is. Let's examine the most prevalent of these to find eye-catching traits.

13.3.1 The rules in this book: Simple and concrete

Getting a sense of what bad code is was the topic of part 1 of this book. To develop this sense, we introduced easy-to-spot rules. These rules are designed to be eye-catching even when our concentration is elsewhere and without much practice.

While these rules are powerful while we are developing our sixth sense, they are not universal. Programmers who have not read this book likely won't consider passing something as a parameter and calling a method on the same object eye-catching and may not even consider it bad. If our team has a shared set of rules like the ones in this book, it is usually easy to do the opposite when we want to make code stand out.

This example breaks two rules. Can you spot which ones?

Listing 13.3 Two broken rules

```
function minimum(arr: number[][]) {
  let result = 99999;
  for (let x = 0; x < arr.length; x++) {
    for (let y = 0; y < arr[x].length; y++) {
      if (arr[x][y] < result)
        result = arr[x][y];
    }
  }
  return result;
}
```

Answer: FIVE LINES (R3.1.1) and **if** ONLY AT THE START (R3.5.1).

13.3.2 Code smells: Complete and abstract

My rules did not come out of nothing; they were distilled from code smells collected from multiple sources like Martin Fowler's *Refactoring* and Robert C. Martin's *Clean Code*. Using code smells is another approach to define symptoms that bad code exhibit. In my experience, most code smells only become eye-catching once we have practiced quite a bit. Some are simple enough to be taught in introductory programming courses and are therefore generally eye-catching to anyone, such as "Magic constants" and "Duplicated code."

Listing 13.4 Example code smell

```
function minimum(arr: number[][]) {
  let result = 99999;                                        Magic
  for (let x = 0; x < arr.length; x++) {                     number
    for (let y = 0; y < arr[x].length; y++) {
      if (arr[x][y] < result)
        result = arr[x][y];
    }
  }
  return result;
}
```

13.3.3 *Cyclomatic complexity: Algorithmic (objective)*

While the two previous methods were intended for humans, there have also been attempts to make computers spot bad code. Again, these are approximations; but because they are calculated, they give a value that a human can use to guide the decision to refactor. The most famous automatic code quality metric is probably *cyclomatic complexity.*

In a nutshell, cyclomatic complexity counts the number of paths through the code. We can count this on the statement level, where **if** has two paths: one where it is true and one where it is false. The same is true for **for** and **while** because we can either enter them or skip them. We can also count on the expression level, where each || or && splits the path in two: one path skips the right side, and one doesn't. Interestingly, this metric also gives us a lower bound for how many tests we should have since we should have at least one for each path through the code.

Listing 13.5 Cyclomatic complexity: 4

```
function minimum(arr: number[][]) {                +1
  let result = 99999;
  for (let x = 0; x < arr.length; x++) {           +1
    for (let y = 0; y < arr[x].length; y++) {      +1
      if (arr[x][y] < result)                      +1
        result = arr[x][y];
    }
  }
  return result;
}                                                  =4
```

Cyclomatic complexity is calculated on the control flow of a method. However, this is not always obvious to humans, especially on the expression level. When humans estimate cyclomatic complexity at a glance, we usually rely on the indentation, since we indent once per **if**, **for**, etc.

13.3.4 *Cognitive complexity: Algorithmic (subjective)*

A much more recent calculated code quality metric is called *cognitive complexity*. As the name suggests, it estimates how much information a human must keep in their head while reading this method. It punishes nesting more severely than cyclomatic complexity since humans need to remember each condition we pass through. Cognitive complexity is likely a closer estimate of how difficult it is for humans to read something. However, in our search for things humans can spot at a glance, this again amounts to indentation.

Listing 13.6 Cognitive complexity: 6

```
function minimum(arr: number[][]) {
  let result = 99999;
  for (let x = 0; x < arr.length; x++) {        +1
    for (let y = 0; y < arr[x].length; y++) {   +2
      if (arr[x][y] < result)                   +3
        result = arr[x][y];
    }
  }
  return result;
}                                                =6
```

13.4 *Rules for safely vandalizing code*

We need to follow three rules when we vandalize code (i.e., make bad code stand out):

1 Never destroy correct information.

2 Do not make future refactoring harder.

3 The result should be eye-catching.

The first and most important rule is that we have to preserve whatever information is already there if it is correct. For example, if a method has a good name but its body is messy, we should not make the name bad to make the method stand out more. We are allowed to remove incorrect or superfluous information, such as outdated or trivial comments.

The second rule states that our efforts should not make the job harder for the next person, who may be ourselves. Thus we should indicate any information we have, including suggesting how we would refactor the code, such as putting blank lines where we would extract methods. Preferably, we should make future refactoring easier.

The third rule states that the resulting code should be eye-catching, ensuring that the code is noticed as a signal and that there is a noticeable gap separating it from the pristine code, as discussed earlier in the chapter. These three rules together make sure we are not creating more problems, since anything that follows these rules can, at worst, be easily undone.

13.5 *Methods for safely vandalizing code*

Having discussed the rules of the game, let's look at some general methods I use to make bad code stand out. I encourage you to find your own methods, fitting what your team considers code smells. But be careful not to break the three rules.

The methods presented here are all safe and easily reversible. Safety and reversibility are essential: these methods are intended for use when I am busy doing something else, so sometimes I misjudge the code. These methods focus on code traits that are either eye-catching to most people or very useful for future refactoring.

13.5.1 *Using enums*

My favorite method to make code stand out as needing refactoring is to put an enum instead of a type code, such as a Boolean. It is usually trivial and quick to add an enum, and enums are easy to spot. As we learned in chapter 4, refactoring enums away, although time consuming, is straightforward. Enums also have the added benefit of being easier to read since they are named.

If we look at our three rules, we first need to consider whether this approach can destroy information. If we are replacing a Boolean, the only possible information would be in the form of named constants. In this case, we can preserve these names as the names of the enum values. But in addition, by making the Boolean into an enum, we add information to the type signatures of variables and methods.

Listing 13.7   Before

```
class Package {
  private priority: boolean;
  scheduleDispatch() {
    if (this.priority)
      dispatchImmediately(this);
    else
      queue.push(this);
  }
}
```

Listing 13.8   After

```
class Package {
  private priority: Importance;
  scheduleDispatch() {
    if (this.priority === Importance.Priority)
      dispatchImmediately(this);
    else
      queue.push(this);
  }
}
enum Importance {
  Priority, Regular
}
```

Changed to an enum

The second rule states that our changes should not make future refactoring harder. Here, we are making it easier since we have a standard flow for dealing with enums: REPLACE TYPE CODE WITH CLASSES (P4.1.3), then PUSH CODE INTO CLASSES (P4.1.5), and finally TRY DELETE THEN COMPILE (P4.5.1) to get rid of superfluous methods.

The third rule says the result should be eye-catching. Enums are easy to spot, although not everybody recognizes them as a code smell. Even so, this transformation is so helpful for future refactoring that we can forego this consideration.

13.5.2 *Using ints and strings as type codes*

In the same vein, sometimes we do not have the capacity to add enums, or we just need to get something working quickly. Here I often use ints or strings as type codes. If we use strings, we have the advantage that the text serves the same purpose as a constant name. A string-type code is also very flexible since we do not need to declare all values up front, so in situations of rapid experimentation, this is my go-to.

Listing 13.9   Strings as type code

```
function area(width: number, shape: string)
{


  if (shape === "circle")
    return (width/2) * (width/2) * Math.PI;
  else if (shape === "square")
    return width * width;
}
```

Listing 13.10   Ints as type code

```
const CIRCLE = 0;
const SQUARE = 1;
function area(width: number, shape: number)
{
  if (shape === CIRCLE)
    return (width/2) * (width/2) * Math.PI;
  else if (shape === SQUARE)
    return width * width;
}
```

As long as we use either named constant ints or strings, we can include all the information we want. Therefore, there is no risk of losing information.

This method is meant to launch the previous one, beginning a cascade. When the experimentation has slowed down, the next step is to replace the strings or ints with an enum. Because we embed the information in the constant name or string content, it is trivial to transform it into an enum. Thus the second rule is satisfied.

We usually check a type code with an **else if** chain or a **switch**, either of which we can spot at a glance. This property is especially true because the strings or constants align vertically since we check the same variable multiple times.

13.5.3 *Putting magic numbers in the code*

Taking this one step further, we also use constants in other ways than as type codes. If I am busy or experimenting or I want to highlight that some code needs refactoring, I don't shy away from putting magic numbers directly in the code. Most commonly, I do this when I am writing code; only rarely will I inline a constant.

Using this technique risks destroying information. Therefore, we need to be careful. If a constant is poorly or incorrectly named, it does not add information, and I have no problem inlining it. If I cannot determine whether the name has information, or I know something about it, I always put a comment wherever I inline the constant, which ensures that I satisfy the first rule.

Listing 13.11 Before

```
const FOUR_THIRDS = 4/3;
class Sphere {
  volume() {
    let result = FOUR_THIRDS;
    for (let i = 0; i < 3; i++)
      result = result * this.radius;
    return result * Math.PI;
  }
}
```

Listing 13.12 After

```
class Sphere {
  volume() {
    let result = 4/3;                        ⟵
    for (let i = 0; i < 3; i++)
      result = result * this.radius;
    return result * 3.141592653589793;  ⟵
  }
}
```
                                                  **Constants
                                                  inlined**

If it turns out the magic numbers should be constants, it is easy to re-extract them. Therefore, we have not made future refactoring meaningfully harder.

The final rule is where this transformation really starts to shine. Almost everybody reacts to seeing a magic number in the code. If our team is aligned about not simply extracting the constants but also fixing the entire method, this approach effectively puts some code in the spotlight.

13.5.4 Adding comments to the code

As mentioned earlier, we can use comments to preserve information. However, they serve a double purpose since they are also eye-catching—at least, they are if we follow chapter 8 and delete most of them. The type of comment that should be a method name can be an excellent signal, as we saw at the start of part 1.

Listing 13.13 Before

```
function subMin(arr: number[][]) {

  let min = Number.POSITIVE_INFINITY;
  for (let x = 0; x < arr.length; x++) {
    for(let y = 0; y < arr[x].length; y++) {
      min = Math.min(min, arr[x][y]);
    }
  }

  for (let x = 0; x < arr.length; x++) {
    for(let y = 0; y < arr[x].length; y++) {
      arr[x][y] -= min;
    }
  }
  return min;
}
```

Listing 13.14 After

```
function subMin(arr: number[][]) {
  // Find min                                    ⟵
  let min = Number.POSITIVE_INFINITY;
  for (let x = 0; x < arr.length; x++) {
    for(let y = 0; y < arr[x].length; y++) {
      min = Math.min(min, arr[x][y]);
    }
  }
  // Sub from each element                        ⟵
  for (let x = 0; x < arr.length; x++) {
    for(let y = 0; y < arr[x].length; y++) {
      arr[x][y] -= min;
    }
  }
  return min;                            **Comments that can
}                                        (and should) be
                                         method names**
```

It is difficult to destroy information by adding something. However, it is possible if the information we put in the comment is deliberately misleading. So as long as we believe whatever we put in the comment is accurate, we should be safe and satisfy the first rule.

Adding comments that can become method names is a great way to signal where to begin future refactoring efforts. Doing so both provides an easy point of entry and suggests method names for the refactorer to use. Rule 2 is upheld as well.

Most editors highlight comments in a different color and sometimes a different style, making them easily noticeable. But even setting that aside, as we follow the advice from chapter 8, comments should become more infrequent, and thereby our eyes will notice them more quickly.

13.5.5 *Putting whitespace in the code*

Another way we can suggest where to break up a method is by inserting whitespace. Like comments, we also used this method in part 1. It differs from comments, though, because we do not need to suggest a method name. Adding whitespace is useful when we can see structure but don't have sufficient understanding to name it. However, in addition to grouping statements, we can also use blank lines to group fields and suggest where to encapsulate data.

As this approach is so closely related to comments, it is also possible to deliberately mislead with whitespace. In the following example, we have deliberately placed misleading whitespace in the expression, causing the expression to be easily misinterpreted. Grouping statements or fields can achieve the same effect. As we are well intentioned, there should be no problems with the first rule.

Listing 13.15 Before

```
let cursor = cursor+1 % arr.length;
```

Listing 13.16 After

```
let cursor = (cursor + 1) % arr.length;   ◁─┐
```
Explicit parentheses needed because modulo binds as multiplication

If we use blank lines to group statements, it is easier to see where to EXTRACT METHOD (P3.2.1). If we are using this approach to group fields, it is easier to see where to ENCAPSULATE DATA (P6.2.3). In any case, blank lines are helpful.

Developers are good at spotting patterns, and blank lines are an easy pattern to spot. They stand out like paragraphs in a book.

13.5.6 *Grouping things based on naming*

Another way we can signal candidates for encapsulation is by grouping things that have common affixes. Most people do this automatically because it is pleasing to the eye. But after reading chapter 6, we know how useful this technique can be for refactoring, too.

Listing 13.17   Before

```
class PopupWindow {
  private windowPosition: Point2d;
  private hasFocus: number;
  private screenWidth: number;
  private screenHeight: number;
  private windowSize: Point2d;
}
```

Listing 13.18   After

```
class PopupWindow {
  private windowPosition: Point2d;
  private windowSize: Point2d;
  private hasFocus: number;
  private screenWidth: number;
  private screenHeight: number;
}
```

Much easier to spot the common prefix window

Applying this method is dangerous in the rare cases where the rule NEVER HAVE COMMON AFFIXES (R6.2.1) does not apply. In any other case, we accentuate information with this technique by making the affixes easier to spot.

Common affixes are the subject of a concrete rule pointing to a specific refactoring pattern: ENCAPSULATE DATA. Therefore, we simply need to follow the patterns and rules whenever we see common affixes, which is easy. As mentioned earlier, people tend to place affixes together instinctively because they are so eye-catching.

13.5.7   Adding context to names

If method and field names do not already share common affixes, we can add to their names to make common affixes more likely. Adding an affix may be a clear signal on its own, but if we need to highlight it even more, we can add an underscore to an otherwise camelCased or PascalCased name.

Listing 13.19   Before

```
function avg(arr: number[]) {
  return sum(arr) / size(arr);
}
function size(arr: number[]) {
  return arr.length;
}
function sum(arr: number[]) {
  let sum = 0;
  for (let i = 0; i < arr.length; i++)
    sum += arr[i];
  return sum;
}
```

Listing 13.20   After

```
function avg_ArrUtil(arr: number[]) {
  return sum_ArrUtil(arr)/size_ArrUtil(arr);
}
function size_ArrUtil(arr: number[]) {
  return arr.length;
}
function sum_ArrUtil(arr: number[]) {
  let sum = 0;
  for (let i = 0; i < arr.length; i++)
    sum += arr[i];
  return sum;
}
```

Adding context to a method name

We have to be careful here that the context we are adding is accurate. On the other hand, even if we end up encapsulating some methods and fields together that should not be together, we can split the class by further encapsulating the two should-be-separate classes.

As with the previous rule, we are moving directly toward the common affixes rule and corresponding refactoring. Also, improving names is always a healthy activity.

Common affixes are clearest when they are together. Therefore this technique goes well with the previous one. However, even if we don't have time to discover multiple methods with the same affix or to group them, we can still make them eye-catching by breaking the conventional casing style, as mentioned in the introduction to this technique.

13.5.8 Creating long methods

If we find that some methods are extracted in an unsatisfactory way, we can inline them to form one long method. Long methods are a warning sign to most developers, making them a great signal that something needs to be done.

Listing 13.21 Before

```
function animate() {
  handleChosen();
  handleDisplaying();
  handleCompleted();
  handleMoving();
}
function handleChosen() {
  if (value >= threshold
     && banner.state === State.Chosen) {
    // ...
  }
}
function handleDisplaying() {
  if (value >= target
     && banner.state === State.Displaying) {
    // ...
  }
}
function handleCompleted() {
  if (banner.state === State.Completed) {
    // ...
  }
}
function handleMoving() {
  if (banner.state === State.Moving
     && banner.target === banner.current) {
    // ...
  }
}
```

Listing 13.22 After

```
function animate() {
  if (value >= threshold
     && banner.state === State.Chosen) {
    // ...
  }
  if (value >= target
     && banner.state === State.Displaying) {
    // ...
  }
  if (banner.state === State.Completed) {
    // ...
  }
  if (banner.state === State.Moving
     && banner.target === banner.current) {
    // ...
  }
}
```

Easier to spot that
they all concern
banner.state

The original methods had names, and unless we are confident that these names are misleading, we should preserve their information. We can do this by using comments, with the bonus of extra visibility.

When methods are not extracted according to the appropriate underlying structure, they can make future refactoring difficult. By inlining such methods, we can reassess and more easily identify the correct structure.

Long methods are not as easy to spot as the other traits we have discussed. However, developers usually notice long methods and note where they are. Developers remember the methods so they can avoid them or because they know such methods are a symptom. Regardless, what long methods lack in immediate spot-ability, they make up for in recall.

13.5.9 *Giving methods many parameters*

Letting a method have many parameters is one of my favorite techniques to signal the need for refactoring. Apart from being obvious at the method definition site, it is also obvious at every call site.

There are two common ways people get around having many parameters. We discussed the first in chapter 7, where we put the parameters into an untyped structure like a HashMap, thereby blindsiding the compiler. Another common approach is to create a data object or struct. Here the values are named and typed. But these classes usually don't align with the underlying structure, so they only hide the smell rather than address it. Both of these ways should be undone.

Listing 13.23 Before version 1: Map

```
function stringConstructor(
    conf: Map<string, string>,
    parts: string[]) {
  return conf.get("prefix")
     + parts.join(conf.get("joiner"))
     + conf.get("postfix");
}
```

Listing 13.24 Before version 2: data object

```
class StringConstructorConfig {
  constructor(
    public readonly prefix: string,
    public readonly joiner: string,
    public readonly postfix: string) { }
}
function stringConstructor(
    conf: StringConstructorConfig,
    parts: string[]) {
  return conf.prefix
     + parts.join(conf.joiner)
     + conf.postfix;
}
```

Listing 13.25 After

```
function stringConstructor(
    prefix: string,
    joiner: string,
    postfix: string,
    parts: string[]) {
  return prefix + parts.join(joiner) + postfix;
}
```

If we make a data object or struct into a long parameter list, we preserve both types and names. If we make many parameters out of a Map, the keys become the variable names, and we even add information in the form of explicit types. In both cases, we are safe from destroying information.

Eliminating a long parameter list often requires quite a bit of refactoring in the form of making classes and pushing code into them to slowly uncover which parameters are coupled and therefore end up in the same classes. However, turning data objects or hashmaps into parameters does not make refactoring harder.

Being eye-catching is where this method excels. As stated, both the definition and all call sites scream for refactoring. There are essentially small road signs spread throughout the code, directing us to the problematic method.

13.5.10 Using getters and setters

Another approach that adds road signs is using getters and setters rather than global variables or public fields. It is easy to encapsulate the data and access it through getters and setters. In turn, these getters and setters should disappear as we enrich the encapsulating class by pushing code into it.

Listing 13.26 Before

```
let screenWidth: number;
let screenHeight: number;
```

Listing 13.27 After

```
class Screen {
  constructor(
    private width: number,
    private height: number) { }
  getWidth() { return this.width; }
  getHeight() { return this.height; }
}
let screen: Screen;
```

This method is also additive: we add code rather than modify or remove it. Thus there is no risk of losing information in the transformation.

Encapsulating is often the first step of refactoring such data. We are not only making it easier, we are also reducing the effort.

Standard convention dictates that getters and setters are prefixed by get or set, respectively. This syntactic convention makes them easy to spot at the definition site and at call sites, similar to using many parameters.

Summary

- We can use bad code to signal process issues, such as a lack of priority or time.
- We should segregate our codebase into pristine and legacy code; the pristine code tends to stay good longer.
- There is no perfect way to define "bad code," but four popular approaches are the rules in this book: code smells, cyclomatic complexity, and cognitive complexity.
- By following three rules, we can safely increase the gap between pristine and legacy code:
  - Never destroy information.
  - Empower future refactoring.
  - Increase issue visibility.

- Examples of concrete ways to apply the rules include the following:
  - Use enums.
  - Use ints and strings as type codes.
  - Put magic numbers in the code.
  - Put comments in the code.
  - Put whitespace in the code.
  - Group things based on naming.
  - Add context to names.
  - Create long methods.
  - Give methods many parameters.
  - Use getters and setters.

Wrapping up

14

This chapter covers

- Reflecting on the journey of this book
- Exploring the underlying principles
- Suggesting how to continue this journey

This chapter first takes a brief look at what we have covered in this book to recall the long journey we have been on. Then I explain the central ideas and principles that led me to this content and how you can employ these principles to solve similar problems. Finally, I provide recommendations for how your journey can naturally continue from this stepping stone.

14.1 Reflecting on the journey of this book

When you started this book, you likely had either no view of refactoring or a very different view than you do now. My hope with this book is to have made refactoring accessible and actionable for more people. I wanted to lower the entry bar to complex concepts such as code smells, utilizing the compiler, feature toggling, and many others. We color the world with the language we use. Therefore I hope I have enriched your vocabulary through the titles of rules, refactoring patterns, and chapters.

14.1.1 Introduction: Motivation

In the first two chapters, we explored what refactoring is, why it is essential, and when to prioritize it. We laid the foundation by defining the goal of refactoring: reducing fragility by localizing invariants, increasing flexibility by reducing coupling, and understanding the software's domain.

14.1.2 Part 1: Making it concrete

In part 1, we went through a reasonable-looking code base and improved it step by step. We used a set of rules to focus our attention and save us from diving into rabbit holes trying to understand the details. Along with the rules, we built up a small catalog of powerful refactoring patterns.

We started by learning how to break up long functions. We then replaced type codes with classes, allowing us to make functions into methods by pushing them into the classes. Having expanded the codebase, we proceeded to unify `if`s, functions, and classes. To conclude part 1, we looked at advanced refactoring patterns to enforce encapsulation.

14.1.3 Part 2: Widening the horizon

After experiencing the workflow of refactoring and forming a deep understanding of what and how to refactor, we raised the level of abstraction. In part 2, rather than discussing concrete rules and refactoring, we examined many socio-technical subjects affecting refactoring and code quality. We discussed subjects relating to culture, skills, and tools, and I provided actionable advice.

The tools we have discussed in part 2 include compilers, feature toggling, Kanban, the theory of constraint, and many others. We covered cultural changes such as approaches to deleting, adding, and vandalizing code. Finally, we explored concrete skills such as uncovering structure and optimizing performance safely.

14.2 Exploring the underlying philosophy

There is a lot of helpful information in this book—too much for one person to keep everything at top of mind. Luckily, you don't need to remember all the specifics to benefit from it as long as you have internalized the underlying principles. Therefore, I want to give you some insight into how I think about and use the rules and other contents of this book.

14.2.1 Searching for ever-smaller steps

This book shares a fundamental opinion with test-driven development and other methods: taking smaller steps dramatically reduces the risk of errors. I never show only the end state, because the journey to get there is where the challenges lie. The ability to break down a large problem into smaller pieces is a significant part of programming. This same ability can be used when we consider a major transformation.

We can find minor transformations that we can chain together to get the major result. Improving through small steps is what refactoring is about.

In this book, we have discussed steps to take when you don't know what the end state is, such as in chapter 13 or all the rules in part 1. All of these steps are small, and they focus on going from something working to something working; this is called *green to green*. Often, this means we have to pass through several intermediate steps where we make only a minimal improvement.

In addition to reducing risk, going from green to green quickly gives us much more flexibility to change course along the way. If we discover something important, we only have to proceed to the next green state before switching. If we get an urgent request for a fix, we can `git reset` back to the last green state and lose a minimal amount of work. We have to reset the refactoring and not simply switch branches and return later, because while we are in the middle of refactoring, we often need to keep track of a lot of loose threads in our heads. If we context-switch away from the refactoring, it is unlikely that we can remember these threads, so the risk of introducing errors skyrockets. We should only ever switch context from and to green states.

We also discussed how to break down transformations that require both code and culture changes into small steps between stable states. In chapter 10, when we explored feature toggling, we looked at the technology and discussed the steps in adopting the necessary culture. On a high level, my recommendation was to build the reflex of putting and removing `if` statements around all changes. Only when this technique is second nature should we proceed to take advantage of the benefits by using it in production. If we tried to jump directly to the end, there is a high risk we would miss some `if` toggles around new code and accidentally release something unfinished or introduce errors.

14.2.2 *Searching for the underlying structure*

We have talked a lot about structure. Indeed, chapter 11 was dedicated to it. When I refactor, I like to imagine myself as a clay sculptor, starting with a lump of clay and slowly molding it to reveal the structure within. I say *clay* because I think code is more malleable and reversible than carving in stone; but overlooking this, Michelangelo expressed the point beautifully:

> *Every block of stone has a statue inside it, and it is the task of the sculptor to discover it.*
>
> —Michelangelo di Lodovico Buonarroti Simoni

To help discover this statue inside the code, I use a nice trick, which is what most of part 1 was about: I use the lines to guide where the methods should be. Then I use the methods to guide where the classes should be. In practice, I take it even further and let the classes guide where the namespaces or packages should be. The trick is to start from the inside and then cascade changes to more and more abstract layers. Therefore, I would rather have one method too many than one too few. One method might be the difference in having a common affix or not, and therefore another class.

14.2.3   *Using the rules for collaboration*

As with everything in the real world, there is no silver bullet; there is no complete and straightforward model. The rules and advice in this book are no different. Thus it is essential to underline that the rules are tools, not laws. It would be a grave mistake to apply them blindly or, even worse, use them to police your teammates. As mentioned in the previous chapter, feeling safe is the number-one priority in a development team. If the rules help you feel safe and confident when refactoring, good. If they are used to hit each other over the head, bad. The rules are a good basis for a conversation about code quality. They are good rules of thumb from which to start. They are excellent for creating the necessity and motivation for learning refactoring.

14.2.4   *Prioritizing the team over individuals*

Continuing, I want to underline the importance of the team. Software development is a team effort. As both DevOps and agile encourage, we should focus on close collaboration. It is easy to fall victim to thinking that individual developers working in parallel increase efficiency. However, this arrangement creates knowledge silos, which are often more detrimental than the benefit from parallelization. Activities such as pair and ensemble programming are an excellent example of beneficial closer collaboration. Properly implemented, such activities help distribute knowledge, skills, and responsibility, leading to more trust and stronger commitment. As an African proverb says,

> *If you want to go fast, go alone. If you want to go far, go together.*
>
> —African proverb

In other words, the team is the method of delivery, not individuals. When people ask me, "Is this line too long?" or "Is this thing bad?" I always ask them these questions:

1. "Do your developers understand it?"
2. "Are they happy with it?"
3. "Is there a simpler version that does not break any performance/security constraints?"

The whole team must commit to the whole codebase that they are responsible for. We want to change code quickly and with confidence, so anything that detracts from doing so should be addressed.

14.2.5   *Prioritize simplicity over completeness*

If you endeavor to come up with your own rules, which I recommend doing, you must adhere to an important design principle. When we see code that feels bad, and we want to create a rule to disallow it, it is easy to fall into the trap of trying to be universal. This approach leads to vague and general rules, much like code smells. These are very useful and impressively specified; however, many fail on the most important criteria: ease of application.

Cognitive psychology describes two systems of cognitive tasks, each with a capacity. System 1 is fast but imprecise. It takes almost no energy to use system 1, so our brain prefers it. System 2 is slow and energy expensive, but it is accurate. A classic experiment illustrates systems 1 and 2 in action. Answer this question: "How many of each animal did Moses take on the ark?" If you said two, it was your system 1 responding. If you correctly spotted that it was Noah who had the ark, you answered with system 2.

We can at any one time do several system 1 tasks, such as chew gum, walk, or drive. However, we can only maintain a single system 2 task, such as talk or text. Multitasking is not a skill humans possess. Some people can do fast task switching. However, since we are not parallelizing anything, there is no practical purpose to do so.

Programming is primarily about problem-solving and therefore is a system 2 task. Throughout the book, I have pointed out that developers are already exhausting their mental capacity on the task they are solving. Thus any rules we want people to execute must be so simple that we can apply them without thinking.

On a scale from "simple but wrong" to "complex but right," if we want behavioral change, we should err on the side of simplicity. Being simplistic can be problematic. However, we can take advantage of another property of humans: common sense. Presenting rules like those in this book with a disclaimer that they are guidelines rather than laws should discourage people from following them blindly.

14.2.6 *Using objects or higher-order functions*

We have used a lot of objects and classes in this book. However, a feature has crept into almost all mainstream languages that spares us from some of them. It goes under many names: higher-order functions, lambdas, delegates, closures, and arrows. A few instances are included in this book, but I have stayed away from them for the most part. This choice is only to make the style as consistent as possible.

From the viewpoint of refactoring, an object with one method and a higher-order function is the same thing; if the object has fields, it's a closure. They have the same coupling. One looks flashier but can also be more difficult for some people to read. Therefore, the same advice applies as earlier: use the one that your team thinks is easier to read. If you want to practice, go through the code from part 1 and refactor it like this.

Listing 14.1   Object

The type signature of the sole method in RemoveStrategy.

```
function remove(
  shouldRemove: RemoveStrategy)
{
  for (let y = 0; y < map.length; y++)
    for (let x = 0; x < map[y].length; x++)
      if (shouldRemove.check(map[y][x]))
        map[y][x] = new Air();
}
```

.check is removed since there is only one method.

Listing 14.2   Higher-order function

```
function remove(
  shouldRemove: (tile: Tile) => boolean)
{
  for (let y = 0; y < map.length; y++)
    for (let x = 0; x < map[y].length; x++)
      if (shouldRemove(map[y][x]))
        map[y][x] = new Air();
}
```

```
class Key1 implements Tile {                  class Key1 implements Tile {
  // ...                                        // ...
  moveHorizontal(dx: number) {                  moveHorizontal(dx: number) {
    remove(new RemoveLock1());      ◁──────▷    remove(tile => tile.isLock1());
    moveToTile(playerx + dx, playery);            moveToTile(playerx + dx, playery);
  }                                             }
}                                             }
interface RemoveStrategy {
  check(tile: Tile): boolean;                 The body from
}                                             RemoveLock1 as a
class RemoveLock1 implements RemoveStrategy    higher-order function
{
  check(tile: Tile) {
    return tile.isLock1();          ◁──────
  }
}
```

**The type signature of the sole
method in RemoveStrategy**

14.3   *Where to go from here*

This journey can continue along many different avenues; the ones that are most natural continuations are macro-architecture, micro-architecture, and software quality. I give recommendations for each next.

14.3.1 *Micro-architecture route*

Micro- or intra-team architecture has been the main focus of this book and is likely the smoothest transition. This field concerns itself with coupling and fragility, all the way from expressions to—but not including—public interfaces and API design. On this route, I like to think there are two paths:

- You can plunge yourself into more sophisticated and detailed smells with *Clean Code* by Robert C. Martin.
- Or you can widen your repertoire of refactoring patterns with *Refactoring* by Martin Fowler.

14.3.2 *Macro-architecture route*

You can also choose to focus on macro- or inter-team architecture. As mentioned in chapter 11, Conway's law dominates macro-architecture, stating that our (macro-) architecture will mirror our organization's communication structure. Therefore, I lovingly dub this the "people route"; to affect the code, we must focus on the people. For a brilliant account of organizing teams and Conway's law, I recommend *Team Topologies* by Mathew Skelton (IT Revolution Press, 2019).

14.3.3 *Software quality route*

The final route is to study software quality. We have discussed quality on many occasions in this book, and it comes in many varieties fitting different needs.

For product teams that deliver software to coding muggles, I recommend learning testing. Refactoring is built into test-driven development, and while this topic is difficult to master, it is easy to get started with. I prefer the classic *Test-Driven Development* by Kent Beck (Addison-Wesley Professional, 2002). While testing is not bulletproof, it targets a lot of the issues users could face.

Platform teams deliver software to other programmers in the form of libraries, frameworks, or extendable tools. For these, I recommend learning type theory. With modern languages, we can express many complex properties in the type system and have the compiler prove their validity. Simultaneously, types help document and guide our users when using our software and ensure that specific properties hold, preventing errors. I recommend the book *Types and Programming Languages* by Benjamin C. Pierce (MIT Press, 2002), which is a gentle introduction to both functional programming and types and gives tools and understanding that can be transferred to other programming paradigms. Type safety is bulletproof; however, it covers only what we teach it.

Finally, the most ambitious readers can study provable correctness through dependent types or proof assistants. Provable correctness is state of the art in software quality. However, it requires tremendous effort to master. Luckily, lessons learned in this area transfer easily to all other programming activities. I recommend *Type-Driven Development with Idris* by Edwin Brady (Manning, 2017), which also builds on functional programming. As of this writing, there is not great demand for the quality that this discipline provides. However, new programming languages for provable correctness are still being invented, such as Lean; so we may hope that provably correct software has its place, as it is bulletproof and covers everything.

Summary

- In pursuit of making refactoring more accessible, we underlined the importance of refactoring and then explored it through an example using concrete rules and refactoring patterns. Then we widened the horizon and discussed many socio-technical subjects affecting code quality.
- The underlying philosophy of this book relies on decomposing large transformations into tiny steps between stable states.
- Recognizing that the structure is often hidden, we use lines to guide where methods should be and methods to guide where classes should be.
- The rules should be used to support collaboration and teamwork; and when refactoring, there is no substitute for common sense.

- The rules and advice in this book are designed with humans in mind, considering their environment and situation. If we want to change behavior, we must prefer simplicity to correctness.

I hope you have found this book both enjoyable and useful. Thank you very much for giving me your attention.

appendix A
Installing the tools
for part 1

We use Node.js to install TypeScript, so first we need to install that.

Node.js

1 Go to https://nodejs.org/en, and download the LTS version.
2 Go through the installer.
3 Verify the installation by opening PowerShell (or another console) and running this command:

```
npm --version
```

It should return something like `6.14.6`.

TypeScript

1 Open PowerShell, and run this command:

```
npm install -g typescript
```

This uses Node.js's package manager (npm) to `install` the `typescript` compiler globally (`-g`), as opposed to in the local folder.
2 Verify the installation by running this command:

```
tsc --version
```

It should return something like `Version 4.0.3`.

Visual Studio Code

1 Go to https://code.visualstudio.com, and download the installer.
2 Go through the installer. When given the choice, I recommend checking these options:

   − Add "Open with code" to the Windows Explorer File context menu.
   − Add "Open with code" to the Windows Explorer Directory context menu.

   These options allow you to open a folder or file in Visual Studio Code simply by right-clicking it.

Git

1 Go to https://git-scm.com/downloads, and download the installer.
2 Go through the installer.
3 Verify the installation by opening PowerShell and running this command:

```
git --version
```

   It should return something like `git version 2.24.0.windows.2`.

Setting up the TypeScript project

1 Open a console where you want the game to be stored.
   − `git clone https://github.com/thedrlambda/five-lines` downloads the source code for the game.
   − `cd five-lines` enters the folder with the game.
   − `tsc -w` compiles the TypeScript to JavaScript every time it changes.
2 Open index.html in a browser.

Building the TypeScript project

1 Open the folder with the game in Visual Studio Code.
2 Select Terminal and then New Terminal.
3 Run the command `tsc -w`.
4 TypeScript is now compiling your changes in the background, and you can close the terminal.
5 Every time you make a change, wait for a second, and then refresh index.html in your browser.

Instructions for how to beat the game are provided in the browser when the game is opened.

How to modify the level

It is possible to change the level in the code, so feel free to have fun creating your own maps by updating the array in the map variable. The numbers correspond to tile types according to the following overview.

0	Air	2	Unbreakable
1	Flux	8	Yellow key
3	Player	9	Yellow lock
4	Stone	10	Blue key
6	Box	11	Blue lock

The numbers 5 and 7 are the falling versions of boxes and stones, so they are not used to create levels. If you need some inspiration, try the following level. The objective is to get both boxes to the lower-right corner, one on top of the other.

Listing A.1   Another level to try

```
let playerx = 5;
let playery = 3;
let map: Tile[][] = [
    [2, 2, 2, 2, 2, 2, 2, 2],
    [2, 0, 4, 6, 8, 6, 2, 2],
    [2, 1, 1, 1, 1, 1, 2, 2],
    [2, 0, 0, 0, 4, 3, 0, 2],
    [2, 2, 9, 2, 2, 0, 0, 2],
    [2, 2, 2, 2, 2, 2, 2, 2],
];
```

The shortest solution for this level is ← ↑ ↑ ↓ ← ← ↓ → → ↑ ← ← ↓ → → → ↑ ← ↓ →.

index

A new online reading experience

liveBook, our online reading platform, adds a new dimension to your Manning books, with features that make reading, learning, and sharing easier than ever. A liveBook version of your book is included FREE with every Manning book.

This next generation book platform is more than an online reader. It's packed with unique features to upgrade and enhance your learning experience.

- Add your own notes and bookmarks
- One-click code copy
- Learn from other readers in the discussion forum
- Audio recordings and interactive exercises
- Read all your purchased Manning content in any browser, anytime, anywhere

As an added bonus, you can search every Manning book and video in liveBook—even ones you don't yet own. Open any liveBook, and you'll be able to browse the content and read anything you like.*

Find out more at www.manning.com/livebook-program.

*Open reading is limited to 10 minutes per book daily